POWER AND POLITICS
IN GLOBALIZATION

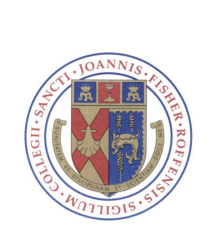

POWER AND POLITICS IN GLOBALIZATION

The Indispensable State

Howard H. Lentner

Routledge
NEW YORK AND LONDON

"Globalization and Power" in Preet S. Aulakh and Michael G. Schechter, eds., *Rethinking Globalization(s): From Corporate Transnationalism to Local Interventions* (Basingstoke: Palgrave Macmillan, 2000). Reproduced with permission of Palgrave Macmillan.

"Civil Society and Conditions of Peace" in Tai-joon Kwon and Dong-sung Kim, eds., *World Order and Peace in the New Millennium* (Seoul: The Korean National Commission for UNESCO, 2000).

Published in 2004 by
Routledge
29 W 35ᵗʰ Street
New York, NY 10001
www.routledge-ny.com

Published in Great Britain by
Routledge
4 Park Square
Milton Park
Abingdon OX14 4RN
www.routledge.co.uk

10 9 8 7 6 5 4 3 2 1

Library of Congress Cataloging-in-Publication Data

Lentner, Howard H.
Power and politics in globalization : the indispensable State / Howard H. Lentner.
    p. cm.
Includes bibliographical references and index.
ISBN 0-415-94884-3 (hb : alk. paper) -- ISBN 0-415-94885-1 (pbk. : alk. paper)
  1. Globalization. 2. National state. 3. Power (Social sciences) I. Title.
    JZ1318.L46 2004
  327.1'01—dc22   2004010578

To Andrew and Mya

Contents

Preface

My attention was drawn to the subject of globalization when, in 1996, my department chairman at Baruch College, Thomas Halper, asked two of my colleagues and me to devise a new course treating the United States and globalization. That task led to my reading and thinking about what had become a buzzword across the academic and policy communities. Subsequent investigations led to a sabbatical research project in 1997–1998 that took me to Malaysia, and to several conferences where I began presenting my views on the topic.

It has been an interesting experience for me to engage with scholars and practitioners from many different backgrounds and disciplines. The topic of globalization has taken me quite beyond the bounds of political science, where I have spent a career, to that rich terrain where interdisciplinary studies engender and fertilize new thought. At the same time, the contribution of this work lies in bringing to bear a clear political perspective and a concern with power. I hope that readers find the views expressed here to be worth considering.

Acknowledgments

My work received encouragement from a number of people, including Henri Goverde and Mark Haugaard of the International Political Science Association Research Committee on Power. Michael G. Schechter and Preet S. Aulakh invited me to their conference on globalization at Michigan State University and selected my paper for publication in their book *Rethinking Globalization(s): From Corporate Transnationalism to Local Interventions* (London: Macmillan Press, 2000). I am grateful to them and to Macmillan Press for permission to reproduce a different version of the chapter from that book, which appears here as Chapter 3. I am grateful to Jung Hyun Shin and Hyun Kim for arranging an invitation to me to participate in a conference held in Seoul, organized by the Korean Association of International Studies and UNESCO. Thanks to Jung-In Kang, Irving Leonard Markovitz, and Bernd Reiter for comments and suggestions on that paper. Together with others, my paper was published in *World Order and Peace in the New Millennium*, edited by Tai-joon Kwon and Dong-Sung Kim (Seoul: Korean National Commission for UNESCO, 2000). I thank the Korean National Commission for UNESCO for permission to reprint my contribution, which appears in this book as Chapter 9. It was in response to an invitation by Eric Borg that I wrote the essay that now forms Chapter 10. I am grateful to him and also to Stewart Clegg, who urged me to present a paper at the Asia-Pacific Researchers on Organization Studies meeting in Sydney; that paper has been reworked as Chapter 7 in this book. A City University of New York Research Foundation service grant provided travel support. The Department of Political Science at Baruch College gave me a small grant, and Kung Wing Au served effectively as my research assistant. Immense thanks are also due to Benedetto Fontana, James Guyot, William Tabb, Gordon P. Means, and three anonymous Routledge reviewers for careful reading of all or parts of the manuscript and for suggestions that improved it.

A number of Malaysians offered generous assistance in helping me to understand their country and its position in the international system. Noorul Ainur

Md. Nor, Noharuddin Nordin (Malaysian Consulate General), and Tan Ah Yong (Malaysian Industrial Development Authority) in New York gave me a helping hand in getting started. Jomo K.S. and especially Zakaria Haji Ahmad proved generous hosts as well as intellectual mentors in Kuala Lumpur. Zakaria was especially helpful in introducing me to others whom I was able to interview.

In addition to some who asked not to be named, I wish to express my thanks to the following people who assisted my research by talking with me about various aspects of Malaysia in the context of globalization: members of the Institute of Malaysian and International Studies at the Universiti Kebangsaan Malaysia, including Rajah Rasiah, Norani Othman, Sumit Mandal, and James Mittelman; Siti Azizah Abad (Ministry of Defense); Noor Faridah Ariffin (Foreign Ministry); Professor Ishak Ismail (MSTE); Razak Baginda (Malaysian Strategic Research Center); Professor Lee Pol Ping; Ashad Hussain (Foreign Ministry); Mohamed Jawhar bin Hassan, Helen E.S. Nesadurai, and Patrick Pillai of the Institute for Strategic and International Studies; Dr. Sharifah Munirah Alatas (ISIS); Paul Chan (HELP); M. Supperamanian (Ministry of International Trade and Industry); Dr. Mohamed Ariff bin Abdul Kareem (Malaysia Institute of Economics); Dato Samsudin bin Osman, Dato Mohamad Datajol Rosli, and Hamzah Bin Md. Rus of Home Affairs; a-Zuhari Yo Dai Thai (Malaysian Industrial Development Agency); Yeow Teck Chai (Malaysian Industrial Development Authority); Mr. Lee (Federation of Malaysian Manufacturers); Irene Fernandez; Professor Chandra Muzaffar (University of Malaya); and Professor Mohamad Abu Bakar (University of Malaya).

It has been a pleasure to work with the competent and efficient Routledge team: Editor Rob Tempio, Editorial Assistant Angela Chnapko, and Project Editor Sylvia Wood. Finally, I wish to express my gratitude to my agent, Richard R. Valcourt.

1
Globalization and Politics

Introduction

The politics of globalization includes two dimensions. The first embodies the practical distribution of power and the constraints imposed by existing arrangements. Those constraints flow from choices that have established and now manage existing structures and processes. The second dimension embraces a more visionary quest for alternative arrangements in the future.

As is true of all politics, both cooperation and struggle are involved, domination and resistance are evident, and contestation abounds. This book deals with present realities and future visions, with both cooperative and conflictive aspects of globalization, and with issues of power and domination in the contemporary world. Certainly, substantial changes have occurred and continue to occur in the modern world. Nevertheless, in my opinion, both the realities and the visions express a good deal of continuity with the past.

Globalization is most commonly presented as an inexorable process that involves bringing the world together through technology. Although the fundamental processes bringing human beings into contact with one another have been at work for millennia, high-speed transport and especially the computer have speeded up the process in the last quarter century or so. Travel, trade, and financial flows now characteristically flow across the globe in voluminous amounts at rapid rates.

These developments are commonly regarded as transforming the world in which we live, but there are four basic assertions about globalization that either restate or modify received ideas about liberal thought. Foremost among the claims is that the state is losing power to the market and has been or will be modified in fundamental ways. This contention restates the Lockean position that society and market relations precede the state. Another claim holds that communities are breaking down and that individuals are becoming increasingly isolated. Traditional liberalism is founded on the notion that rational individuals formed contracts and constituted civil society, which Locke equated with the state. With the increase of the market and other contractual relations, traditional communities and societies faded before free thought in which different ideas of morality and reason emerged, and individuals were no longer constrained by social conventions and traditions.

Another assertion promotes the formation of new identities and novel social and political formations, indeed the creation of a transnational civil society. Given both the absence of constraints and the individualistic origins of society and government, aspirations for universal freedom of association, identity, and contractual relations have always been implicit in the liberal consensus, and aspects of the globalization debate claim that these aspirations are now being brought to fruition.

Still another assertion foresees the development of a broad human project of global governance that includes a universal legal system and intervention nearly everywhere on behalf of human rights or humanitarian principles. Although consistent with the universalizing tendencies of traditional liberalism, in some ways this last claim flies in the face of the others, for governance requires state power both for its formulation and its enforcement. Whatever diversity exists among those regarding globalization as inexorable, the basic argument tends to treat politics largely with an outlook geared to the future.

Two implications flow from such a treatment: analysis tends to have an ideological or at least normative orientation, and analysts tend to assume that politics in the future will less and less resemble what has gone before. Furthermore, as the very term "globalization" itself suggests, many analysts assume that a politics of the globe, however fragmented or inchoate, has already emerged and that the world can be treated—at least to some extent—as a unit in which some sort of new form of politics is already being practiced.

In my judgment, developments in the world are not inexorable. Without denying that technology has an impact on the lives of people all over the world, I argue that the arrangements for channeling and using resources are chosen by people who act within political and social contexts, all of which exist within conditions structured by power. That means that people, using their material resources and ideas, have conflicted and cooperated with others to establish extant arrangements. Moreover, they continue to contend to preserve, modify, or drastically alter the arrangements. Thus, to understand the conditions of globalization, one needs to examine the array of power underlying them, the agents who propel and contend over them, and the values and aspirations at work in contentions over managing the arrangements.

The fundamental problem of politics stems from the simultaneous existence of human striving for autonomy and community. Aristotle's assertion that "man is by nature a political animal" includes the notion that individuals seek to lead a good life but they are enabled to do so only within a good state. Such a state requires institutions, the rule of law, citizenship in which recognition is accorded individuals, justice which in the first place entails equality, and some purpose or end. Although ultimately the purposes of the individual are served by the political community, those purposes are not merely matters of human needs for food, clothing, shelter, and so forth, but encompass something larger.

Such larger purposes that forge a unity among free individuals and political units are lost in the liberal views, based on Locke, that figure most prominently in contemporary thinking about politics and civil society. In general, liberal thinking promotes merely the interdependence of individuals who cooperate with and assist one another through a division of labor. At best, the state provides the elementary services of law and order to facilitate the pursuit of individual, group, and corporate interests. No common interest or larger purpose brings people together into a common endeavor. To the extent that a common good can be identified, it grows out of selfish pursuits, as Adam Smith averred, and does not result from distinct deliberation and formulation of definite public purposes. Neither does it allow for essentially antagonistic interests between different groups. A peculiarly American emphasis on individualism goes further in claiming increasing scope for autonomous persons to act without restraint by either government or society.

In the mid-nineteenth century, Hegel tried to recapture the larger purpose within which people lived by distinguishing between civil society, a realm of particular interests supported and regulated by a governmental apparatus, and the state, a realm of freedom in which a universal societal purpose enabled individuals to transcend mere needs and to choose beyond them. Despite his intriguing solution to the fundamental tension between autonomy and community, Hegel's understanding has not been widely adopted.

If liberalism has produced an excess of individualism and a reduction of community feeling, history is filled with many examples of community domination squeezing individual autonomy. One interpretation of the bloody history of the twentieth century that remained quite popular in the wake of World War II construed it as a struggle between tyranny on the one side and respect for the individual on the other.

Within states, politics consists of constituting arrangements for continued deliberations about policies as well as ongoing monitoring of the enforcement of those policies. Arrangements include the building of institutions and rules by which discourse can be conducted, determining who should be included among the ranks of citizens, and principles and procedures to be employed in coming to decisions. In addition, some understanding of the basis of legitimacy—the right to rule and the obligation to obey—has to be formulated.

All states include violence, some in their formation, others in rule without politics, still others providing for the monopoly by the state of the legitimate means of violence to be used in maintaining order and enforcing law. Thus politics consists of both nonviolent deliberation and the use of force at different stages in the lives of states as well as the pursuit and administration of justice. For losers in deliberations and for dissenters from systems of domination, their autonomy may be sacrificed to community rule, often through the use of violence. Furthermore, all states retain at least the potential and, more often than not, the capability to employ violence in their relations with other states.

But the tension between autonomy and community prevails in the relations among states as well as within them. It is here where globalization and politics intersect, and in the present world violence and imposition of the strong on the weak tend to prevail over politics, although the discourse of globalization hardly notes it. Developments within the context of globalization, such as the worldwide rationalization of production and convergence through the spread of best practices as well as cultural exchange, follows in the wake of the rise to systemic domination of a coalition of liberal states.

Although globalization is the term of choice in contemporary discourse it obscures the fact that the world remains divided into states, which are aggregates of power with independent decision-making centers. In part, the matter tends to be hidden by the application of the term "state" to very loosely organized entities that lack the conditions and attributes that characterize states and are thus open to domination. Sometimes these entities are referred to as failed states. Except for these and minuscule, very weak units it is politics among states, not politics within a global entity, that operates in the world. Furthermore, many observers interpret the increasing connections across state boundaries as erosion of borders; still others treat their speculations about the future as settled facts, leading them to assume that the world will one day, usually soon, be integrated into a single unit.

What Is the Politics of Globalization?

The examination of the politics of globalization pursued in this book does not assume the inevitability of global integration and then formulate views about global governance. My analysis aims to understand the background and politics of the contemporary world in which globalization trends contain responses to many different political questions and in which contenders struggle for power. Ideas and conceptualizations themselves are tools in contentions over domination and resistance. This approach differs from that which assumes that the world is undergoing a fundamental transformation that makes it sensible to treat the globe as a unit.

In perhaps the most thoughtful book on the subject, Held and his associates (1999, p. 49) take such a tack when they write:

> Today, virtually all nation-states have gradually become enmeshed in and functionally part of a larger pattern of global transformations and global flows.... Far from this being a world of 'discrete civilizations', or simply an international society of states, it has become a fundamentally interconnected global order, marked by intense patterns of exchange as well as by clear patterns of power, hierarchy and unevenness.

In setting out a formulation that posits either the existence or inexorability of such a global order, politics then tends to be treated as an ideological struggle for control of the future. Held and associates (1999, Table C.1) describe three distinct "political projects" for "civilizing and democratizing contemporary globalization." The first, "liberal-internationalism," aims for "reform of global governance" based on an ethic of "common rights and responsibilities." The second, "radical republicanism," stresses "alternative structures of global governance" guided by an ethic of "humane governance." And the last, "cosmopolitan democracy," strives for "reconstruction of global governance" founded on the notion of "democratic autonomy." Although discrete, each of these distinct alternatives assumes the inevitability of a future characterized by global unity.

If, instead, the world is treated as an international system undergoing some change that increases interconnectedness but that does not amount to profound transformation, analysis of the politics of globalization proceeds along quite different lines. Rather than perceiving an inevitable development, this view notes that the most powerful countries, coordinated in a coalition led by the United States, promote a liberal ideology of free trade, unfettered financial flows, direct investment, and other objectives. These powerful countries, furthermore, advocate a neoliberal ideology that aims to reduce the involvement of states in economic production by privatizing state-owned enterprises and to put into place states that are open to the influence of those powerful countries operating both directly and through the market. To facilitate this project, both intergovernmental and nongovernmental organizations, together with rules and regimes that may be put into place, provide institutional support. In short, this concert of leading states promotes an international community. Observers often regard the direction of developments to equal either the actual or the potential integration of the world.

But the direction of things relies upon power and purpose, the fundamental components of politics. The leading powers' policies shape international institutions and procedures, and then they push smaller countries to join in those arrangements. But as the powerful promote community, the weak aspire to autonomy within whatever community may be formed. To be sure, the powerful hold out incentives—the promise of development and the threat of economic collapse—but, unless the weak are sufficiently autonomous to enter into agreements freely, their range of choice is severely constrained. The issue resides not so much in separation as inclusion on the basis of choice. Small or weak countries aspire to gain the advantages of participation in the regimes of free trade and investment. On the other hand, they do so not to be submerged in an order dominated by the more powerful but rather to gain wealth and power themselves. However, they can gain such enhancements only by engaging in the larger cooperative schemes.

Just as surely as there are tensions and disagreements between the strong and the weak, divisions occur within the coalition of the leading countries. Frequently, disputes break out that amount to conflict over important issues such as trade rules or intervention policies. Very few conflicts hold the potential for war among the major powers, although the status of Taiwan provides a deep conflict between the United States and China that has to be handled in a particularly delicate way so as to restrain the dogs of war.

One also needs to note that, although each weak country seeks autonomy in the face of domination by a system of rules fashioned by the leading powers, this conflict does not array a coalition of the weak against a concert of the strong. Instead, in parallel with the situation of the individual in society, each country strives for autonomy against domination but also for cooperation in order to achieve those purposes that cannot be achieved autonomously.

To elucidate that struggle, the following discussion analyzes the discrete political issues at play in the contemporary international arena. These include matters of power, institutions, ideas and ideology, authority, democracy, human rights, law, justice, equality, regimes, legitimacy, sovereignty, citizenship, civil society, and violence. Analyzing present arrangements in each of these matters describes the shape of politics in globalization as it occurs. This approach may be contrasted with the debate over future policy.

Foundations of Globalization

Although theoretical concepts offer useful insights and directions for inquiry, specific human arrangements are always historical. That is to say, in inquiring into the issues that have been resolved in the building of globalization, it is important to remember that what exists today has emanated from previous experience. Certainly events like the Cold War come to an end, and conditions afterward differ from those that prevailed during its existence, but present conditions nevertheless have been shaped by arrangements and decisions made in the past. Furthermore, both the past conditions and the circumstances emanating from them have been experienced differently by different persons and separate countries. At some level of generality, for example, colonialism had common characteristics for all colonies and colonists; nevertheless, each suffered or enjoyed separate experiences and has developed in the post-colonial period in at least semi-autonomous ways. Thus the following analysis adheres to historical specificity and aims to describe the conditions supporting globalization. Should those change in substantial ways, the course of the future is likely to veer into a different direction than it seems to be heading now.

Power

As the fundamental concept of politics, power has been thought of in many ways. One prominent conceptualization stresses the domination of one person or entity over others, whereas another emphasizes the construction of power through interactive speech that leads to acting together (Arendt 1958, 1970). A favorite of political scientists focuses on the specific acts by which one individual or group induces another to do things that the other would not otherwise do (Dahl 1957). In a more modern formulation that draws on the French writer Foucault, Clegg (1989) stresses that power relations are reproduced through the accession of individuals to structural power and that sometimes people resist rather than cooperate in their own submission. Waltz (1979) treats power as a fund of capabilities that enables the more powerful in general to work their wills with greater regularity than can the weak. Violence seems intimately related to power (Weber 1948; Schelling 1960, 1966), although Goehler (2000) distinguishes between transitive power, which includes violence, and intransitive power, which does not. Any historical narrative about power arrangements is likely to touch on various of these formulations, for each reveals a facet of a complex set of relationships (Haugaard 1997).

In elucidating contemporary power arrangements in their historical specificity, many things need to be taken for granted. Modern science and the modern period of enlightenment comprise one dimension of the world in which we live. Scientific knowledge and its technological applications have contributed to the immense productive capacity of industry, commerce, information, and finance. Growth of the world's population, which reached one billion only in 1850 then three billion almost exactly a century later only to double before the end of the twentieth century, can largely be attributed to a reduction of the death rate through public health measures based upon modern science and technology. On the other side, the expansion of military force over the past two centuries has also occurred as a product of science and technology. Faith in human improvement and progress forms part of the enlightenment character, and modern democracy as well as conceptions of humanitarianism and human rights flow from an enlightenment commitment to the individual human being as central to social organization.

In addition, some basic forms of political organization provide a backdrop for the world's contemporary situation. Even though it frequently offers a target for transformationalists in today's world, the state and its sovereign constitution give fundamental shape and outline to the political organization of the world. From its origins in the fifteenth century, the state has provided the blueprint for political organization. In recent history, the political choice of societies emerging from colonialism turned universally to the state form. Bringing the matter forward to very recent breakups of empires, specifically the Soviet Union and Yugoslavia, successors have taken the form of states. The reason for these choices is not far to seek, for the state affords a mechanism for making autonomous political and policy decisions in a world of other states. Moreover, this advantage of the state gets reinforced by the institutions and mechanisms of international politics, such as the United Nations and other organizations that are founded by states and dedicated to perpetuating them (Lentner 1996).

Another background feature for contemporary history is provided by the nation and modern nationalism. Despite some dispute about whether nations emanate from primordial origins (Smith 1986) or are modern inventions (Greenfeld 1992), we can assume that modern nationalism dates from the time of the French and American revolutions. Both of these revolutions incorporated the idea that citizens, enjoying some fundamental rights within their respective political systems, formed the basis upon which the polity was legitimated. This democratic ideology served to mobilize citizenries into state structures. Furthermore, modern nationalism continued to be reproduced throughout the nineteenth and twentieth centuries first in Europe and the western hemisphere and later throughout the world. Nations are linked to states through the ideology of nationalism which seeks a state for every nation (Gellner 1983). As events in the Balkans in the late twentieth and early twenty-first centuries attest, nationalism and state-seeking persist vigorously.

Because of the condition of anarchy that stems logically from the principle of exclusive jurisdiction within a territory that is sovereignty, and the potential for war among states, the modern era has also seen a quest for institutionalized cooperative arrangements among states. From traditional treaties, states have formed both worldwide and regional organizations to provide mechanisms for coordinating policies and implementing agreements. Particularly in the post-World War II period, states have shaped a thick melange of organizations for many different purposes, and these organizations provide venues for policy coordination, dispute settlement, negotiating agreements that may take the form of treaties, and mechanisms that are often substituted for forthright state action. Some, such as the European Community, entail both long-term and complex cooperative mechanisms.

With these background features in mind, the distribution of power in the world early in the twenty-first century can be described by a brief historical narration of the last century and a half. Shortly after the midpoint of the nineteenth century marks the beginning of this narrative, for the major powers that have dominated much of world history entered into a phase of competition at that time. In addition, it was then that a new era began, when chemicals, electricity, the internal combustion engine, and other scientific applications formed the most visible manifestations of the second phase of industrialization.

Among the new contenders for world power, the United States had a head start, although it assumed new energy in its Civil War and the aftermath. Germany and Italy united for the first time, thus becoming new aggregates of power in international politics, although only the former ranked among the leading powers. After foreign pressures were exerted on it in the 1850s, Japan forged a new and vigorous political and economic system with the so-called Meiji Restoration in 1868. Even Russia entered the modern era with its abolition of serfdom in 1861 and its industrialization policies before World War I. Each of the major powers was driven by a distinctive ideology and set of constraints, but every one strove for a situation in which its own values and concerns could be achieved. Unsurprisingly, these incompatible strivings led to mortal conflict.

As each of these states entered the twentieth century, their aspirations clashed with established powers such as France and Britain and with those of the other aspirants. In addition to their ambitions, these rivals also formulated conceptions of how the world should be run, and these clashed on many battlefields. The twentieth century turned out to be history's bloodiest, in part because of the industrialization of war and in part because of disputes over how to rule the world. The twentieth century can be interpreted as a clash between competing capacities for industrial production and the employment of weapons in war, or as a fight between the competing ideologies of fascism and communism, on the one side, and democratic liberalism. In triumphing, the United States outproduced its rivals, and its ideology of democracy and capitalism won out over competing systems of value. Simultaneously, twentieth-century wars so weakened the traditional powers that their empires collapsed and the entire world became divided into territorial states recognized by others even in cases in which they lacked the capacity to function as states. Some of these previously subordinate states began in the mid-twentieth century to emerge with some potential in the long run for becoming major powers, specifically China, India, and Brazil.

In the early years of the twenty-first century, no other state stands in equal or near equal power with the United States, and no opposing ideology that offers an alternative to liberal democracy and capitalism is linked to a power base sufficient to challenge the dominant order in the world. This position makes the United States especially safe from the sort of devastation that might be inflicted by another power, and it leads to such influence that others have decided to join with the United States in a concert that lays down the rules for managing the world. Two incentives constrain other states to cooperate: there are positive benefits to be derived from participating in the liberal political economy and from the security protection of such a powerful country, and it takes little imagination to figure out that a fairly stable order in the world, whatever the irritations of remaining deferential, offers both comfort and predictability that would be missing should American power contract or American policy shift away from identifying its interests with the broader stable world order.

Institutions

In addition to its power and identification of its interests in a global context, the United States has also led the way to gaining the cooperation of other states through institutional arrangements that make the coordination of policies easier and steadier (Ikenberry 2001). Institutionalization has followed a pragmatic and quite diverse course.

In the late nineteenth century, the United States helped to found the Pan-American Union as a means of gaining the cooperation of western hemisphere states. At the same time, the United States retained its discretion to intervene in those same states when its interests led it to act unilaterally. Regarding China, the Open Door notes proposed cooperation of the powers in order to retain American access to Chinese markets. In contrast, with respect to Spain, the United States unilaterally decided to fight a war in Cuba and to impose a constitution on the successor government and then to wrest Puerto Rico and the Philippines from their previous colonial owner, making them American colonial possessions.

Following the turbulent interwar period and then the rocky Grand Alliance of World War II, the United States first sought to institutionalize worldwide international relations through international organizations. These included the United Nations, the International Bank for Reconstruction and Development, the International Monetary Fund, and the International Trade Organization, the last substituted after Congress failed to endorse it by the General Agreement on Tariffs and Trade. When the scheme for global cooperation foundered, particularly with reference to a German settlement, the United States together with Canada and most of the Western European countries forged the North Atlantic Treaty Organization. Less extensive arrangements in Asia tended to be accomplished by bilateral treaties. In the Middle East, informal ties with various countries including Israel and Saudi Arabia demonstrated the pragmatic and diverse character of American diplomacy.

With many strands in its bow of international instruments, the United States could choose to play its notes of national interest with a variety of partners or alone, as fit the circumstances. Thus, in 1956, the United States turned against its NATO allies Britain and France in the Suez crisis, and employed the United Nations. On the other hand, in 1999, faced with a recalcitrant United Nations Security Council, the United States drew its now nineteen NATO partners into its war against Yugoslavia over the Kosovo issue. In between those actions, the United States defied all its organizational allies and instruments and fought largely alone against North Vietnam in the 1960s and early 1970s. Similarly, in 1965, Organization of American States allies were drawn into an American intervention in the Dominican Republic; whereas the North American behemoth intervened unilaterally in Grenada in 1983 and in Panama in 1989.

With the pattern clearly established, it then becomes necessary to explain why international institutions are sometimes used and sometimes avoided, and at other times manipulated for different objectives. A beginning of an explanation lies in the recognition that the foremost institution in the world is the state. Although states possess significantly different capacities, the stronger states remain the fundamental units upon which international politics operate. States act with a combination of cooperation with others in a community and guarding of their own autonomy. For the weak, submission to the will of the strong may comprise the single option; for the strong, a range of choice persists. And for the strongest, the choices available are often quite wide-ranging.

Thus the United States can even decide not to act. From 1991 to 1995 American policy makers dithered over the breakup of Yugoslavia and accompanying wars, most prominently the extended one in Bosnia in which several "safe havens" were established by its European allies and the United Nations. More dramatically, in 1994 the United States not only made a decision not to act during the massacre resulting in genocide in Rwanda over the course of four months but also ensured that others would not intervene for lack of transport equipment available only from the American military. For most states, a failure to act in the face of pressures leads to others taking action against them, often with costly consequences. Given its unique power position, however, the United States is able more often than not to refrain from action with impunity.

Although the state persists as the most fundamental institution, the existence of cooperative international institutions entails that they have to be taken into account when authorities choose to act in international politics. In addition to providing instruments to be employed, international institutions may sometimes impose costs. For example, violations of trading rules to which a state has agreed may be followed by the imposition of retaliatory sanctions by trading partners under authority of the agreed trade regime. Military intervention in another country might precipitate a military response under authority of an international organization, such as the UN's reaction to Iraq's invasion of Kuwait in 1990. For major powers, such costs comprise a part of their calculations in determining whether to act and which action to take. Sometimes, costs can be minimized by cooptation or diplomatic and informational deflection. For example, in deciding to intervene in Caribbean countries, the United States usually attempts to bring along some of its fellow members of the Organization of American States or seeks either the endorsement or invitation of small regional countries. This is to say that for powerful countries the costs incurred from membership in international organizations are generally either minimal or can be offset by quite inexpensive supplementary actions.

The international institutional arrangement most frequently cited as a constraining force is the European Union, which has gone farther than any other international cooperative arrangement to embed states in sets of obligations that are costly to break. Given the underlying commitment of the United States to European integration (Lundestad 1998) and the decisiveness of that underpinning to the success of regional cooperation, the central issue for continued globalization is what direction would the Europeans take should the United States decide to withdraw its organizational presence from the continent.

In my judgment, developments in Europe would go in one of two directions, either of which would support the persistence of the state as the fundamental political unit in the world. The Europeans might decide to speed up and deepen their institution building, choosing a single executive and adopting a single foreign and security policy. In that case, Europe would be transformed into a very powerful state, a superpower like the United States. As an alternative direction, the European Community might disintegrate into its constituent entities, the nation-states of Germany, France, Britain, Italy, Spain, and so forth. Meanwhile, the European Community can be thought of as an extraordinary international organization that exacts higher costs than most from members tempted to deviate from agreed practices and rules. In addition, the EU has exercised substantial influence on applicant countries from eastern Europe.

Furthermore, institutionalization in Europe remains unique, for no other region in the world approaches the depth of organizational coordination achieved there. And, while some writers hold up Europe as the model for the future of the world as a whole, no evidence exists for parallel global patterns developing. Other regions have followed different paths, and neither do they offer models for the world as a whole or even for other countries (Cumings 1987).

Certainly, private corporations from the leading industrial countries have, in the conditions established by American military power and policy with an assist from other major states, continued to spread their activities of investment and trade through much of the world. With the introduction of the personal computer and rapid travel, individuals from those same states interact more extensively among themselves and with privileged persons in less developed states. These obvious facts and exceptionally interesting phenomena, however, have not transcended the basic political units and institutional arrangements that manage power in the world.

Ideas and Ideology

Although some people seek, acquire, and employ power for its own sake, with no other purpose than to impose their will on others, most power wielders link power to purpose. That is to say, most of those possessing power are imbued with and represent values that they strive to achieve. Moreover, they think and act in certain ways and must employ schemes that link specific objectives with means for achieving them. Patterns of thought and action stem from ideas that embody the ends to be achieved and the means for satisfying them. An ideology is a system of ideas linking ends and means, explanations of reality, and usually a plan or program for action to put the ideas into effect. Except in the most extremely predatory states, ideas tend to be embodied in institutions. Furthermore, when states act internationally they tend to project the values, ideas, ideologies, and means that characterize their intrinsic societies. Very powerful states, then, identify their own characteristics as preferable, and they act to reproduce their ideas and attributes in those places where their influence reaches. Inferentially, an observer may read back from an international set of arrangements to the main powers whose ideas it reflects. Ideas become effective, of course, largely because they are linked to material power.

Although many of the ideas associated with globalization phenomena have been passed on from previous eras that contributed components, the prevailing concepts in the post-Cold War period when the term has become such a buzzword derive from liberalism, specifically capitalism and democracy. But American society in particular offers other ideas to the discourse about ruling and managing the international system. These include pluralism, or the idea that nongovernmental groups should participate in public affairs, and privatization, or the idea that private entities such as firms and NGOs tend to be more effective than governments in implementing public policies. In addition, such broad conceptions as universal human rights, global governance, and international community stem from an unexamined liberal consensus (Hartz 1955).

During the Cold War the United States and the Soviet Union competed in a contest between two universalizing ideologies that sought comprehensively to organize every society on the basis of their respective principles of democratic politics and free markets on the one side and authoritarian politics and command economies. Alternatives, such as the Japanese developmental state with "soft authoritarian" politics and capitalism (Johnson 1995), existed, but they did not figure in the dominant discourse of the period, and they have not fared well since in competition of ideas. With the end of the Cold War, a novel ideology has taken hold, although it is not uncontested. This ideology, neoliberalism, promotes market principles above all, emphasizing minimal government, privatization, equal treatment of domestic and foreign investment, free trade, and unconstrained markets.

Although some scholars argue for the independent existence of ideas as explanatory variables in analysis (Goldstein and Keohane 1993; Wendt 1999), the departure from ideas by the powerful when it is convenient or feasible offers evidence that brings such a position into dispute. Instead of regarding ideas as separately existent entities, one might better treat them as embodiments of power and as rhetorical devices. The powerful do organize themselves according to ideas that they prefer, and they frequently employ ideas to justify their preferences. On the other hand, the United States more often than not proclaims the idea of free trade but then adopts protectionist measures to shield its own producer and consumer groups. Neoliberals expound the virtues of free markets but seem never reluctant to mount rescue operations of both public and private entities whose activities jeopardize financial or commercial interests.

Authority

When power is exercised by some people over others in circumstances in which both sides agree that there is an obligation to obey, the wielders act with authority. In states with established governments and ordered societies based on justice, authority tends to be recognized to such an extent that citizens obey laws even when they disagree with them, and violators of law recognize that they are doing wrong in the face of legitimate authority.

It needs to be made clear that authority does not exist in those circumstances in which action requires the agreement of the actors, such as international interventions done in implementing a resolution of the United Nations Security Council, whether it is done with or without the consent of the state on whose territory the action takes place. Neither does authority exist in an action in which one or more states acts to coerce a state, even though the acting states rhetorically invoke the "authority" of the international community or an organization that adheres to formal procedures.

The basis upon which those running a political system claim authority to rule and those subject to it find an obligation to obey forms one important line of inquiry in political philosophy as well as an important practical issue for political leaders and followers. In today's dominant discourse democracy, or the election of leaders by citizens, prevails as the main justification for ruling and obeying. Until they lost confidence in themselves, the communist leaders of the Soviet Union justified their rule by the claim that they possessed special insight into the dynamics of history. Developmental states rely on their accomplishments in economic growth to legitimize their rule and expectations of obedience. Kings claim divinely endorsed succession and thus obedience to the representative of God; theocratic rulers profess to rule in the direct name of God or a prophet. Hobbes and Locke regarded some sort of social contract to shape the basis upon which command and obedience should be based. Plato and Aristotle regarded some sort of justice or the provision of the conditions for pursuing a good life as the foundation for rule and compliance. Claims that they act on behalf of specific nationalisms provide the justification for some leaders to demand the obedience of those identifying with their respective nations.

What all of these rationales have in common is the quest for some intellectual or moral basis upon which to found systems of rule. This is the dimension supplementing violence that Gramsci (1971; Bobbio 1988) included in his concept of hegemony. Although in some circumstances for short periods of time violence alone may afford a basis for rule, the long term and the need for stability require an intellectual or a moral foundation. In addition, as Machiavelli indicated, effectiveness also must be evident for authority to prevail.

In the world of the early twenty-first century, many efforts are expended to advocate for international authority and to build authoritative institutions on a worldwide level. Such efforts are often put forward under the rubric of global governance. Frequently advocates present the idea that given the inevitable march of globalization there exists not only a need but a requirement that broad rules and regimes transcending the state must be put into place to reflect the inexorability of developments. The spirited activities of nongovernmental organizations are offered as evidence that the state no longer monopolizes authority in international relations, and a new ideology of civil society in which NGOs are termed CSOs (civil society organizations) has arisen in an attempt to legitimize the aspirations to power of advocacy groups.

When one examines the specific mechanisms by which international institutions are put into place, however, one notes that treaties among states persist as the mechanism for founding organizations and setting rules. Furthermore, the operation of the organizations, their resolutions, and the rules are made effective only by the actions of states or of entities that the states have authorized to act. Thus the search for authority in a globalizing world leads directly to states.

Of course, some states are not constituted on the basis of authority; other states continue ineffective. But well-ordered and legitimate states clearly possess authority. Their leaders rule with confidence and competence; their citizens obey routinely. The same cannot be said for any international organization.

Democracy

The term democracy has often been used cynically, a tribute to the power of the idea. Several communist states, East Germany, for example, called themselves "people's democratic republics," even though they remained repressive states with secret police and without contested elections or the freedoms to speak and organize that are essential to the practice of democracy.

In the years since the collapse of communism the term, rather than being invoked cynically, has tended to be employed instrumentally and rhetorically. Most often, democracy has been conflated with pluralism, and the peripheral secondary aspects such as petitioning governments are treated as the whole of democracy.

Such a rhetorical shift tries to provide legitimacy for the activities of self-appointed groups that advocate their views in public in attempts to influence such intergovernmental organizations as the World Trade Organization or diplomatic forums. As noted above, a new rhetoric that presents such groups as civil society organizations is a further attempt to legitimize advocacy as democracy, even though no democratic political institutions are in place and democratic consent is largely absent in the circumstances. For at least some advocates, there is an explicit attempt to raise the status of self-selected groups to the level of recognition as legitimate participants in governance. For example, some people wish for treatment of lobbyists as if they were governments:

> NGOs are, more and more, performing part of the functions traditionally performed by governments (viz. representing people's interests). There should be an appropriate way for tax payers to have the option of paying a certain amount of their taxes directly to CSOs of their choice. *(Kaul 2001, p. 5)*

Although such discourse became increasingly common in the years just before and after the turn of the century, it tends to hijack rather than highlight the essential meaning of democracy.

If, instead of treating democracy rhetorically one deals with it analytically, the term has to be treated in the context of an institutionalized political system in which those who govern are chosen from time to time by those who are governed. Thus democracy requires that elections must occur and that there be citizens who possess the freedom to speak and to organize themselves into parties that contest the elections. In addition, democracy rests upon a culture in which both elections and governmental decisions are made by majority rule, in which losers accept the legitimacy of the choices, recognizing that they retain the rights necessary to advocate, organize, and run in elections to accomplish change. Citizenship entails membership in a state in which recognition is given to citizens by one another and by the authorities of the state. Governors, those who wield the power of the state, must be responsive to the citizenry in listening to those who express grievances or advocate new laws and policies; in case they fail to be sufficiently responsive, the voters may turn them out of office in subsequent elections.

In this sense, the institutionalization and practice of democracy has grown. As stipulated by Huntington (1991), modern democracy has advanced in three waves occurring, respectively, in the late eighteenth century, following World War II, and forward from the 1970s. Even though a recession in numbers of democratic political systems has succeeded each increase, there has been an overall historical addition. For the citizens of those countries, the practices of democracy offer opportunities to enhance both their autonomy and their political effectiveness as members of a community. They can help to shape the policies that affect them, and they are able to oppose state activities deleterious to the well-being of both the society and the individuals comprising it. For example, Drèze and Sen (1989) have demonstrated that famine has never occurred in circumstances in which citizens have access to a free press as a means of bringing conditions to the attention of authorities.

On the other hand, even democratic political systems cannot entirely prevent individuals and groups from pursuing their particularistic or selfish interests dressed up in the regalia of public advocacy of policies to serve the common good. Neither can such a political system entirely stop elites from rent-seeking, corruption, and other activities that serve their personal and group interests. All that a democracy can do is to structure an arena within which the parties—individuals and groups, elites and masses—can struggle over policy. Much of the activity in the struggle turns out to be self-serving. From time to time, however, actual community interests and public purposes can be formulated and served.

Another claim for democracy that has achieved some prominence avers that liberal democratic countries form a separate peace (Doyle 1983, 1986). This assertion not only posits that liberal democratic countries never go to war with one another but also implies that, with the increase in the numbers of democratic polities, fewer wars will occur in the world at large. Additionally, in the related thesis put forward by Singer and Wildavsky (1993), the world can be divided into separate zones, respectively, of peace and turmoil.

These Manichean views contributed to the American policy discourse in the 1990s that divided the world dichotomously into cooperative states and those either not fully integrated in the imperium or rogue states. Moreover, a Manichean view prevails in determining against which states violent and interventionary actions may be taken. Excluded are powerful states and those fitting current definitions of democratic states. Other states, weak and nondemocratic, are subject to violent and peaceful interventions by the powerful states and their instruments, the international intergovernmental organizations and NGOs. Although the justifications for such interventions range fairly widely, depending upon the circumstances and interests involved, the powers mainly justify their interventionary actions by referring to human rights, law, and justice.

Human Rights, Law, and Justice

In the late nineteenth century advocacy groups in liberal societies promoted the expansion of international law to include peace and to constrain some of the effects of modern technology such as by outlawing hollow-nosed bullets. Some societies also sought to develop international regulations to govern treatment of prisoners of war. Following World War I such efforts were extended to forbidding the use of poison gas and even to outlawing war in the Kellogg–Briand pact. This last as well as other treaties and informal agreements testify to the success of such efforts in inducing governments to make formal arrangements. In addition, some agitation led to the widespread belief that opinion had hardened in opposition to targeting civilians in war. Thus, while air power strategists such as Douhet and Mitchell were formulating visions of winning wars exclusively by broad-area aerial bombing, public opinion and leaderships in the liberal countries thought that a norm prohibiting the deliberate terror bombing of civilians prevailed.

As Guernica and then Coventry and London, and then Hamburg and Dresden and Tokyo and Hiroshima and Nagasaki were bombed from the air, and civilians and property were alike incinerated, it was impossible to hold that there was any effective extant constraint on the deliberate massacre of civilians. These acts of war were replicated within German society and territories that Germany conquered in the genocide against the Jews and other groups deemed undesirable by the Nazis. Similarly, Germans, Soviets, British, Japanese, and Americans mercilessly killed prisoners and soldiers who had surrendered. Dower (1986) has portrayed how the Americans and the Japanese did so with venomous hatred based upon racially stereotyping the enemy. In light of atrocities of the Second World War, it was difficult to claim that there were effective restrictions on the brutality of warfare.

Then, in Vietnam, the United States used aerial bombing against civilian populations and, in some cases, massacred civilians at close range, as in the My Lai incident. Similarly, in Sudan over the course of thirty years, in Nigeria during the Biafra secession war, in Angola's civil war, in the wars associated with the disintegration of Yugoslavia in the 1990s, in the Russian suppression of Chechyna, in the 1994 Rwanda genocide, in the DR Congo at the turn of the century, and in the Sierra Leone rebellion in the late 1990s and early 2000s, civilians continued to be targeted by soldiers.

What became known as ethnic cleansing in the 1992–1995 Bosnian war repeated actions that had occurred in the United States in the nineteenth century when the American army (acting on orders of the national government, which was responsive to and supported by the white population) removed Indians to reservations. In less dramatic but parallel terms, the United States maintained throughout much of its history racial segregation of black citizens and tolerated private terrorism of blacks by lynching, torture, and other forms of intimidation. Of course, this way of life succeeded centuries of slavery.

Opposition to these practices has been sustained over the last century and a half, expressing values similar to those embodied in the doctrines of globalization. Even during times of slavery, abolitionists militated against slavery; some advocates of equality and civil rights opposed lynching, segregation, and so forth. There appears to have been little if any opposition to the ethnic cleansing of indigenous peoples from European-derived areas in the Americas.

Such liberal aspirations as treating people as equals and tolerance for nondominant groups, as well as bringing under control the weapons and practices of war that have grown up in the industrial era, also inspired advocates in international politics. The massive violations that had occurred in World War II prompted renewed, and official, efforts to punish perpetrators of so-called war crimes and crimes against humanity or any other violations of the laws of war. These efforts began with the trials under ex post facto law of some Nazis and some Japanese officials. At the same time, the victors who conducted these trials ensured that the Japanese emperor remained isolated from any blame for the actions committed in his name; in addition, for intelligence-gathering reasons, the Americans screened the Japanese Unit 731 from any accountability for the atrocities that its personnel had committed. Of course, no personnel of any of the victors were brought to trial for killing prisoners, shooting surrenderees, machine-gunning or bombing civilians, or any other acts of war.

Building upon the precedents of the Nuremberg and Tokyo trials, the liberal states have promoted expansion of the concepts of prosecutable war crimes and crimes against humanity. Largely dormant during the Cold War, these positions have become stronger in the wake of the liberal triumph; a war crimes tribunal was created to deal with actions done during the Bosnian war, and a similar tribunal was added following the Rwanda genocide. In 1997, the movement expanded with the signing of an agreement in Rome to create an international criminal court designed to punish those acting in unacceptable ways in wartime.

Meanwhile, in 1948 the United Nations General Assembly passed the Universal Declaration on Human Rights, and many other resolutions embodying basic liberal ideas have subsequently been passed. In addition, a number of formal agreements incorporating liberal principles of justice have been signed.

Advocacy and action in the post-Cold War period have gone forward through the activities of the United Nations, many nongovernmental organizations, and some governments, in trying to give effect to liberal principles by intervention to suppress conflict in weak states. Obvious failures in Somalia, Bosnia, Rwanda, East Timor, and elsewhere leave the fate of the attempted application of liberal legal principles internationally in an ambiguous condition. Although a widespread movement has been able to sustain interest in such activities, despite the failures, only the course of time and events will determine whether they advance as liberals gain increasing power, or retreat in the face of such brutal realities as the setbacks before and during World War II.

Clearly, the application of liberal principles will continue to be unlikely to be brought to bear against powerful states such as Russia or by others against the United States, or against such recalcitrant states as Iraq and Afghanistan. Only violence, against which the liberal principles are arrayed, will determine domination in such areas. The invasions and consequent toppling of regimes in Afghanistan in 2001 and in Iraq in 2003 offer testimony to the employment of violence against recalcitrant states.

Sovereignty

Much of the debate over the promise of the triumph of liberal principles all over the world, both with reference to the market and to the extension of liberal views of international law, has been conducted in a vocabulary in which the concept of sovereignty figures centrally. As occurs with respect to many words employed in public debates, people assign varied meanings to the term sovereignty. Krasner (1999) summarized usages into these broad categories: (1) the legal principle of exclusion of others from a territory, (2) recognition by others, (3) control of transborder transactions, and (4) effective exercise of legitimate authority within domestic jurisdiction. The first two involve legality whereas the last two entail control. An important thrust in globalization advocacy argues that states have lost a good deal of control over transborder transactions to market forces; another aspect of the debate attempts to make exceptions based on legal or moral grounds for intervention by powerful states on the territories of weak states. This last line of argument seeks to transfer legitimate authority to international organizations and institutions operating under agreed and established procedures, that is, to extend liberal principles of governance to international relations.

Too often the legal principle of exclusive jurisdiction is conflated with autonomy, and the logical corollary of exclusive jurisdiction—international anarchy—is conflated with conflict. As Waltz has emphasized, anarchy means that no authoritative government exists above states, leaving each state with the autonomy to decide how to cope with the pressures from the international system and the actions of other states. Thus international politics presents the same sort of tension, replicated throughout social life, between autonomy and engagement with a community, although the bonds of community and the constraints of law and practice are substantially weaker in international relations than those that exist within a well-ordered state.

Nevertheless, the increased volumes of trade and financial transactions, and information and cultural exchanges that comprise globalization pressures present novel tensions. Governments dedicated to economic growth face the advantages offered by foreign investments and, on the other hand, the vulnerabilities incurred by opening up their economies to external competition. They face the sometimes agonizing choices of disciplining their own societies' malpractice or waiting for interventions by IFIs to blame for imposing needed discipline. For some countries, the transformation from the Cold War bipolarity to the single-centered international system in its wake has required more self-reliance and discipline because strategic allies no longer offer the shelter that community often did in the context of major power competition.

Conclusion

The view of globalization and politics presented above has tried to illuminate the conditions and choices that underlie current arrangements and to provide a brief glimpse of some of the visions held by the advocates of a globalized integrated world, as well as a critique of those visions. Current circumstances prevail because of the dominant, unchallenged power position of the United States and the liberal coalition that it leads. At the moment, no significant challenger has appeared on the horizon, nor has any alternative conception of ruling the world. As long as American power and policy commitment remain, the extant circumstances are likely to continue to be reproduced and strengthened, but, should the United States falter or should its allies lose confidence, then circumstances might undergo substantial change. In short, I have argued that globalization does not constitute an inexorable juggernaut leading the world onward. Instead, phenomena and pressures associated with global integration rely upon specific historical power arrangements and political choices made by specific agents.

Obviously, not everyone agrees with that analysis, for the globalization discourse is quite a varied one. The variety of understandings comprises the subject of the next chapter.

2

Alternative Conceptions of the Contemporary World

Introduction

Post-Cold War uncertainty provided fertile ground for a variety of analytic perspectives that contended to give conceptual shape to the new era. Fukuyama (1989) gained considerable notice when he presented his thesis that history had ended, and Huntington's (1993, 1996) claim that the world was entering a period in which broad civilizations defined the faultlines for international conflict engendered an extensive debate among scholars and policy makers. Less prominent but very important for analysis are perspectives presented to the scholarly community.

Three distinct viewpoints organize the scholarly debates. Realists emphasize continuing power shifts and concerns with security (Brown et al. 1995). More optimistically, a liberal position gives a more prominent place to international cooperation, to international institutions, and to private entities and activities, and, thus, economics. Some liberals advocate global governance (Keohane and Martin 1995; Finkelstein 1995). Finally, a critical theory perspective challenges the premises of rationality and materialism shared by the first two approaches and asserts that new sorts of communities and institutions can be constructed (Wendt 1994, 1995, 1999; Ruggie 1998) by willing human agents.

Particularly with reference to the first two positions, the lines are not wholly fixed, for some realists (Waltz 1993) expect that in future states will compete much more in economic than in military terms, thus diminishing their concerns with relative gains that give more advantages to one country than another. Even some of those embracing the constructivist school of thought regard material interests—mixed in uncalculated proportion with ideas and norms—to be strongly determining causes of state behavior (Katzenstein 1996; Wendt 1999).

There is broad agreement on two matters: the breakdown of the bipolar global structure (Mearsheimer 1990) and the spread of a primarily economic but multidimensional globalization process (Kennedy 1993; Held et al. 1999). In addition, the sustained and impressive economic growth in East Asia is indisputable (Gilpin 1987, 2000, 2001) even in the wake of the 1997–1998 economic crisis. Beyond that, however, contention reigns among the three analytical perspectives.

Some believe that politics has been transformed so profoundly that a new politics with world citizens attentive to global issues has come into play and that states are parochial and narrow (Luard 1990). Others perceive that the control of modern technology affords the United States the tools of military and political domination in a world of competing states (Nye and Owens 1996). At the same time, Nye also portrays the world as complex, including other arenas in which military prowess does not apply (Nye 2002). Certain writers see the future in Atlantic or Western European developments (Kupchan 1996; Ruggie 1993), whereas others think that they observe the decline of the West and the rise of East Asia (Weede 1996). Perceptions range from complex and fragmenting turbulence in the world (Rosenau 1990) to possibilities for constructing a world state (Wendt 1994).

One of the most prominent interpretations of the contemporary world goes by the name of globalization. This term encompasses a wide range of views drawn from a variety of traditions. Some advocates, especially those from business and business-oriented economics, stress that not only does change characterize the world's contemporary condition but that the direction of change is increasing the roles of the market and of transnational linkages among individuals and groups and diminishing the roles and functions of states. Undoubtedly, communications and transportation technologies have tended to form new linkages across state borders, increase international trade and investment, and create cultural phenomena neither linked to territorial space nor confined to originating groups. Nevertheless, it does not necessarily follow that states are in the process of disintegration or that sovereignty has been rendered obsolete.

The State, Modernity, and Postmodernity

Broadly speaking, this book examines the hypothesis that globalization pressures contribute to state diffusion, state formation, and state building. This proposition opposes the more conventional, alternative hypothesis which holds that states are being diminished, weakened, and eroded by globalization.

Part of the quarrel of these two views about empirical reality finds its roots in theoretical and conceptual differences over the state and the nature of the international political economy. The most commonly accepted conception of the state is Weber's (1978), in which the state forms a coercive apparatus distinct from civil society and holds a monopoly on the right to use legitimate violence within a defined territory. Widely adopted by such writers as Evans, Rueschmeyer, and Skocpol (1985), this twentieth-century definition of the state replaced an older conception in Western political philosophy that effectively ended with Hegel (1952) and Rousseau (1973) in which the state formed not simply a coercive apparatus but also embodied a rational deliberative process and encompassed civil society which remained as a component of the state. For Hegel (1952) and Rousseau (1973), civil society expressed the particular, or selfish, interests of individuals, an ethically neutral, marketlike association (Habermas 1987, p. 39). The tension between the particular—embodied in civil society—and the universal is resolved by Hegel in the institutionalized state. In Rousseau, similarly, individual and common differences were noted, but a general will giving expression to the interests of the state as a whole seems achievable.

More recently, Hegelian and Rousseauian ideas have been adopted by writers such as Giddens (1987), although mediated to a large degree by a Marxist, materialist understanding rather than a Hegelian focus on ideals and ethics. Taking a sociological approach derived from Durkheim (1986), Giddens stresses the broad state functions of providing deliberation and surveillance.

Another view, expressed by Cox (Cox with Sinclair 1996), emphasizes that change emanates from the forces of production in civil society and from the international environment. In turn, the changes foster different kinds of states.

Nevertheless, a liberal conception of the state has reigned since the nineteenth century as the foremost view. In this perspective, the state appears as the sphere of domination, whereas the market, civil society, is treated as the realm of freedom. Division occurs among the supporters of the liberal perspective between those who would reduce the state to an absolute minimum and those supporting an active interventionist role for government. The Great Depression marked one dividing line, before which those supporting an expansive market and a minimal state reigned and after which supporters of an active government prevailed. In the wake of World War II, Keynesian perspectives dominated but were slowly undermined. In a period that began in the early 1970s there was a rising hostility toward the state by supply-side economists and ideologues. With the election of Margaret Thatcher in Britain and Ronald Reagan in the United States, a new version of liberalism, called neoliberalism, gained prominence, and a "Washington consensus" (Williamson 1990; Kamarck 2000) centered on fomenting an expanded market and a minimal state took hold in official policy matters. More recent thinking stresses the importance of the state as essential to economic development (World Bank 1997), and originators of the "Washington consensus" have to some extent revised their thinking about appropriate policy reforms (Williamson 2003).

Habermas (1987, pp. 38–39) argues that the separation of political rule and the capitalist economy emerged in the nineteenth century as an empirical development with which philosophers have grappled; and he regards as "tendentious" Hegel's solution, based on a principle of subjectivity, of bringing the individual and the universal together in a "higher-level subjectivity of the state over the subjective freedom of the individual." Habermas (1987, p. 40) prefers "a democratic self-organization of society" that mediates the universal and the individual "by the higher-level intersubjectivity of an uncoerced formation of will within a communication community existing under constraints toward cooperation," which sounds something like Rousseau's general will and Giddens' deliberation. Habermas' normative position clearly supports the democratic state as the only available institution to defend modernity:

For a society to influence itself in this sense it must have, on the one hand, a reflexive center, where it builds up a knowledge of itself in a process of self-understanding, and, on the other hand, an executive system that, as a part, can act for the whole and influence the whole. (p. 357)

Until now, the democratic, constitutional nation-state that emerged from the French Revolution was the only identity formation successful on a world-historical scale that could unite these two moments of the universal and the particular without coercion. (pp. 365–366)

Habermas' project not only illuminates the discourse of modernity but also brings light to bear on what is known as post-modernity, another strand of thought involved in the treatment of globalization. Post-modernity's origins may be found in Nietzsche (Habermas 1995, Ch. IV) who, together with his followers, criticizes modernity and rejects the concept of reason and the philosophy of the Enlightenment. In other words, post-modernism represents less a new stage of history than a renewed attack, under different guise, on modernity. Like Habermas, who defends modernity, Berman (1992, pp. 46–47) argues on behalf of "the progressive drives and universalistic hopes that are close to modernism's heart." Citing the vitality and diversity of creative work in many realms of culture, Berman avers, "The fact that modernist work can go on thriving in so many different modes is a sign that the modernist project is as viable and fruitful as ever."

These arguments suggest that continuity rather than discontinuity more accurately frames contemporary life. Despite technological change and increasing economic integration throughout the world, the world early in the twenty-first century more nearly resembles conditions of a century earlier than it differs. After considering the claims of post-modern critics who deny it, one still concludes that reason remains a fixture of human endeavor. Thus globalization trends comprise a continuous process rather than a discontinuous one. Even though the term may have emerged as a buzzword only in the 1990s, the phenomena that it denotes go back much farther. The telegraph and the computer fall on the same continuum of rapid communication among people over long distances, even though the capacity and dispersed use of the computer mark impressive changes.

What has changed in the last 150 years or so is the rise to dominance of the United States and a coalition that supports a liberal international political economy. During the course of the twentieth century, the anti-Enlightenment forces of fascism were defeated by force and the predatory forces of communism, by production, leaving liberalism triumphant. Relative power and hegemonial leadership have grown, but an ideological thread has remained consistent.

Despite the shifting stresses on the balance of state and market among liberals, the basic conception that the state should remain minimal while the market should expand formed an important component of American ideology during the Cold War. In such historic undertakings as the Marshall Plan, the United States promoted this view of the state. Even greater reliance was placed on the market in American relations with Latin America. With the end of the Cold War, this dominant view has been given practical flesh as private foreign investment and finance have mushroomed to proportions difficult to have imagined in the years following World War II. A certain irony attaches to this development, for the spread of liberal ideology and the proliferation of free markets associated with globalization have resulted from the growth of power of the hegemonic states (Huntington 1981, pp. 246-259).

Writers in the field of international politics have stressed the importance of states as repositories of power (Morgenthau 1973; Waltz 1979) in relationship to one another. Gilpin (1987, 2001) emphasized this power in the creation of systems of international political economy but also pointed out the reciprocal effects of economics on politics, noting that the strength of hegemonic system founders may be undermined by the process of uneven development whereby competitor states may rise to a position of challenger to the hegemon. Others have compared states and markets as possessors of power (Stopford and Strange 1991), arguing that somehow firms within markets may gain greater control over outcomes than states. Indeed, the argument gets carried so far as to be formulated as "the retreat of the state" (Strange 1996). On the other hand, some writers make a crucial distinction between developmental and predatory states (Evans 1995), a difference that has been accepted more broadly (World Bank 1997). Almost as an afterthought in the post-Cold War period, developmental states may also be contrasted with centrally planned economies, for they are invariably conceived as states with market economies.

Thus the distinction between developmental and predatory states turns out to be a modern one. Predatory states are those in which an independent civil society remains weak or suppressed and the wealth accumulated in the economy is appropriated by a small elite that monopolizes power in the society. In contrast, a liberal state is one in which two distinct realms, government and economy, exist in tension. Whatever its flaws, the liberal state has proven its superior productive capacity that increases wealth in a society. It is the spread of this principle of political and economic organization of society that is often referred to as economic globalization.

Inasmuch as markets are central to thinking about globalization, it remains important to be clear about the juxtaposition of states and markets. Much of the thinking about globalization fudges fact and preference by regarding the spread of market mechanisms as inevitable but, at the same time, advising governments that they "must" allow such mechanisms to operate (Rosecrance 1986), thus conceding that states control access to their territories and retain autonomous choices regarding their participation in capitalist economic systems. Clearly, states that take advantage of the benefits of globalization processes are developmental states, not predatory states or states characterized by centrally planned economies.

In this context, the conventional globalization thesis holds that states recede in the face of market pressures, public governing mechanisms being replaced by private systems of regulation (Sassen 1996) and state-based governance being substituted by international or global governance institutions (Keohane 1989; Commission on Global Governance 1995).

In stark contrast, this study demonstrates that developmental states grow over time in strength vis-à-vis markets, and the more successful of them improve their positions in the international system relative to other states. Moreover, through institutionalization, successful developmental states also gain capacities to improve citizen welfare, provide security, and make available increased amounts of public goods that engender the conditions for additional wealth production. None of these capacities accrues to private firms and market mechanisms, although these do contribute to the wealth and well-being of citizens and their states, which accumulate resources at the individual, family, firm, and state levels. In other words, rather than undermining states, markets contribute to conditions that require their strengthening.

The histories of the United States and other leading countries demonstrate that effective governments provided the bases for the growth of national markets. In the United States, consolidation of states' debts after the Revolution and territorial expansion through purchase and conquest prepared the way for a national market. Even in those cases where private activities led the way, as in frontier settlements, it was necessary for the national government to establish order and to legislate rules under which private activities could flourish. Despite the complex economic integration tying the country together, a Civil War broke the United States apart. It then took a Union triumph in the clash of arms from 1861 to 1865 to lay the groundwork for unleashing the massive industrialization process that brought the United States to the position in 1914 of the world's wealthiest country (Maddison 1995). Subsequently, as the economy continued to expand, government at all levels of the federal system took on additional tasks and became increasingly institutionalized. Following World War II, the hegemonic position of the United States in the noncommunist world enabled it to promote the internationalization of markets, and the end of the Cold War marked the demise of all effective alternatives to the liberal arrangements advocated by the dominant liberal coalition.

In the sense that other models that provided for greater government management of the economy have been eclipsed, the contemporary world does provide greater scope for private activities, for markets to operate. However, that occurs internationally only because powerful states have created the conditions for it and promote the extant arrangements. Should the world evolve to the place in which private activities actually supplant the strong institutionalized states that guarantee the operation of markets, then markets would begin to erode and eventually collapse, for strong states remain essential to the operation of markets.

Greider (1997, p.18) observes that the global economy has a tendency to divide "every society into new camps of conflicting economic interests." On the other hand, it is in the nature of particular interests to be divided, so that globalization pressures merely work their effects in somewhat novel ways on normal, specific interest cleavages within societies. Those cleavages need to be managed by states that provide institutions for conflict resolution.

In the contemporary world, many states have shown themselves incapable of maintaining social cohesion, and ethnic nationalism emerged in the 1990s as more prominent than previously. Part of the problem in this pattern lies in the undeveloped stage of state formation. States have entered into the international system and been recognized by other states in a juridical sense (Jackson and Rosberg 1982) but remain in a stage of formation as very incomplete empirical actors in an effective governing sense. Even when fissures emerge along ethnic and nationalistic lines, groups quest to build states as the mechanisms by which they can achieve their aspirations. If one takes states as given and not in need of construction, and particularly should one hold a hostile attitude toward the very conception of state, then any weaknesses that appear in the world seem to offer evidence that other forces or actors are gaining at the expense of states. From a developmental perspective, however, in which states are built and decay, these other entities are not contenders against the state but rather there exists a flow in which interdependent participants wax and wane.

Interdependence does not imply that the participants are functionally equivalent, for they are not. As profit-seeking entities, firms remain particularistic, with no responsibility for a common good. The philosophical foundation of a liberal, free-market economy, laid down by Adam Smith (1970/1776), avers that the common good is promoted by the selfish interacting behaviors of individuals and firms pursuing only their own interests.

On the other hand, states are organs of deliberation (Giddens 1987) and givers and enforcers of law and regulation, with the participation of and on behalf of their citizenry. States provide the public goods—such as infrastructure, macroeconomic management, currency, and rule of law—that make it possible for complex markets to operate. Additionally, states maintain relations with other states and accumulate and exercise the power in order to protect their relative positions in the international system (Waltz 1979).

Not everyone agrees with such an analysis of functional differences, and normative preferences are often far apart. These varying attitudinal stances also affect views of globalization. In the state formation view adopted in this study, a regard for states as aggregates of power (Waltz 1979) remains central both as an analytical concept and as a normative preference, for only states have the capacities to accomplish public purposes and to provide the public goods necessary for complex economic activity to go forward. At the same time, states offer deliberative processes and other governing mechanisms for the pursuit of justice, and they remain institutions that can provide both security and welfare for their citizens, activities that fall outside purely economic functions.

On the other side, some writers express intense hostility toward the state, regarding it as an obstacle to an economically more rational system. For example, Ohmae (1995, p. 131) writes that states "combine things at the wrong level of aggregation." His analysis does not indicate what "wrong" means, but the context makes it clear that his focus rests on the firm and on economic activity. He regards much state activity as economically irrational, indeed, even criminal. In sharp contrast to Hegel's notion that the state operates in the service of common good, Ohmae (1995, p. 130) refers to "often extortionate demands [from interest groups] ... [including a] common level of public services."

In this study, the view that the state is diminishing or eroding is rejected. My view is that Waters (1995, p. 33) is wrong when he argues that "states are now surrendering sovereignty to international and supranational organizations as well as to more localized political units." In my judgment, Waters (1995, p. 122) is completely mistaken when he offers this opinion: "If states survive globalization then it cannot be counted the force that it currently appears to be." One reason that this viewpoint has gone astray is that the author has not recognized that states are essential for globalization to take place.

My study adopts a position close to that of Panitch (1996, p. 109) when he writes, "[T]he state has ... been a fundamental constitutive element in the very process of extension of capitalism in our time." Strong institutionalized states have provided the foundation for the emergence and expansion of national markets; and hegemonic states remain the essential underpinning for the growth of international markets.

Moreover, states provide the essential framework within which deliberative processes of public decision making can occur. The stance of this study shares the view of White (1995, p. 113) when he declaims, "[T]he national state remains the only viable real-world framework for the democratic political system." In addition, with only a different emphasis on causation, this undertaking argues along lines similar to those of White (1995, p. 119) when he declares, "The most decisive point is that historically the national state is itself a creation of the globalization process.... As the globalization process continues to grow and develop, so will the national state."

States clearly have to cope with tremendous pressures emanating from the international political economy, other states, firms, and nongovernmental organizations. The conventional interpretation of globalization would hypothesize an erosion of the state as a result of these pressures. In contrast, my state formation interpretation expects that states will increase in strength as they are built over time and face the pressures.

Here is the definition of globalization that I employ. It excludes other meanings that have been used in different contexts. Globalization means increasing connections across the world. Although the connections focus most fundamentally and substantially on political and economic matters, they extend to cultural exchange in many directions and from many sources, transfer of technology from more scientifically advanced societies to others, sharing of ideas broadly through mass media and other channels such as religious organizations, rapid spread of communicable diseases, and the international transmission of illicit goods and services as well as violence. This view rejects the alternative meaning in which fundamental arrangements are being transformed (Held et al. 1999; Cerny 2000), with power and authority flowing away from the state and toward firms, associations, and international organizations such that the world may be thought of as a single coherent unit.

In my conception, globalization may be dated from the mid-nineteenth century and regarded as a set of processes that, with the exception of some interruption between 1914 and 1945, have been largely continuous (Lentner 2000b). Thus, as used here, globalization is neither an ancient nor a very recent phenomenon nor a new period of history after the Cold War (Friedman 1999). Globalization expresses developments in a modern international system (Hirst and Thompson 1996), in contrast to a global one, for the globe cannot be treated usefully as a unit (Waltz 1979, 1986, 1993, 2000). To try to do so leads to substantial misunderstanding.

Outline of Book

Following the introduction, the book is divided into three parts. This chapter and the succeeding two examine a variety of perspectives on power and change in the contemporary era. Another major part describes the system of hegemony of liberal states, including the liberal international political economy, management in the contemporary world, and developmental states. In the third major part, the relations between the rich and strong on the one hand and the weak and poor in the connected world are analyzed.

The themes of this book are explored systematically, first by examining in the next chapter the issues of globalization and power in order to understand the nature of the contemporary world and its governance system. Basically, the argument is that the international political economy remains international rather than global, with power continuing to reside with states that provide the foundations for the operation of an international market. Despite the wide range of activities of private firms and organizations in an increasingly integrated international economy, states have to perform a range of tasks for markets to operate effectively. Moreover, politics involves moral choices, a task for which the state is equipped, whereas markets possess no function for making ethical determinations. The politics of the international political economy involves maintaining dominant groups within the major countries forming the dominant, or hegemonic, coalition worldwide.

Although the dominant liberal ideology elides differences between states and markets and between global and domestic problems, Chapter 4 takes up the division between international and state problems. Examined from a global perspective, political economy exhibits inequality, unevenness, disparate power, and diversity. Moreover, various sorts of organizations operate internationally in addressing such political and economic issues as preservation of the natural environment, population growth, migration of people, trafficking in drugs, criminal activities, spread of disease, war, internal disorder, and so forth. In addition to states, international organizations, firms, and nongovernmental organizations participate in the politics and economics of international relations. Specific state problems take on quite a different coloration from international ones, for state-building and maintenance of position in the international system carry quite different overtones from great power-denominated stability and other management considerations in the international system as a whole.

Hegemony in the liberal international political economy forms the content of Chapter 5, in which the main outlines of the paramount arrangements for managing the international system are presented. This chapter describes the three main regimes for security, trade, and finance that have been put into place by the leading powers under the auspices of United States leadership. In addition, economic integration schemes such as the European Union and trends in economic development throughout the world are analyzed. Finally, the chapter examines the mechanisms of management of the international political economy and coping with such phenomena as humanitarian crises, failed states, and backsliding states.

Chapter 6 describes the ways in which power is managed in the contemporary world. Continued maintenance of the hegemonic structure requires the active support and military power of the United States and its allies in the international system and the spread and maintenance of the liberal state form to other countries. The chapter examines the foundations and conditions for the extensive roles given to private enterprise, voluntary groups, and individuals in the contemporary world. Sources of authority in the world are also identified.

Within the context of the liberal international political economy, developmental states form and are built. In Chapter 7, developmental states are contrasted with centrally planned economies and predatory states. Then the chapter traces changes over time through imitation, institutionalization, and increasing autonomy. As states are built, they take on increasingly complex functions that are analyzed here in terms of the legal order and public goods that they provide as well as developments in citizenship and democracy. In addition, many other functions or tasks that states perform are examined. These include political functions to provide security, order, and human rights. Additionally, states carry out economic functions related to education, entrepreneurship, planning, technology, and savings and investments.

In Chapter 8, the matters that developmental states undertake in responding to globalization pressures shape the agenda. Specifically, developmental states have many tasks relating to the international economy and in forging their respective positions within it. In addition, states engage in complex politics that shapes their ability to act both domestically and internationally. Furthermore, states negotiate with both other governments and with foreign business interests; and they deal with nongovernmental organizations.

The subject matter of Chapter 9 comprises civil society in the context of globalization. The chapter treats each of two concepts, civil society and conditions of peace, in turn, discusses the relationship between them, and offers an explanation of the underlying structural power conditions that give rise to the present situation. Chapter 10 takes up the matter of citizenship within the context of globalization discourses. The analysis makes the points that politics is fundamental to the processes of change occurring in the world and that the dynamics stem from the most powerful centers and are shaped by the politics of those metropoles. The dominant discourses about globalization do not simply describe developments in the world but also present facts within ideological frameworks based on assumptions about trends in the world. The chapter enumerates the requisites for continued globalization and treats the problem of recapturing the notions of public space and common good within the context of the states that remain requisite to further globalization. To provide a deeper empirical analysis of state responses to globalization pressures, Chapter 11 details primarily the case of Malaysia, with some reference to other East Asian countries. This case demonstrates that both state and civil society have grown and that state institutionalization and effective functioning have proven essential to economic success.

The final chapter summarizes the argument and briefly interprets the events of the post-September 11, 2001 period in the context of my overall themes. Finally, I reiterate these basic themes: first, evolving globalization and growing states have coincided; second, developmental states remain critical to both order and democracy; and third, secure and prosperous states form the backbone of international cooperation. From these, it becomes apparent that continued international economic cooperation and prosperity rely upon strong states. Instead of fading away, states will remain essential to further globalization.

3
Globalization and Power

Introduction

Globalization remains a contested formulation in contemporary social science discourse. Like any other phenomenon involving politics and economics, globalization involves power relations. Before exploring the relationship of globalization and power, I discuss the scope of globalization and present a useful analytical formula. Then, this chapter addresses several primary questions. (1) What is the nature of the system of political economy in the world—global or international? (2) How is the system managed or governed—by the market and/or global institutions or by the powerful states? (3) What is the direction in the flow of distribution of power in the world—toward accumulation by states or by other entities?

The argument in this chapter offers the following answers to the three questions. Despite phenomenal changes resulting from technological innovations that have substantial impacts on globalization processes, the nature of the political economy system continues to be international, based upon states, rather than global. Thus, increasing linkages originate within particular states and have impacts in others that respond. The international political economy is sustained by a hegemonic arrangement in which markets operate within a system of management governed by powerful states and the institutions they have created for their use. In response to the third question, analysis has to be more complex, for the direction of power distribution includes a number of dimensions. Among them are the state-market and more general public-private distributions, the inequality of states and the constraints arising from that unevenness, the related question of the historical conditions of peace, and, finally, power distributions among groups and the impact on individuals. A further analytical complication flows from the causal complexity in which globalization often has effects on power distribution but also globalization itself results from certain arrangements and shifts in political power.

Finally, inasmuch as politics always involves choice among morally loaded alternatives, there follows a brief exploration of normative considerations associated with the phenomena of globalization and the justificatory implications of alternative ways of organizing and managing globalizing processes and pressures. Because economic units have no legitimate moral authority and international organizations lack effectiveness except as instruments of the powers, states remain the efficacious mechanisms for deliberation and choice on important matters of public policy. States also endure as effective agents in the international political system relating them with one another.

It needs to be said that the chapter gives only minimal attention to the cultural dimensions of globalization. Although many people in the world experience broad and varied opportunities for enriching their lives through exposure to music, art, and other cultural phenomena drawn from many different indigenous bases, these experiences do not appear to constitute a central feature of the structural power arrangements that underlie and sustain globalization. Nevertheless, later in the chapter I comment briefly on some potential meanings of cultural globalization with respect to power.

The Scope of Globalization

Although the term has become a buzzword in the 1990s, almost no one regards globalization as an exclusively post-Cold War phenomenon. Waters (1995, p. 62), who treats it broadly and thinks that it implies the undermining of the state, writes, "Globalization is at least contemporary with modernization and has therefore been proceeding since the sixteenth century." Robertson (1990, p. 26) thinks that the "national society in the twentieth century is an aspect of globalization" and refers to "the accelerated globalization which began to occur just over one-hundred years ago." Robertson treats as the major components of globalization, in addition to national societies, "the system of international relations, conceptions of individuals and of humankind." In another place, Robertson (1992, pp. 6–7) writes, "... overall processes of globalization ... are at least as old as the rise of the so-called world religions two thousand and more years ago."

In contrast, Albrow and King (1990, p. 1) argue that "globalisation is the present process of becoming global: globality itself lies in the future, but the very near future." They perceive "a cosmopolitan culture," whereas Featherstone (1990, p. 10), calling attention to a local-cosmopolitan dichotomy (for example, most tourism is local, in enclaves of the familiar) suggests "that there is little prospect of a unified global culture, rather there are global cultures in the plural...." Featherstone (1995, p. 13) thinks that "with more voices talking back to the West, there is a strong sense that modernity will not be universalized. This is because modernity is seen as both a Western project and as the West's projection of its values on to the world." He sees "a strong tendency for the process of globalization to provide a stage for global differences not only to open up a 'world showcase of cultures' ... but to provide a field for a more discordant clashing of cultures."

Whatever and whenever its origins, in its post-modernist interpretation,

"Globalization as a concept refers both to the compression of the world and intensification of consciousness of the world as a whole.... [T]he main focus of the discussion is on relatively recent times" (Robertson 1992, p. 8). For purposes of analysis in this book, let us date it from shortly after the mid-nineteenth century with the rise of modern industrial powers, new technologies of transportation and communication, growth of international exchange of goods and capital flows, and modern migration patterns.

Leaving aside culture, globalization includes various meanings and refers to several discrete areas of economics: rationalization of production on a worldwide basis, increased levels of international trade, and unrestricted capital flows in a system of global finance. In a common expression, the present world is witnessing the formation of a single world market. Changes occurring over the past thirty or so years in the international economy also have had serious implications for domestic economies in which (1) the welfare state has been weakened, (2) labor unions have declined, and (3) inequality has grown.

These changes raise a number of questions. As noted in the previous chapter, various writers have put forward claims about transformational changes in the world. Clearly, changes are occurring in the international political economy, but the more extreme views on globalization that see the demise of the state, the rise of nongovernmental agencies exercising authority, and the triumph of the market in a global stateless society do not seem warranted (Offe, 1996). Polanyi (1944) attributed the collapse of nineteenth-century civilization to its attempt to create an ungoverned market, and his analysis is recalled by Cox (1992, p. 145) and others who foresee the rise of a transnational social movement that will create a new basis of politics as the answer to the triumph of the market. As shown below, I dissent from this view, for the institutional mechanism by which groups can protect themselves from market and hegemonic state pressures lies at hand in the state. Hopes for transnational social movements based upon class or other group interests appear to be utopian, especially in the face of existing institutional means for aggregating and representing group interests.

Before moving to a useful formulation of global phenomena, another issue, indeed, a confusion, arising from the globalization literature needs to be addressed. A number of observers use a formulation like that of Axford (1995, p. 10) in which he refers to "the universalistic logic of world capitalism versus the particularistic logics of nation-states." Framing the matter in this way inverts the Hegelian concepts of the particular—referring to selfish, individual, and group, or limited interests—and the universal or common good. Surely, firms in a capitalist order neither aspire, nor are they expected to seek, to serve any interest beyond their own profitability, a quite narrow, particularistic endeavor. On the other hand, states aggregate interests and resolve societal conflicts through deliberation in search of a common good that serves the public interest. If there ever were to be a global state, one could speak of universalistic logic, but capitalism by its nature is particularistic. To conflate universalism and capitalism is to confuse the geographical reach of particularistic interests with a global political order that might aspire to embody universalistic, or common, interests.

Liberal readers do not accept this Hegelian formulation because they adhere to Smith's (1970/1776) view that the common good flows from the unrestrained pursuit of particularistic interests. However, Carr (1964/1946) refuted this perspective by pointing out that such a posture embraces the notion of a natural harmony of interests, whereas, in reality, the interests of different persons and classes very often conflict. Although it may sometimes be possible to achieve a harmony of interests, such an accord needs to be striven for and does not constitute part of the nature of things. Carr also pointed out that dominant groups, and states, have a tendency to claim the universality of their own values and to identify their interests with a common good (also see Waltz 1979). They are able to do so, however, only because of their great power.

I treat globalization as a set of pressures operating across the international system with which states cope. In this perspective, neither markets nor international institutions can operate without states, and accumulation of power and preservation of relative positions remain central considerations. From this perspective, I address the three primary questions stated at the beginning of the chapter: the nature of the system of political economy, its management, and the flow of distribution of power in the world.

Nature of System of Political Economy: International, Not Global

Although it is conceivable that the world could become sufficiently integrated as to compose a single market and/or a single polity, that integration has not yet occurred. Should that image become reality, analysts would be justified in treating the world as a unit. To the present, however, the conditions making it so have not developed, and the conditions that do exist conform to a model of an international political economy. For example, multinational enterprises continue to be nationally based, and firms continue to rely on national market shares more than on international trade. Even firms that trade heavily often are engaged in intrafirm trade. Regulation of firms tends to be done by state governments, and states provide all of the underpinning for supplying money and guaranteeing property rights. In an analysis that examined the convergence thesis by comparing economies, firms, production practices, and policies, Berger and Dore (1996) and their colleagues revealed the great diversity of national practices that continues in and among the industrialized countries.

Hirst and Thompson (1996, pp. 2–3) make clear several points. (1) "In some respects, the current international economy is less open and integrated than the regime that prevailed from 1870 to 1914." (2) "Genuinely transnational companies (TNCs) appear to be relatively rare. Most companies are nationally based and trade multinationally on the strength of a major national location of production and sales. . . ." (3) ". . . [F]oreign direct investment (FDI) is highly concentrated among the advanced industrial economies. . . ." (4) ". . . [T]rade, investment and financial flows are concentrated in the Triad of Europe, Japan and North America and this dominance seems set to continue." (5) "These major economic powers . . . thus have the capacity . . . to exert powerful governance pressures over financial markets and other economic tendencies." Although from an economic point of view the concentration of FDI remains logical because of the promise for unconditional returns to investors, the concentration does provide political power as well. Again, from an economic perspective the capacity to govern does not always translate into effective governance because economic costs might accompany such action. Nevertheless, the capacity remains in reserve.

Hirst and Thompson sketch ideal types:

> A *globalized economy* ... distinct from that of the international economy.... Distinct national economies are subsumed and rearticulated in the system by international processes and transactions. The inter-national economy, on the contrary, is one in which processes that are determined at the level of national economies still dominate and international outcomes emerge from the distinct and differential performance of the national economies.... Thus while there are in such an economy a wide and increasing range of international economic interactions ... these tend to function as opportunities or constraints for nationally located economic actors and their public regulators.

In a global economy, TNCs would be global and not subject to state governance. States could not impose their own regulatory objectives.

They argue that the international trading system has been most open when there has been a hegemonic power, in the contemporary period, the United States. If the globalizers are right, this will end. In the 1990s, when they wrote their analysis, however, the United States maintained military hegemony,

> in the sense that its strength ensures that no other state can use political power to restructure the international economy.... The US also remains the largest single national economy and the powerhouse of world demand.... the dollar remains the medium of world trade. (Hirst and Thompson 1996, p. 14)

All of these observations remain true in the early years of the twenty-first century.

As put by LeHeron and Park (1995, p. 5), "... enterprise and governance form a relation, that is they are mutually constituted by and constitutive of each other...." They claim, "The role of the state was critical for industrial changes and spatial restructuring in the rapid industrialization phase of the Asian NIEs during the 1960s through the 1980s.... Government policy is still significant for industrial changes and restructuring."

Eichengreen (1996) presents a historical development view of the international monetary system ("the glue that binds national economies together"), showing the shift from a liberal system before World War I to capital controls in the interwar period and to neoliberal arrangements since the 1970s, and argues that national decisions tended to respond not to common circumstances—as would occur if there were a unified global system—but to arrangements decided by other countries. He also stresses the continuous cooperation of the leading countries under the Bretton Woods monetary system and notes that this cooperation occurred as "part of an interlocking web of political and economic bargains" among allies (p. 135).

Similarly, Helleiner (1994, p. 8) stresses that the globalization of finance resulted from the decisions of the leading states (United States, United Kingdom, and Japan) "to grant more freedom to market operators through liberalization initiatives, (2) to refrain from imposing more effective controls on capital movements, and (3) to prevent major international financial crises."

Apart from understanding that the system is international rather than global, one must treat certain issues concerning choice. First, where do choices lie? And second, what kinds of choices are available? There are several levels of decision making.

At one level, it is important to note, the international political economy features liberal rather than nonliberal arrangements. Were nonliberal states to comprise hegemonic power in the world, different arrangements would prevail. Had Germany and Japan won World War II, or had the Soviet Union triumphed in the Cold War, the construction of the international political economy would appear far different than it does under American and allied hegemony. Within that liberal hegemonic system, however, there are other levels of choice that accrue only to states.

For example, levels of regulation or deregulation of sectors of an economy and concessions of relative liberalization and loosening of control over firms by governments are state decisions. Within the international economy, states have to make the choices involved in relative liberalization and protection of their own economies in the context of international exchanges. Creating the entire context of economic activity, the construction of such regimes as the GATT and WTO, relies upon state negotiations and decision making.

Once established, liberal systems still have to be parsed in terms of levels of importance of choices. As Kapstein (1991/1992) has written, such fundamental choices as the 1985 Plaza Accord to realign major currencies are of necessity made by states. Central banks take decisions that set the terms within which other participants in money markets, investment, and trade operate.

Once these three levels of framework for the operation of a liberal economy are in place—that is, within the confines of a liberal system—markets, firms, and nongovernmental organizations have scope to operate. Within this context, often, nonstate entities have greater control over outcomes than do the states that set the rules and the boundaries within which economic activity ensues (Strange 1996). Once this realm generates economic activity, there may be reciprocal effects on states and on the liberal structures within the international political economy. Those effects, of course, generate the need for continuing management and governance. When nonstate activities press on the boundaries of state-controlled interests, state officials may act to correct markets. For example, the G-7 finance ministers and central bankers "hinted" in April 1997 they might intervene in currency markets to halt the rise of the dollar against the yen as a means of dampening down Japan's trade surpluses (Sanger 1997).

As currency markets in Southeast Asia were roiled in late 1997 and the South Korean economy began collapsing through a series of bankruptcies and a profound debt crisis, governments and IFIs turned their attention to rescue packages. In particular, a $57 billion arrangement was put together to prevent the South Korean situation from melting down, for that would threaten the entire world financial system. To be sure, efforts at constructing a bulwark in Korea in order to stave off an attack on Japan that would eventually challenge Western Europe and the United States enlisted the cooperation of private banks that had extended loans to Korean firms. Impetus and coordination, however, necessarily came from governments and their international institutions. In cases like this, private markets obviously possess the power to attack and even bring down the financial systems of strong countries; but, just as obviously, the constructive work of impeding damage to other economies and of supporting the interlocking structures of international finance in order to prevent worldwide collapse rests with states.

Without the establishment of the liberal system, its maintenance by state-provided public goods, and its continued management by the hegemonic powers, there would be chaos and very little scope for private enterprise and unregulated activities by private firms, nongovernmental organizations, and individuals. Thus, the matters in which the market has control over outcomes occur only within the constraints afforded by states. These matters hold considerable significance, and private firms certainly generate wealth efficiently. Nevertheless, their ability to act and the confines within which they operate have to be managed in order for them to remain effective and to make their contributions.

What kinds of choices remain available to different actors? As in any system of power relations, choices are more constrained for those in the most submissive positions. Individuals without skills in poor countries lacking effective state apparatuses have little choice, although refugees in foreign war zones are even more constrained. Laborers in firms tend to be increasingly constrained vis-à-vis management even in developed countries. Aggregates of wealth whether held by individuals like George Soros or by industrial firms like Boeing Aircraft or banks like Citibank operate with fewer constraints and can, thus, make decisions about the disposition of their own resources that can have quite wide-ranging consequences. More constraints hem in weak states than strong ones, although even weak ones control access to their territories by firms and individuals. Like every other entity, major powers face severe constraints, but they retain choices of quite formidable proportions.

How Is the System Managed or Governed?

Helleiner (1994, pp. 112–113) emphasizes, particularly through his case analysis of the management of the debt crisis in the 1980s that the system of international finance relies fundamentally on the actions of states for its survival. Moreover, the US government, he points out, did not act on behalf just of the private sector in supporting financial liberalism in the 1970s and 1980s. He gives two national interest reasons:

To begin with, administration officials realized that a more open, liberal international financial order would help preserve U.S. policy autonomy.... In the short run, they perceived speculative capital movements as an important central tool in the U.S. strategy of encouraging foreigners to absorb the adjustment burden required to correct the country's current account deficits....

A more liberal international financial system ... also ... would preserve U.S. policy autonomy in the long run.... The dollar's position as a world currency, for example, would be preserved.... The unique depth and liquidity of U.S. financial markets also ensured that private investors, if given the freedom to invest globally, would continue to underwrite U.S. deficits through their holdings of attractive U.S. assets.

Generally, the international economy is sustained by a system of hegemony underwritten by US military and economic power, allies' power, and the interests of the United States, Western European powers, and Japan; and it is managed by the G-7 and the G-10 (Bank for International Settlements in Basel). Discrete regimes operate in different issue areas, and these do not always mesh, but the basic pattern of hegemony—liberal ideas underwritten by power—characterizes the international system of political economy in the first decade of the present century.

In trade, rules set by the powerful are embodied in the GATT/WTO regime, but the United States acts beyond that regime to champion its own rules, as it has done in the Strategic Impediments Initiative, the Clinton administration's results-oriented bargaining with Japan, and the Helms-Burton Act which continues a tradition of the American exertion of extraterritorial control. Such domination of the rules is sometimes defended on the grounds that the United States is moving in the same direction as the international regime although with greater force and speed (Garten 1995).

The same argument cannot be applied to the shifting terms of trade that disadvantage some states as others benefit. For example, Caribbean countries have lost trade to Mexico under terms of the NAFTA. In addition, an increasing movement by the powers to protectionist measures seems underway and may be accelerated if troubled Asian economies try to address their problems by exporting more to the United States market only to be met by the resistance of demands from American workers and others for protection.

In a global economy, both trade and finance should be moving in the same direction, but this is not the case in the contemporary world. While trade barriers are moving in a nonliberal direction, finance seems to be increasingly free-wheeling. Although the 1980s debt crisis was managed by states, new problems of management and regulation may be arising in the field of the new financial instruments that fall under the rubric of derivatives. What needs to be remembered is that, should any crisis arise out of nongovernmental activities in this or another field, governments will be the ones that will be called on to mount a rescue effort, as happened in late 1997 and early 1998 with respect to Asian economies. Because of that anticipation, states are likely to continue to monitor developments as best they can to avoid a crisis.

Such management activities often lie in the background, but states have other broad management challenges in the areas of the natural environment and of security, war, and turmoil. Even when the powers largely abandon their management to NGOs, small states and state-backed political forces are likely to become the effective managers.

With the successful conclusion of the Uruguay Round and the establishment of conflict-resolving mechanisms in the World Trade Organization, some movement toward international governance has occurred in the area of trade, although tough disputes tend to be negotiated outside the formal mechanisms. On the other hand, governance in the area of international finance continues to rest firmly upon states, although they achieve results through cooperation. Kapstein (1994, pp. 80–81) explains,

> International cooperation among central bankers rests . . . on home country control. . . . [A] model of governance in which the responsibility for defining national financial institutions . . . and regulating them is placed on the state. Under home country supervision, states look to one another, as opposed to some supranational or multilateral entity, to legislate and enforce any agreements that have been collectively reached. As a result, the linkages between states and their national banks have not been broken by globalization, and in some respects they have even been strengthened.

Thus, the essential tasks of management of the international system are carried out by states. Within established confines, there may be, as Strange (1996) and Sassen (1996) argue, private governance activities occurring. These, however, happen only because of and within a deeper, state-driven structure of governance. Without that structure, markets would engender crises leading to failure of the liberal order. With it, states act to preserve the liberal international political economy.

Distribution and Accumulation of Power

Partly from hegemonic interests and partly from a shift in power within countries, free market liberalism has been put into practice. Primary influence over economic policy within the leading industrial countries has transferred to a coalition of bankers and neoliberal economists such as Milton Friedman and Friedrich Hayek and their followers from a coalition of Keynesian economists, labor unions, social democrats, and New Dealers. In part, this has resulted from a disillusionment with embedded liberalism of the post-World War II period. Certain powers have flowed to firms, banks, and so forth, but the maintenance of the system requires continued surveillance and action by governments.

In calculating the direction of power flows in the face of pressures for global integration, several distinct issues need to be addressed. First, the relative control by states over market forces forms the agenda of a good deal of the literature on globalization. In the last quarter century, the powers have tended to concede to firms and to the market increased freedom of action. Nevertheless, state management continues to make itself felt.

Second, in addition to their relations to markets, states stand juxtaposed to one another. Uneven development remains a phenomenon in the present era as it has in the past. At a moment in history when security seems abundant in a hegemonic liberal order, states may have the luxury of approximate unconcern with the security implications of relative gains but they nevertheless regard their positions and those of potential adversaries in comparative terms. Although true of all states, the status quo, liberal powers in particular continue the race to maintain their positions lest their privileges and the order that they underwrite be threatened.

Third, the power balance within states needs to be weighed, particularly to identify the dominant groups whose ideology supports the hegemonic order of political economy. Because the prevailing order that concedes to market forces the power to operate ultimately rests upon the political commitments of states, the support for the liberal regime needs to be protected. As Ruggie (1996) has noted, if states allow the erosion of embedded liberalism through the free flow of market power across state boundaries and the market redistributes wealth in the dramatically unequal fashion that it has a tendency to do, then deprived citizens may withdraw their support for the liberal regime.

Fourth, the analysis needs to examine the stability of extant communities and, especially, the formation of incipient communities and identities not tied to states. These consist of two types, fragmented identities and transnational identities. In the post-Cold War period ethnic nationalism has shown itself to be the strongest force in community identity, and, of course, it is a phenomenon that reinforces the state (Gellner 1983). Islam, too, does not challenge the state, although certain tendencies within it advocate a form of state in which any boundaries between society and state are blurred under a regime of shari'a. On the other hand, evidenced also in the contemporary world is the identity politics of gender, age, sexual orientation, and so forth that does not necessarily but might provide a device for the fragmentation of power within states, reducing its accumulation at the state level. Moreover, in a movement some refer to as the growth of an international civil society there are traces of transnational identity across national boundaries based on democracy, human rights, post-modern culture, and so forth. The logical consequences of these identities on power flow in the same stream, for they imply the removal of power from the nation-state to others.

The final issue of power distribution concerns the whole matter of preserving hegemony from challengers. It is the preponderance of power by the status quo powers that insures the environment for liberalism. Choices have been made by those leading states to devolve power to the private sector in the interest of production. What, then, could disrupt the necessary preponderance that preserves the liberal system? Four things seem to be candidates for undermining or overturning the system. First, the United States, the mainstay of the worldwide system of economic cooperation, might decide to end its forbearance and embark on a campaign of aggression. Writers as far apart as Waltz (1993) and Ruggie (1996) have called attention to this possibility, however unattractive they may find it. The Bush administration's waging preventive war against Iraq in 2003 may portend such action on a repeated, though infrequent, basis. Second, a revisionist power might accumulate sufficient resources and standing to challenge the rules laid down by the liberal states. China appears to be the prime candidate for such a role, although such potential does not seem imminent and lies off in the future. Third, despite the continuing yet oft-questioned success of Keynesian management to offset downturns, it seems improbable that capitalism has entirely lost its cyclical tendency for busts to follow booms. Continued ascendancy of political groups who fiercely hold to tenets of unfettered private enterprise and to anti-government postures would make it more likely that residual Keynesian proclivities would diminish, almost ensuring a severe market contraction. In such an event, it seems more likely than not that each state would turn to looking out for itself. Finally, the system might be undermined by the resistance to inequality within states by disadvantaged groups that might demand autarchy and protection as well as redistributive policies within their own countries. At the very least, as Ruggie (1996) has warned, there may be an erosion of support for the liberal system.

Power Distributions Regarding States and Markets

As Evans (1995, 1997a) has so eloquently argued, states and private firms both contribute to industrial development and are mutually empowering, so both must remain strong for economic transformation within states to occur. Heilbroner (1990), too, stresses the two realms necessary for the effective functioning of capitalism, the public realm of the state and the private domain of enterprises. Tensions between these spheres remain inevitable, with each seeking to sustain autonomy yet, at the same time, needing the other for the maintenance of prosperity through the effective functioning of the system. Evans neatly captures the mutual although distant relationship in his phrase, "embedded autonomy."

Although construction of effective economic systems relies on the activities of both realms, maintenance of prosperous markets ultimately turns on political decisions. Given the histories of some obvious failures, clear preference needs to be given to political choices that sustain autonomous public realms against "rent-seeking" or "predatory" state arrangements and that create the conditions for healthy private sectors to perform activities not done well by centralized bureaucratic apparatuses. Examples illustrating obvious errors in different directions are provided by the Soviet Union and Zaire. The former chose to concentrate the power of economic decision making in a centralized bureaucracy that provided sustained industrialization over a number of years but eventually lacked the flexibility to adapt to new phases of industrialization, ultimately to decline rapidly from the early 1970s. In contrast, Zaire's leaders after 1965 opted for a rent-seeking state that served no public interest, essentially appropriating accumulations for a predatory elite that allowed the infrastructure and government services sectors to decline. Power went only to the state in the Soviet case and in Zaire to a small private elite that had captured the governing apparatus.

Standing in sharp contrast are many success stories in which, with considerable institutional and policy variation, public authorities and private firms chose arrangements under which power increased in both realms. From Western

European welfare states to the more conservative United States to the various exemplars of the East Asian "miracle," many countries have prospered under effective states and energetic private sectors.

Neither centrally planned economies nor predatory states provide either attraction or impetus for international trade and investment. Thus sustenance of international economic activities that spread technology and investment requires that power remain in the hands of those determined to provide public services and to regulate markets to preserve them. Because states are the organs of deliberation that ultimately decide such matters, the important outcome of keeping the balance of power between the realms that will sustain the liberal capitalist order depends upon maintaining the hegemony of liberal states and upon control and wisdom of governing decisions within those states by those committed to the liberal order.

With the collapse of the Soviet Union and its alternative order in Eastern Europe, a strong challenge to the liberal order was removed, and there is no other center of power in the world that immediately threatens to substitute centrally planned economics for market economics. Neither does any predatory, rent-seeking state provide an alternative to liberalism. Indeed, rent-seeking remains inconsistent, both in theory and practice, with the accumulation of power that could provide the basis for such a challenge. By its nature, rent-seeking endures as a self-enriching activity done at the expense of accumulating wealth for the fulfillment of larger purposes. Although other predators might imitate such rent seekers as the Suharto family of Indonesia, neither the command economy nor the rent-seeking regime offers a model with wide appeal for adoption to replace liberalism.

Within liberalism, those supporting the ideological position that markets should be allowed to triumph without state support or interference reached their maximum strength at some time in the 1980s. Since 1993, when the World Bank published its *East Asian Miracle*, the dominant ideology within the liberal order has been accepting of the empirical studies pointing to a continued important role for the state in promoting economic development and continued prosperity. Later in the 1990s, the Bank strengthened this emphasis (World Bank 1997).

Power Distributions Among States

Liberal states maintain their dominant positions in the international political system, managing the international political economy through coordinated and largely institutionalized action. Within that arrangement, the United States remains central and hegemonic within the cooperative joint enterprise (Nye 1990). Without a challenger on the horizon, there appears little prospect that war over systemic change (Gilpin 1981) will occur soon.

Completion of the Uruguay Round and the establishment of the World Trade Organization, together with other efforts that promise continued sustenance of cooperation among the dominant liberal powers, portend a stable future for liberal hegemony. Expansion of the North Atlantic Treaty Organization, however dubious it may appear to some observers (Mandelbaum 1996a; Steel 1998), demonstrates United States' commitment to a stable liberal order, as do the adjustments of United

States-Japan security arrangements that were made in 1993 and 1996. All of these activities appear to demonstrate the triumph within American politics of those supporting liberal internationalism and the turning back of any incipient "new isolationism" (Ruggie 1996).

Moreover, the strength of the dominant coalition continues to increase, as additional states join that coalition. Not only are Eastern European states adopting liberal policies but they are also seeking institutional association with the dominant coalition through membership in the European Union and the North Atlantic Treaty Organization. Meanwhile, South Korea in December 1996 became a member of the Organization for Economic Cooperation and Development. Of course, states seek membership in the coalition for the benefits of stability and prosperity that it confers. Should those benefits appear to be jeopardized, states would be placed in a position that required them to rethink their membership. In 2004, jeopardy does not appear imminent.

Politics and Economics Within States

Both market and political pressures have been working for some years to erode the post-World War II bargain that Ruggie (1982) termed "embedded liberalism," in which a liberal international order did not require state authorities to refrain from erecting welfare systems and other protections of citizens from the buffeting of international market forces. Domestic barriers have come under assault from the operations of multinational enterprises operating in a milieu that encourages the rationalization of production on a global basis and from bankers and currency speculators taking advantage of the decline of currency restrictions and the rise of computer technologies that support global banking activities.

Domestic protections have also come under political assault from governments, such as the powerful actions of the United States against Japan under terms of Section 301 of the 1988 Trade Act. Ideological campaigns against welfare have also made their mark.

Despite their absorption of much of the ideological trimmings of neoliberalism, Bill Clinton in the United States and Tony Blair in Britain still represented the rearguard defense of embedded liberalism. Political battles on the issues of reducing protections and welfare transfers in the European countries and in Japan are likely to remain on the agenda. In the end, though, the threat that complete removal of protections would probably lead to withdrawal of support for the liberal international order remains a formidable barrier to the complete abolition of embedded liberalism. Should that projection prove erroneous, however, and the alternative of withdrawal of support for the liberal order come to pass, that order is likely to collapse, with great uncertainty about what would follow. The nightmare driving the post-war order has been the "beggar-thy-neighbor" policies of the 1930s, and the reenactment of that disastrous course remains a probability should those holding the most extreme neoliberal positions gain power in the leading states, especially the United States.

Rodrik (1997b, p. 33) warns against "complacency toward the social consequences of globalization," for he envisions two dangers that might arise from it. The first is the same as that noted by Ruggie, but the other focuses on the potential for new class divisions arising from the beneficiaries and the victims of globalization. To avoid such an unpleasant circumstance, he advocates the continued maintenance of social safety nets. Identity politics also promises increasing fragmentation.

Fragmented and Transnational Identity Politics

Strength proceeds from unity as well as from material forces at the disposal of aggregates of power. Should the unified communities supporting rule in the dominant states become fragmented, the power at the disposal of those states would prove less usable for coherent purposes, and the liberal order that they serve might be weakened or collapse. Two tendencies in modern identity politics have been noted: fragmentation within polities and the construction of new transnational identities.

Axford (1995, p. 200) canvasses the phenomenon, arguing that "[g]lobalization dissolves the physical and psychological boundaries of place, and either liberates or threatens those identities in some way tied to particular locations." Drawing on Giddens (1990, 1991), he notes that "this aspect of modernity ... allows for connections" across the globe. Axford (1995, p. 206) goes further in arguing that the formation of identity through "cultural manufacture" marks the critical distinction between modern and postmodern politics. As he notes, different versions of globalization perceive in the process the engendering of rootlessness, on the one hand, and a great potential for the creation of virtual places and entities (pp. 217–219).

The rootlessness of the modern world has become even more apparent with the collapse of communism and increased migration. However, the widespread turn to religious fundamentalism in the Muslim world, in former communist countries, and in the western hemisphere suggests that quite traditional forms of identity are taken on by those at sea in a changing time.

Insofar as individuals seek solace, religion provides a traditional shelter. However, politics and states remain the effective mechanisms for protecting aggregates of people and for making common decisions. Thus, not only are these political mechanisms essential to maintaining the requisites to sustain market economics, they are indispensable for protecting citizens from the worst buffetings of market forces, nongovernmental terrorism, and other threats. Fragmented, isolated individuals with free-floating identities do not constitute the basis for a politics of common good; they could only submit to market forces, to criminal enterprises, or to totalitarian politics hostile to the relatively unfettered market.

A different approach to identity, which perceives or hopes for new groups forming across national boundaries, emanates from two sources. In the post-Cold War context, liberal groups have mounted extensive nongovernmental international activities and seek the formation of an international or global civil society (Braman and Sreberny-Mohammadi 1996). Some Marxists, on the other hand, foresee the development of new groups across state boundaries that will provide the basis for a reaction and resistance to the forces of globalization (Cox 1991; Cox with Sinclair

1996; Gill 1997), although the obstacles to this development have been pointed out by "post-Marxists" who nevertheless retain a utopian optimism about such a project (Macdonald 1997).

Beginning with the 1992 Rio conference on development and the environment, nongovernmental organizations and individuals have convened meetings parallel to the large United Nations-sponsored, intergovernmental conferences held almost every year during the 1990s. Such meetings do provide occasions for face-to-face interactions among individuals from many different cultures and may even lead to political activities within their respective home countries. However, even less authority resides in these nongovernmental associations than in the inter-governmental activities taking place simultaneously.

A stronger case for the development of an international civil society can be constructed from the immense, and often heroic activities of nongovernmental humanitarian and relief organizations that occur in areas of turmoil in the world (Bennett et al. 1995). Despite the publicity that presents such activities as wholly private, they tend to be funded largely by governments. To the extent that they are supported by private contributions, the contributors are subsidized by governments through tax schemes. For example, in the first four months of 1997, the US government, although largely devoid of a policy and with hardly a presence, obligated $133,093,414 for humanitarian assistance in the Great Lakes region in Central Africa, most of it by grants to private relief organizations (U.S. Agency for International Development 1997). That relief effort was carried on by entities that were hardly simply instruments of government policies, but neither did they constitute an aggregate of power independent of governments. As substitutes for government policies, their activities give rise to quite serious questions of democratic accountability. Moreover, they clearly acknowledge their inability to perform such important political functions as separating fighters from innocent civilians (Crossette 1997), and the failure of governments to act leads to such moral disasters as the protection by humanitarian agencies of the perpetrators of genocide.

Modern means of communication do provide a vehicle for the formation of a class of cosmopolitans who identify across national boundaries, but there is little evidence that this class of people constitutes a significant number. Neither is there any evidence that either power or authority can be attributed to it. Power with respect to the computer has tended to lie with governments and corporations. Despite the frequent invocation of the idea of virtual communities, the Internet was created and sustained by governments, and a struggle for influence a decade or so after the end of the Cold War has been mounted by large corporations. Thus, in the contemporary world, as has been the case for some time, the foremost shape of identity remains the nation; and the foremost repository of power remains the state, despite the substantial evidence that has appeared to illustrate large private aggregations of power. In the post-Cold War period, with its relative absence of fears of general, major-power war, space has been opened up for other experiments in identity formation (as socialism provided a class identification before 1914) but these experiments as yet have not resulted in any significant aggregations of power strong enough to match states or corporations.

Potential Disruptions

There is nothing inevitable about human affairs, and the existing liberal order provides no exception to that rule. Neither is the future foreseeable, and extant arrangements might be modified in ways that one cannot guess. Still, it is not difficult to imagine a number of possibilities that could prove fundamentally disruptive to the liberal international political economic system prevailing in the early twenty-first century.

The first of these, the end of American forbearance and a campaign of aggression by the United States, appears only vaguely in incipient plans at waging preventive war. An inability to transform Iraqi society quickly after the swift victory there is likely to act as a brake on the prosecution of other preventive wars by the United States for some time to come. On the other hand, circumstances often change very rapidly in politics, leading to speedy decision making and rapid response to threats and dangers. The attacks against the United States on September 11, 2001, illustrate how fast policy can shift (Harries 2002). Further modifications in circumstances might promote other dramatic changes in policy.

A second source of potential disruption of the liberal order would be the appearance of a revisionist power with sufficient accumulation of resources to challenge the hegemonic arrangements. Despite evidence of revisionist aspirations, no challenger appears on the horizon, for no country possesses the capacity to mount a believable challenge. In the long run, China could conceivably champion an alternative world order, but that seems not to be its ambition at present, for its aggregate power is not yet sufficient to support any realistic prospect of achieving any such ambitions.

Should economic integration continue to develop, a third source of disruption would be provided by a worldwide depression in which prices turn downward and states turn inward. Given the complexity of current economic arrangements in trade, finance, and foreign investment, it does not lie within the knowledge of economists or other prognosticators to predict if and when an economic downturn might occur. One could also take the position that the contemporary world economy has such unprecedented characteristics that old thinking about business cycles does not apply. Prudence, though, encourages observers to recall a history of depressions and not to rule out a collapse in the future.

Finally, the operation of the market without compensating governmental redistribution might produce such an unequal distribution of wealth that deprived groups might respond by demands for redress or structural changes to protect them from further depredations of the international market. A revolt of deprived groups, thus, would provide a fourth source for disruption of globalization processes. Some observers believe that such groups would form a global counter-response to those privileged by globalization; I believe that new transnational formations are much less likely than the placing of demands on states for redistribution and protection. Occasional protests by worker groups, such as French farmers during the endgame of the Uruguay Round negotiations or the French electorate that returned a Socialist government in June 1997, augur a future should governments decide not to perform their social welfare functions and allow markets to operate unhindered. At the very least, there remains a potential for withdrawal of support for the liberal international order if the instrumental purposes—greater prosperity and richer lives—of that order do not continue to materialize.

Normative Considerations

In the post-Cold War period, interest has grown in the political effects of ideas and norms (Goldstein and Keohane 1993; Katzenstein 1996; Ruggie 1993; Wendt 1994, 1995, 1999). The authors of these texts do not claim that material interests derive from norms or that power needs to be set aside. Rather, they confront the "givenness" of material interests and argue that both identities and interests are constructed through a process in which ideas and power interact. For the most part, they do not establish the mix or relative weights of these ingredients in the shaping of identities and policies.

For purposes of the move toward integration of a world market and communications net, the essential problem to grapple with is whether the legitimacy of the liberal international political economy rests on the dissemination of liberal ideas or whether that dissemination results from the hegemonic position of the powerful liberal states that dominate the system. In making his distinction between hard and soft power, Nye (1990) stressed the "transformation of power" based on a system of interdependence, but he emphasized that the new forms of power would be used essentially to pursue American material interests. He has made even clearer that the information means that others perceive as creating new worlds may be used to maintain domination (Nye and Owens 1996). Carr (1964/1939) was interested in power, morality, and change in international relations. He performed a service in pointing to the limitations of realism and to the advantages of ideas, commenting on the propensity of those with power to make universal claims for their own norms and ideas and, in the end, in asserting the need for a compromise between power and morality. The mix of power and morality in contemporary international politics can be viewed from the vantage point of important recent events.

The moral disaster that occurred in the wake of the 1994 massacre in Rwanda and succeeding events gave the appearance that there was a growing liberal tolerance for genocide. During the spring and early summer, some 500,000 to 800,000 or more Tutsi and moderate Hutu people were slaughtered in Rwanda. During that mass murder, the United Nations reduced its presence in the country, and the United States government weaseled by avoiding the term "genocide," referring to the slaughter as "acts of genocide" (Gourevitch 1995). When the Rwanda Patriotic Front invaded to drive out the government that fomented the genocide, the killers and their families and supporters fled to neighboring countries, particularly Zaire. There, the "international community" mounted a "humanitarian" relief effort run largely by United Nations refugee and relief agencies and nongovernmental organizations, although some American and other governmental military aid was provided to assist in the delivery of food and supplies (Minear and Guillot 1996).

However, the relief agencies did not possess the capacity to separate Hutu fighters and political leaders from innocent refugees, thus finding themselves in the position of feeding, clothing, housing, and treating those who had committed the genocide. Additionally, the agencies yielded to the organization of the refugee camps by the Hutu leadership, who also used the protection and sustenance provided to prepare for a new invasion of Rwanda. Not until partly unrelated events in Eastern Zaire led to the dismantling of the refugee camps did the festering predicament come to an end, although not without its own moral ambiguity.

No unusual insight is required to recognize the moral failure that accompanied the efforts of agencies acting on good intentions. The problem that needs to be unraveled is why the moral failure was allowed to happen. Part of the explanation lies in the nondemocratic, nonaccountable nature of such operations. Had democratic governments taken specific rescue and relief actions with their own armed forces and civilian employees, their citizens would have observed and reacted. However, international agencies and nongovernmental organizations, bureaucratic units all, acted to carry out their respective missions in competition with the others. Those missions tend to be very constrained, requiring the agencies to respond to political pressure and direction without reflection on larger political issues. Their activities, although subsidized by states, allow states to sidestep responsibility for addressing the political and moral implications inherent in a problematical situation. Nongovernmental organizations, in particular, cannot be held accountable in the liberal climate that treasures privatization and treats the state as little more than a minimal mechanism for supporting economic activity.

Neither nongovernmental organizations nor international organizations have the purpose or the capacity to act as broad organs of deliberation and choice, for none is democratic. Although the Rwanda fiasco clearly reveals the ability of states not to function as moral deliberators, states at least have the purpose and the means to act as mechanisms of moral choice following open public debate and deliberation.

If states and international institutions refrain from facing such profound moral questions as the perpetration of genocide, then they can as easily ignore less egregious and less visible ethical choices in the future. Fundamentally, at least the means to make such choices ought to be preserved. Presenting an "apocalyptic scenario," Attali (1997, p. 61) points out that, should the market economy ultimately come to dominate and drive out democratic politics, "Western civilization itself is bound to collapse." Attali urges compromises to address the fundamental questions that need answers in order to avoid such a calamity. Even more modestly, I suggest that it is important to defend the state and ensure that states continue to hold sufficient power to seek justice as well as prosperity and safety for their citizens.

Conclusion

As in all human arrangements, power undergirds the status quo: globalization occurs because those advocating and enforcing liberalism possess the power to dominate. Tendencies to integrate an international economy were prevalent in the late nineteenth and early twentieth centuries under a gold standard that, as long as it was accepted by political leaders, disciplined domestic macroeconomic policy. Full acceptance of such market principles, nevertheless, did not stop the deep anti-liberal forces of fascism and communism that rose to confront liberal democracy. Although the history of the twentieth century may be read as the triumph of liberal democracy over those anti-liberal challenges, no guarantee provides assurance that liberalism will always sustain the reign that it holds in the early post-Cold War period. In the long run, a challenger state with sufficient accumulated power may confront the order put into place by liberals. Such a challenge might be as effectively met by the liberal states as they and their allies were able to do in the two world wars of the twentieth century, although the risks of losing would be uncertain and the high costs of winning would be inescapable.

A shorter run threat might stem from misunderstanding the power con-siderations underlying the liberal international order. Capitulation to market forces on a global scale out of a retreat from politics and from misunderstanding of the foundation of power upon which liberal dominance rests could lead to the undermining of the order and to its replacement by aggregates of corporate and criminal power or by totalitarian political rulers against which individuals would be helpless. Thus, to preserve the international political economy and to protect citizens against the depredations of the market, it remains necessary to protect and enhance state power to make decisions, to regulate firms, and to redistribute wealth.

Both the long- and the short-term challenges may be addressed most effectively by extending consideration to the interests of those states, such as China and the Islamic states, that make somewhat different demands on the system than the liberal states alone. If those nonliberal units were brought into partnership with the liberal order, through diplomatic and institutional compromises, continued political nurturing of the liberal international political economy would remain more probable. Moreover, the domestic political support within the democracies might be sustained for the liberal international order by the continued workings of politics at both the international and domestic levels in which a range of values, not just the efficiency of the market, would figure in the debates and deliberations over public policies.

4
World Problems
and Specific State Problems

Introduction

One of the confusions stemming from the conventional view of globalization portrays the world as being transformed from a state-based international system to a globally based arrangement. Such a perspective arises from giving exaggerated emphasis to the effects of the reduced costs of transportation and communications that have occurred over the course of the last century and a half and to the spread of the international system across the globe. From that focus, some observers make great inferential leaps from facts like instantaneous communications to speculations about an imagined world community. Moreover, in the private sector, some multinational firms have moved from basing their investment and operating strategies in a single country to spreading their manufacturing and distribution activities across many states. Confusion arises from conflating scope of activity by individual firms with a presumed structural unity within which they operate. Clearly, firms are not the basic structural units that form the fundamental organization of the world. Nor does the globe form the unit of organization. States comprise the international system in which they and other entities conduct relations and operations (Giddens 1987; Jackson and James 1993; Offe 1996).

Furthermore, that international system persists as an unintended arrangement that flows from the relations of unequal units (Waltz 1979). Many measures illuminate the inequality. Even before the intense buildup of arms in the United States that began in President Jimmy Carter's last year in office and Ronald Reagan's deficit-building defense budgets, the United States and the Soviet Union controlled about eighty percent of the world's armaments. In 1991 the imbalance in capabilities of the two sides in the Iraq versus United States-led coalition resulted in a brief battle in the Gulf War that ousted the Iraqi army from Kuwait, split the Iraqi nation, and devastated Iraq's infrastructure. The allies suffered very few casualties, and no material damage occurred outside Iraq other than in Kuwait, which the Iraqi army had occupied for a time. That particular inequality increased even more in the following twelve years, as evidenced by the quick battle with fewer forces in the American invasion and conquest of Iraq in 2003.

From consumption of products and energy to investments in research and development, the United States, with only four percent of the earth's human population, surpasses other countries by sufficient margins that it persists autonomously without depending very much on others. Often, American policy makers seek to achieve goals in the international environment that require others' cooperation, as it has in forming its alliances, the regime governing world trade, and the campaign to suppress terrorism. Such policy aspirations do require concessions and compromises, but no other country can maintain such an independent posture as the North American giant.

Because the United States casts such a wide shadow in world affairs, Americans in particular often find it difficult to differentiate between specific American problems and world problems. After all, their spokesmen use such terms as "the world community" in which to wrap their country's policy preferences. In light of its widespread power and interests, the United States frequently identifies its interests with those of the system as a whole. Despite this conflation of state and worldwide perspectives, it remains important for clear analysis to keep the distinction. Thus this chapter insists on distinctions among states and between individual states' perspectives and broader ways of looking at things. In discussing these different outlooks, the analysis also indicates the place of international intergovernmental and nongovernmental organizations in coping with problems of coordination and cooperation in the world. Mainly, the chapter attempts to illuminate the ways in which states' problems diverge and how these separate interests interact in the international arena where coordination and cooperation occur.

Inequality of States

States share some fundamental characteristics, giving the international order a certain coherence. For example, state organization based upon territorial boundaries and formal legal jurisdiction of governments over the populations within those boundaries provides a fundamental pattern of order in the world. Furthermore, the principle that each of those governments exercises a legitimate monopoly on the use of force within the boundaries persists not simply through its practice but also as a result of recognition by other governments. Nevertheless, inequality continues to mark the state system.

The ramifications of inequality extend so widely that the empirical facts of diversity may be regarded as equally significant as the basic similarities of principle. Although most states contribute in some measure to shaping the international system, very few powers shape the most fundamental structural features. Waltz (1979) not only established the theoretical significance of small numbers of powers but also derived the important differential implications of multipolar and bipolar structures. For example, he worked out the logic and invoked the supporting case studies of the dangers of miscalculation implicit in multipolar structures versus the greater danger of overreaction in bipolar ones. In a bipolar structure, he argued, no uncertainty exists concerning which country the adversary is, but each adversary has a tendency to overreact to the diplomatic and military moves of the other. This part of Waltz's theory, then, accounts for such behaviors as American and Soviet interventions in Angola in the 1970s, where neither had a vital or important national interest.

Despite their fundamentally adversarial relationship, the superpowers engaged together at times in attempts to formulate common guidelines within which they could manage their relationship. These efforts occasionally proved effective, for example, in agreeing to the 1972 Anti-Ballistic Missile Treaty, which lasted for more than twenty-five years, although the United States in 2002 withdrew from it in pursuit of both theater and national missile defense systems. Such successes resulted from symmetry in the two countries' military capabilities at the time and their parallel interests in stabilizing the nuclear deterrence standoff as well as in saving money. That collaboration was jolted, however, in the following decade when the United States, under another, less constrained president, decided to increase its military spending to unprecedented levels, revealing an underlying inequality between the superpowers. That inequality had affected prior efforts at joint management, for example, in their failure to come to terms during the Nixon-Brezhnev years on effective rules of engagement in the Third World. Because the United States retained such a superior position economically, its strategy aimed to link Soviet behavior in peripheral countries to bilateral economic ties, and presidential advisor Henry Kissinger in particular thought that the Soviet Union could be rewarded and punished economically for its activities or restraint in the Third World.

The Soviets, in contrast, sought to compartmentalize their strategic relationship with the United States and their activities in the rest of the world. Lacking economic strength, they relied on military instruments to pursue their search for influence in the Third World. Thus inequalities in material resources importantly shaped their foreign policies. Furthermore, the superpowers found it possible to cooperate in the arena, anti-missile defenses, in which their capabilities and capacities to act approached equality; but they were unable to find common ground in those other areas, economic intercourse and Third World interventions, where their material capabilities persisted in unequal measure.

Even larger and more obvious ramifications of inequality pervade the relations of more disparate states. In the post-Cold War period, European allies of the United States in the North Atlantic Treaty Organization (NATO) have been unable independently to engage in military activities requiring substantial projections of force, for only the United States possesses the airlift capacity to transport large numbers of troops and equipment over long distances. Of greater moment, American control of the information technology required for modern battle management precludes others from mastering local theaters of combat, unless the United States should be willing to share its command of such resources (Nye and Owens 1996).

In the economic sphere, differences—not just standards of living of populations but also accumulation potentials of states—are remarkable between such countries as those in East Asia and poorer and declining entities in Africa. Apart from obvious disparities of wealth, life chances for people living in the respective countries, and possibilities of developing into mature economies and states, very weak states remain vulnerable to intervention by neighbors and larger states and to internal breakdown and domestic warfare for control of the meager power and spoils available. Although poverty alone does not necessarily imply such awful consequences, it remains a contributing cause to political incoherence, vulnerability, and turmoil. In contrast, prosperity contributes to stability, tranquillity, and strength.

These qualities advance the autonomy that allows states to act effectively in dealing with other states as well as with firms and other entities operating in international affairs. The fundamental structure that constrains everyone's behavior is primarily shaped by the distribution of capabilities among the major powers; however, other countries face opportunities and challenges in coping with others. Those that maintain their internal coherence and strength can often have important effects in their regions as well as in broader international affairs. For example, Malaysia provides important leadership within the Association of Southeast Asian Nations (ASEAN), and it has consistently supplied troops for United Nations peacekeeping missions deployed in the post-Cold War period. In contrast, poor and divided, weak states cannot exercise influence in international arenas and may themselves become targets of the depredations of others. Two West African states, Liberia and Sierra Leone, provide post-Cold War examples of the awful misfortunes of such weak countries. Both suffered not just civil wars but also brutal looting and rapacious interventions by neighboring states.

Unequal material and political resources not only affect states' abilities to exert influence in their international environments and reduce their vulnerabilities to interventions by other states but also condition the consequences of broader forces operating generally. In cases of major air pollution, for example, wind currents as well as geographical location in relation to the sources of such pollution result in very different effects on different countries. Although such problems present concerns across the globe, the differential impacts promise that each country will calculate effects on itself and that international cooperation on common policies will be difficult to achieve.

In addition to material resources and political coherence, states remain unequal in their cultural diversity. Although culture tends to be fraught with immense analytical difficulty, different societal arrangements, systems of belief, patterns of logic, mythologies, and value structures appear to shape the choices that the leaders and peoples of different countries make. A culture's placing a high value on education for its citizens and a historical tradition of equality among classes, in a case like that of South Korea, probably contributed to the myriad choices made that led to the immense increase in material wealth that the country enjoyed in the latter part of the twentieth century. Difficulties for such an analysis arise immediately when one notes that North Korea shares the same culture but has followed a very different material and policy path.

Max Weber's thesis that the Protestant ethic contributed mightily to the rise of capitalism in Europe has been substantially weakened by the extraordinary triumph of capitalism in Japan and other Asian countries. Lee Kuan Yew's trumpeting of a system of Asian values has been scorned by other Asians, particularly in the wake of the 1997–1998 Asian economic crisis. Samuel Huntington's theme of civilizational faultlines has drawn quite damaging criticism, and his claims of backwardness of the Islamic world have been belied by the technological and material advance of such Muslim countries as Malaysia. Still, uneven development has occurred, and the rapid growth of some countries contrasted with the economic and political decline of others cannot be attributed entirely to different material forces or to broad international or global systems. Each country makes choices, and those choices are partly shaped by cultural traits.

To examine such matters carefully, one needs to study specific countries with distinctive traits (Lentner 2003). Such case studies may be painstaking, but they offer a solid avenue on which to ride toward knowledge of how culture affects choice. During and following the Cold War, many scholars turned their attention to cultural aspects of the Soviet Union and Russia in order better to understand the choices that were being made. Surely part of the explanation of Soviet choices lies in the material base, but the interesting question that poses itself is: Why did the material base collapse? Economists can give part of the answer in pointing to the slowdown in productivity growth. However, that begs the question of why productivity did not increase; and the answer may be found in part in the rigidities of communist ideology and Russian cultural practices that got in the way of making a transition to an information-based phase of industrialization that more flexible capitalist, democratic countries had begun to make and were in the process of moving along.

Material inequalities and cultural differences, thus, have extended ramifications with regard to the choices that states make as they seek to maintain their positions in the international system. Beyond the implications for choice, inequalities of position also result in uneven consequences of broad trends in the world for different states. Although it remains true that certain developments such as environmental degradation, communicable diseases, drug trafficking, and political violence including wars have wide-ranging effects that extend beyond the borders of discrete states, those effects have quite different impacts on countries. In part, different impacts result from location along the path that developments follow. For example, diseases do not occur everywhere simultaneously; they start in one place and spread to others. Countries with advanced public health facilities most likely will prove less vulnerable to the spread of plagues than those with only primitive conditions. Similarly, war and disorder work their effects quite unevenly, with fighting, combat casualties, and civilian damage wreaking havoc in zones of war, often producing refugees who flee to neighboring countries which, although affected, incur costs sharply reduced from those imposed on the belligerent areas.

These four—material inequality, geographical location, cultural distinctiveness, and divergent vulnerability—and the resulting differences in ramifications for different countries produce for each country a discrete perspective on global processes. From the viewpoint of a less developed weak country, broad and rapid international financial flows may appear more threatening than promising. In contrast, countries with major private credit providers are more likely to perceive possibilities for increases in wealth. Both may concern themselves with the need for regulation of financial flows, but each will bring to the bargaining table its own set of interests and concerns. In the end, moreover, the leaders of each country know that they need to interpret their country's interests and be prepared to act for them by their own efforts should cooperation fail. Frequently, the costs and benefits of cooperation among states favor collaboration to achieve common or parallel interests. Nevertheless, the conditions under discussion point to the difficulties of achieving cooperation. Beyond impeding agreements to work together, the conditions often provide incentives to defect from compacts reached. As a result, implementation of cooperative pacts achieves as much significance as the signing of accords in the first place.

Given this situation, many efforts have been expended to build institutions involving common norms and rules and international intergovernmental organizations. Because threats often menace more than one country at a time and opportunities offer advantages to many, states regularly achieve cooperation. At the same time, the institutions and organizations that are built persist as mechanisms for the coordination of policies and possess little, if any, autonomy themselves but remain instruments of states, mainly the more powerful ones.

International Organizations and Institutions

In order to achieve those objectives and conditions that individual states cannot accomplish alone, states form organizations and build institutions together with others that are similarly constrained to cooperate internationally. The rhetoric employed to gain the cooperation of others in striving for one's ends results in much misunderstanding about the nature of such organizations and institutions. Because discrete states' interests diverge, leaders use such symbols as world peace, international community, and other phrases to include other countries in promoting their endeavors. Most prominent discourse tends to be generated by the leading states which more often than not set the common agendas. Still, diplomats from small states declare themselves in favor of democracy within organizations, by which they mean that one state, regardless of size of population, should have one vote. They may also declaim on behalf of equality, arguing that, although weak and often incapable of bearing responsibilities, they should count as much as heavily populated, rich, and powerful states that do have the capacity to carry out tasks. In addition to using rhetorical devices, leading states also seek broader legitimacy for their actions as a means of lowering the costs of carrying out their ventures.

This line of argument does not intend to convey the impression that all diplomatic discourse within international organizations and institutions is cynical. That is not the case, for often threats do impinge upon many states, and mechanisms such as the United Nations Security Council do afford the means for coordinating the policies of interested states and formal decision procedures for ensuring that various states are able to voice their views about joint actions being considered. In the logic of the situation, however, each state strives to achieve its own interests. Furthermore, this tendency of thought calls attention to the distinctive aspects of formulating cooperative undertakings in international organizations: separate and compatible foreign policies, rhetoric designed to gain cooperation and influence, a legitimation process, and the clearly distinguishable dimensions of declaratory policy and implementation. In such places as Rwanda, Bosnia, Kosovo, and so forth, the means to implement what are rhetorically referred to as profound resolutions as often as not fail to materialize because states possessing the wherewithal to carry them out determine not to deploy their resources.

Just as major powers pursue policies through international organizations, so do smaller states use those organizations for their own purposes. For example, some states prove willing to dispatch their troops in peacekeeping operations as long as the financial costs of doing so are picked up by wealthier states. Bangladesh has gained a reputation for such actions. Others cooperate in such endeavors in order to sustain their reputations as committed partners in maintaining orderly international regimes. Thus a country such as Malaysia has sent troops to every post-Cold War United Nations peacekeeping operation, with the obvious instrumental payoff of reflecting on the country as a reliable participant in the prevailing liberal world order.

International organizations not only afford mechanisms for states to pursue their international objectives and to coordinate their policies with others; they also provide cover for states aiming to avoid dealing with extremely difficult or intractable problems. One glaring example involves the care of refugees from areas of war and turmoil, a problem that grew exponentially in the post-Cold War period. By relying upon the United Nations High Commissioner for Refugees and other agencies such as the United Nations International Children's Emergency Fund, the powers can avoid becoming embroiled in very sticky problems germane to the politics of the refugee-engendering countries and the receiving countries. Especially since the end of the Cold War, international nongovernmental organizations have provided additional means for powers to insulate themselves from inconvenient situations.

International Nongovernmental Organizations

From liberal societies spring many private groups, a number of which take an interest in matters affecting other countries and widespread problems. Some groups act primarily as advocates for specific causes. Among the more well-known such groups stands Amnesty International, an organization that opposes the repression of civilian political activists, torture, and the death penalty. Many private associations lobby governments, firms, and intergovernmental organizations on behalf of protecting the natural environment. Advocacy activities of such groups have grown to include broad participation in, or parallel to, international intergovernmental organizations. Many groups are credentialed to present their positions to the United Nations

Economic and Social Council (ECOSOC) and they post representatives to New York. Additionally, nongovernmental organizations have held parallel meetings in the vicinity of United Nations conferences, seeking to affect the official deliberations and the general public discussion of the issues involved.

Other groups engage in relief and humanitarian activities in zones of natural disasters and wars. For example, the International Red Cross enters into combat situations, ministering to the medical and health needs of the personnel of all belligerents. Another prominent organization, Doctors Without Borders, dispatches professional medical personnel into areas of violent conflict to dispense medicine and health care to the sick and wounded. The International Rescue Committee assists refugees by providing temporary food and shelter and then in seeking resettlement and starting to plant crops and build structures. Oxfam and Catholic Charities mount massive feeding programs for refugees and people displaced or downtrodden by war and natural disasters. These and many other private humanitarian organizations contribute tremendous amounts of work and assistance to millions of miserable people under adverse and grossly deplorable conditions. Efforts exerted by workers rise sometimes to the heroic and often to the admirable. In the post-Cold War period these activities have proliferated, especially in Africa and Southeastern Europe.

The prominence gained by nongovernmental organizations as both lobbyists and operators in international relations has led some observers to regard them as important and independent actors that, in some ways, displace states or at least add a significant new dimension to international life in the form of a civil society. Although that view is not without merit, it tends to mask the connections between these private actors and states and to inflate the position of nongovernmental organizations in international power arrangements. One estimate indicates that states subsidize the budgets of international nongovernmental organizations at the level of sixty percent of their revenue (Lehmann 1990).

More directly, nongovernmental organizations often conduct their activities under contract with governmental agencies such as the United States Agency for International Development (USAID), with the clear implication that their work has been authorized by a government and that public functions have simply been privatized. As a result, citizens have increasing difficulty in establishing accountability, for this situation divorces public action from direct lines of authority and responsibility. When a private organization carries out governmental functions, it cannot be held accountable in a political process. Instead, accountability has become an administrative matter, in which the private group is responsible only to the government agency. However, the pretense persists that the group engages exclusively in private voluntary activities. Such obfuscation also provides a cover for a government to withdraw from activities with which it wishes not to be saddled.

World Problems

With the increased awareness engendered by contemporary communications, some observers perceive as global and worldwide current and impending manifestations of certain developments, particularly those concerning the environment, population growth, and migration but also including crime and drugs, disease, and war and disorder. Although none of these matters can be claimed to be new in human affairs, their dimensions appear different now than before; and the increasing connectedness of people in different parts of the world allows selected examples of them to be placed as issues on an international agenda.

Most prominent among these concerns, several environmental matters have gained increasing attention since the rise of green parties in Europe and environmentally concerned interest groups in the United States and other countries in the early 1970s. The most alarmist of these movements have receded in the face of analyses and empirical developments that place the concerns in a balanced context. For example, neo-Malthusians engaged in a rhetoric that greatly exaggerated what some of them called the "population bomb" (Ehrlich 1968) that portended exponential growth of the human population and the stripping of the earth of its resources. Some alarmists argued that the earth would soon run out of room for all the people on it.

Despite providing a distorted formulation of the problem, Sowell's perspective gives some balance to the issue. Taking "the American dream" of providing a family of four with a quarter-acre plot in the suburbs, the Chicago economist offered the perspective that the entire population of the world could easily reside in the state of Texas. Although the world's population did double from 3.0 billion in 1952 to 6.0 billion in 1999, the rate of increase has fallen in response to a variety of political actions to stem the growth. In the developed countries, it has become common for birth rates to fall behind replacement rates, population growth coming entirely from net immigration. Moreover, health and reproductive programs have taken hold in most less developed countries, leading to substantial reductions in birth rates.

A second alarm was sounded in 1971 with the publication of the Club of Rome-sponsored study, *The Limits to Growth* (Meadows et al. 1974), which forecast the exhaustion of the world's "finite" resources and falling standards of living if drastic measures were not taken to cut both production and consumption and to end "waste." Julian Simon (1981) offered an analytical refutation of these claims by showing that natural resources are not finite, that market forces would ration goods should they become scarce, that the prices of commodities steadily fall, and that substitutes provide the services that natural resources offer. Simon's argument has been vindicated by the empirical evidence showing an increase in the known quantity of such commodities as petroleum, the falling price of any basket of primary products, the substitution of such commodities as copper wire in telephone communications by fiber optics and wireless telephony, and the rising standard of living in the more than thirty years since the Club of Rome's dire predictions of decline.

To a large extent, the debate about natural resources has shifted to a focus on renewable resources, and the discourse about population has been redirected from raw growth to migration and displacement. Furthermore, the discussions about environment have been restructured into a balanced consideration of economic growth and environmental protection, symbolized by the fashionable term, coined by the Brundtland Commission's *Our Common Future* (World Commission 1987), "sustainable development."

Undoubtedly, the world faces certain broad problems concerning the environment and the need to provide for a growing human population. That the latter places stresses on the natural environment cannot be doubted. At the same time, industrial production places immensely greater strains on it than does population. Nevertheless, problems can be addressed more effectively if they are carefully stated, understood in historical and related contexts, and analyzed in realistic rather than utopian political frameworks. Given the notorious proneness to error that projections have, it also seems more prudent to be clear about what is unknown and therefore cannot be solved, if at all, until sufficient information and greater insight become available.

Another caution needs to be stated before attempting an analysis of these various world problems. Despite the increasing evidence that certain problems—global warming is one—may have worldwide repercussions, the effects on different geographical areas and places with distinctive economic conditions are bound to be widely divergent. In addition, attempts to take advantage of or to ameliorate local effects of such global phenomena will be determined in part by an existing distribution of power; power arrangements, in turn, may be reshaped by the uneven effects across the globe. Thus, even should one be able to state the problem with precision, one also needs to understand that a complex and reciprocal relationship will exist among the global problem formulated as a natural or scientific phenomenon, local natural conditions conducive to accepting or rejecting the effects of the global phenomenon, and political power exercised through extant and changing arrangements. With those cautions, I turn to an analysis of several global issues.

Environment

Going back to the first human settlements, economic and military activities have inflicted damage on the natural environment. Very ancient agricultural techniques such as slash-and-burn farming destroy natural vegetation in order to create spaces for systematic crop production. Centuries ago, China was denuded of its forests. As the United States was settled, pioneers cut down the oak forests of New England and plowed under the grasslands of the Midwest. More recently in the post-World War II period, Costa Rica removed over seventy percent of its rainforest to make way for coffee production and cattle raising, in large part to satisfy the North American market for caffeine fixes and hamburgers. Today, Brazilians and Indonesians burn rainforests in order to prepare the way for economic production. These activities across the centuries and millennia represent the continuity of human striving for sustenance and betterment. From an economic point of view, the costs of human material improvement were borne by nature.

Discontinuity came into focus as the industrial revolution, especially the massive developments since 1850, imposed greater stresses on the natural environment as consumption increased immensely in the advanced industrial countries. In addition, observers pointed to the externalities of production that inflicted great damage on nature and appeared to be transferring costs from the living generation to its successors. The unprecedented economic prosperity that grew in the post-

World War II period introduced not just new technologies and new devastations of the environment but also engendered among many citizens a new consciousness of the damages and costs involved. Thus new political concerns were placed on the agendas of the industrialized countries and of the world. In part, the new consciousness in the industrialized portion of the world produced political aspirations to cut back on economic development, a project that threatened to make permanent the division of rich and poor countries.

Leaders in the less developed countries countered this incipient project in the run-up to the United Nations conference scheduled for Stockholm in 1972 by insisting that the meeting should be dedicated not exclusively to the environment but also to development. Their success was evidenced both by the agenda that included both items and by the siting of a newly created international organization to deal with environmental problems in Nairobi. Similar tensions manifested themselves at the second conference held in Rio de Janeiro in 1992, even after the attempt to resolve them by the phrasing "sustainable development."

Concerns with the natural environment range across a number of matters, but attention has focused mainly on destruction of the natural environment by industrial pollution and accidents such as oil spills and nuclear power plant meltdowns, depletion of the ozone layer, global warming, exhaustion of renewable resources, and destruction of animal and plant species.

Some of these problems have been effectively addressed. For example, the United States has led the way in regulating industrial pollution through emissions-control legislation and providing for the clean-up of toxic wastes. Certain other countries have passed similar laws (Paarlberg 1997). In addition, the adoption of international agreements in Vienna in 1985 and Montreal in 1987 to phase out chloro-fluorocarbons (CFCs), which caused the depletion of the ozone layer, led to the happy result that the hole in the ozone layer in the southern hemisphere has begun to recede. One of the deals made at the 1992 Rio Summit conference included the trade of preservation of forests for debt relief.

On the other hand, it seems more likely that responses to such problems as global warming will occur in the future on a country-by-country basis, as the effects become known, despite efforts to coordinate policies under the Framework Convention on Climate Change and the Kyoto Protocol. Perhaps the most important consideration in this speculation is that global warming will affect different countries in dramatically different ways. For example, while the low-lying coastal regions of Bangladesh may be inundated, permanently driving farmers away from the source of their livelihood, Russia may finally surmount its endemic agricultural deficit as new lands become cultivable and old fields increase yields in the new climatic conditions. Such differential impacts of global warming promise that adjustments are more likely to be made on a per-country basis than through collective action. Thus, even with respect to a problem that may more easily be defined as global than many others, facing it and attempting to find solutions or means of adjustment turn out to be the responsibilities of individual states, although it remains imaginable that those states' specific adjustments might be eased by international cooperative arrangements.

The tension that arose between the rich and poor countries, which respectively gave priority to preserving the environment and promoting economic development, emanated in part from a mistaken understanding of the causes of environmental degradation. Neo-Malthusians tended to frame the issue as one of increasing human populations pressing upon limited nonrenewable resources. That formulation resulted from two errors: resources are more abundant and the services they provide more fungible than such analysts estimated; and greater pressures on resources stem from high levels of industrial production and mass consumption in the rich countries than from increasing populations in the poor parts of the world. In effect, the mistaken analysis led to a project that entailed placing the burden of costs of consumption by the rich on the poor. Unsurprisingly, the poor rejected the project and insisted on their own economic growth. That misunderstanding of the relationship among population, economic development, and environment led to advocating counterproductive policies, for it is enrichment and rising standards of living—not poverty and reduced levels of living—that tend to produce declining population growth rates. Thus inequalities in wealth in the world are matched by inequalities in birth and death rates as well as in resulting unequal rates of population growth. Once again, accurate analysis requires attention to different states and avoidance of misplaced emphasis upon the globe as a unit.

Population and migration

Slowly increasing over the millennia, the human population of the world began faster growth as modern science and the industrial revolution contributed to health, higher standards of living, and enhanced expectations of longevity. By producing more goods and providing increased opportunities for employment, the industrial revolution sustained the livelihood of larger numbers of people. In addition, the application of public health measures and the spreading of public sanitation contributed to a significant lowering of the death rate, which paved the way for very large increases in the population. Public health measures and conception control devices offered the instruments for reducing the birth rate, and public policies promoted family planning to restrict the number of children. Although both facilitative and coercive measures have had some effect in reducing the birth rate in most countries, the most significant population control measure has proved to be rising standards of living and the increased expectations engendered by the most highly productive and high consumption societies.

Thus, in the latter part of the twentieth century, it became common for the advanced industrial countries to be characterized by a population profile in which the birth rate remained below that needed for replacement of the extant population. At the same time, these countries' wealth and economic opportunities attracted immigrants from poorer countries whose populations exceeded the ability of their production systems to afford jobs and adequate living standards. Therefore, what may be considered to be a global population problem turns out to be an international one in which the stresses of one society tend to be alleviated, at least in part, by the abundance of other societies.

This development has led to a shift of analytical emphasis from population growth to migration. However, the change does not deal directly with the stressed societies; instead, it calls attention to inequalities among states and brings to the fore a concern with economic growth and development in the poorer countries. This concern is treated in Chapter 7. Furthermore, the refocused emphasis does not capture many of the dimensions of the issue of human migration.

Humans have always moved from place to place, sometimes temporarily but more frequently on a permanent basis. People from Southeast Asia moved up to Japan, and Asian migrants peopled North and South America some 10,000 years ago. Mohammad's founding of Islam soon sparked a movement out of Arabia to North Africa and into the Iberian peninsula. Following Columbus' voyages in 1492 and after, Europeans began moving to the western hemisphere, and they soon began bringing slaves from Africa to replace the decimated indigenous populations. In the middle and latter part of the nineteenth century, Europeans flowed across the Atlantic to people the western hemisphere.

Today, Koreans, Palestinians, and Filipinos regularly migrate to the oil-rich Southwest Asian countries; Central Americans and South Americans as well as Mexicans migrate to the United States to perform those low-level, poorly paid, but necessary tasks needed for the smooth running of a complex modern economy, and they are joined by Africans, Asians, Russians, and others; Bangladeshis, Indonesians, and Burmese go to work in Malaysia and other wealthier countries of Southeast Asia; and Turks and Greeks and other southern Europeans and North Africans emigrate to the rich northern European countries where they find employment opportunities and new lives.

Added to these migrations, a contingent of highly educated, specially skilled workers from many less developed countries move to the advanced industrial countries who employ them in such positions as scientists, computer programmers, university teachers, and so forth. Because the costs of transportation have been so drastically reduced, there has emerged in the contemporary world also a small group of persons who permanently reside, on an alternating basis, in two countries.

In addition to these broad movements impelled by economic incentives, another category of migration stems from political turmoil, war, civil strife, and related dangers to life. Although the production of refugees and displaced persons has also characterized episodes recurring throughout human history, the twentieth century proved especially cruel by generating millions upon millions of people driven from their homes. In Europe in mid-1945, for example, some fifty million people found themselves wandering in the aftermath of World War II. Throughout the Cold War, people fled in droves from political violence: in South Asia following the partition of British India in 1947; in the Fertile Crescent following Israel's declaration of independence in 1948; in China following the triumph of the communists in 1949; in Korea during the war from 1950 to 1953; in Hungary in 1956; in Vietnam and Cambodia in the 1970s; and so forth, and so forth. Turmoil and war both during and after the Cold War generated millions upon millions of refugees and displaced persons, with an estimated 21.8 million refugees living away from home in 2002 (UNHCR 2002). The large numbers of the late twentieth and early twenty-first centuries result from another general development of the era.

War

War has become popularized through total war and guerrilla tactics, with the result that many more civilians than soldiers are killed in combat in the contemporary era. From early in the twentieth century total war involving whole populations has become the norm in an industrial age in which the factory worker producing munitions contributes as much to a war effort as the soldier who employs them on the battlefield. With the reach provided particularly by aircraft, then, civilians and infrastructure have become military targets. In one sense, the apogee of targeting civilians was reached in World War II with the firestorm-creating bombing of London, Hamburg, Dresden, Tokyo, and Hiroshima. In another sense, the destruction of infrastructure in Iraq in 1991 and in rump Yugoslavia in 1999 have been done with far fewer civilian casualties than in earlier wars.

Guerrilla warfare, which deliberately elides the distinction between combatants and civilians, has also contributed to the pass to which the human race has come at the beginning of the twenty-first century. Techniques of terror that had once been directed at undermining governmental authority, as in the murder of school teachers and mayors during the war in Vietnam, have been transposed into brutalization of civilians for possibly supporting a government, as in the hacking off of farmers' hands in Sierra Leone in 1999. In 2001 civilians were deliberately targeted by the nongovernmental organization Al Qaeda based in Afghanistan when hijackers flew airliners into the World Trade Center towers in New York and the Pentagon in Virginia.

Even though these characteristics of war at the turn of the century engendered significant movements of people, whose plight occasionally was brought to the attention of the publics of the advanced countries, none of it can reasonably be thought to be global, for the larger global characteristic occurs in the differences among people in different countries.

Contrast the American bomber crew with the civilians who must remain on the ground. Nearly impervious to injury from hostile gunfire or other combative action, the bomber crew enjoys a rich diet, comfortable housing, luxurious vacations, expensive and intellectually rich educations, access to high art and varied popular culture, all in a secure country with healthy friends and family, in short a good life. None of these advantages adhere to the civilians on the ground in a poor country in turmoil: they face hunger, death and injury from gunfire and other combative action, homelessness, despair, poverty, disease, separation from friends and family, in short a nasty and brutish life.

The central characteristic, viewed from a global perspective, then, is inequality and difference on a series of dimensions. It remains, thus, difficult to find a useful conceptualization of world problems, for politically the world is not a unit, and on most dimensions it is not a unit. Politically, economically, culturally, and socially, the world remains an international one, with separate states interacting within certain novel forms in increasingly connected ways. For the most part, however, whatever imaginative aspirations some observers may have for a global unit, descriptive analysis is served more effectively by framing the problems as specific state problems. Such framing raises an entirely new set of puzzles and questions.

Specific State Problems

Specific countries participate in the international economy and cooperate in multilateral endeavors, but they do so in order to increase their own autonomy. For example, since 1978 China has turned increasingly to the global arena to acquire markets, investments, and technology, but it has done so not by submerging its own interests and national life within a homogeneous worldwide system. China participates in cooperative arrangements in order to continue to build its independence and strength, to bring about the unification of the country which had been partly divided by imperialist action between 1850 and 1949, and to extend its influence to other matters in the world where it determined its interests are involved. Although involvement in cooperative endeavors with other states does bring with it certain constraints, these pale in comparison to the burdens under which China operated when it was weak and subject to penetration by the leading powers and to military defeat in 1894-1895, in World War I, and again in the 1937–1945 period. As China grows economically and acquires modern, effective military capabilities, its autonomy will increase even in the context of operating within the constraints of globalization processes.

Those constraints do require certain adaptations in China's domestic economy, legal system, and society in order to take advantage of the opportunities offered by the international political economy. All the evidence, however, indicates that China as a coherent state retains its ability to choose how to deal with the pressures emanating from abroad and that it is increasing the capabilities that will make the choices effective.

That such a giant and ancient civilization as China should retain its autonomous ability to choose how to deal with the conundrums of international politics might be thought to be exceptional, that smaller, weaker, less deeply based states have lost their autonomy. To illustrate that small vulnerable countries also retain their autonomy and in fact enhance it through globalization processes, Singapore offers a superb example.

The location of Singapore provides both a strategic asset and the key to its economic growth. Under the British Empire, the island housed a fortress for the protection of the Malay Peninsula and the Strait of Malacca, although the Japanese easily captured it from the rear at the onset of World War II in Asia. Its economic development occurred as a result of changes in the international economy that were taken advantage of by innovative and energetic residents. With the opening of the Suez Canal in 1869 and the advent of steamships Singapore became a main port for the Malayan trade (Huff 1994, p. 8). A burst of commercial activity based upon the staple products, tin, rubber, and petroleum ensued and lasted through

1960. Following independence and a short-lived union with Malaysia, Singapore turned to manufacturing, and its economy grew at the remarkable rate of an annual average of 10.3 percent from 1966 to 1980 and then during the eighties at the annual rate of 7.2 percent. By 1990 Singapore's per capita income was US$11,160 (Huff 1994, pp. 30-31).

Although its economy was transformed after independence, it grew from a fairly high base, and it was able, through extensive government direction, to take advantage of favorable developments in the international political economy. By responding to international developments, Singapore added services as a third important sector supplementing staple port activities and manufacturing. These services included transport and communications services that made Singapore a shipping and air traffic center, tourism, and—most important—financial and business services (Huff 1994, p. 38). More recently, the country has invested in biotechnology research and development facilities (Arnold 2003).

Few states have enjoyed such success as Singapore's, although many have experienced substantial economic growth at differential rates. Inequality remains the central characteristic of the international system in which states with varied histories and distinctive cultures exist in different circumstances and face assorted challenges and opportunities. Although convergence appears to occur in general (Barro 1997), growth takes time and is shaped by many different factors. Among these is the prior experience, often of colonialism, that has paved the way to present levels of production.

For example, Cumings (1987) has demonstrated that South Korea and Taiwan acquired strong bureaucratic traditions from the Japanese through the first half of the twentieth century, and South Korea had the further experience of a semi-colonial relationship with the United States for a long time. One result of the Korean war was the militarization of the society, but another was the elimination of the power of the landlord class. Partly through the support of the United States, South Korean government direction of the economy was established. In South Korea, the government is distinguished by its ability to implement its policies because of the existence of a "hard state" (Koo 1987).

Another determinant of differential growth is comparative advantage, which in Singapore's case was derived from location. During the operation of the product cycle in which manufacturing moves from its place of origin to other countries, cheap and skilled labor offers a temporary comparative advantage. Some countries benefit from their resource endowments, such as fertile agricultural soil, climate, or mineral deposits. Each of these nevertheless needs to be managed, directed, and shaped by an effective government determined to achieve economic development.

Such governmental direction can often go further by selecting industrial and commercial sectors to enter, thus to an extent shaping comparative advantage. Without the natural resources of iron ore, Japan and then South Korea chose to and did become leading producers of steel and automobiles. Korea then entered the shipbuilding business and became the world's leader. Singapore's choice to enter the financial services sector followed a similar logic. All of these choices emanated from effective governments that took advantage of world markets rather than restricting themselves to their national markets. At the same time, such a choice means that the country must compete with producers everywhere. That implies that behind the choice lie such attributes as imagination and courage as well as a commitment to the public good of the nation.

Not every country is endowed with an elite possessing such attributes. Some leaderships make wrong choices even when dedicated to development, but others do not possess any conception of public good at all. Instead, they are personally self-serving and use their state apparatuses as mechanisms of exploitation and self-enrichment; they lead predatory states.

Although general trends in the world at large are generated by the more powerful states and present both opportunities and challenges to others, those trends have significantly different impacts on different countries because they operate through national filtering processes that vary immensely. In observing and analyzing what goes on in the world, then, one is well served by recalling that, although from one perspective problems may be viewed from a worldwide angle, each country confronts its own circumstances in its own way. It copes with the constraints of its own past and its endowments as well as with the constraints of the international system and the distinctive objectives of other states having an interest in its affairs. If there is any single dimension that makes a difference in how successfully a country is able to cope, it is an effective state, with all that that includes.

Conclusion

Despite a pronounced tendency within discussions about globalization and the contemporary world to assume that an integrated worldwide system is in the process of being formed, it is well to remember that a political system structured by unequal states remains extant. That implies that it is worthwhile to treat separate matters in distinct ways and to cling to distinctions that make a difference in the world. The fundamental nature of the international system stems from its composition by separate, mostly independent, sovereign states. Sufficient common interactions occur to make it reasonable to discuss collective matters. At the same time, it remains important to keep in mind that those matters tend largely to be shaped by the most powerful states in the system, and those leaders have a well-established tendency to frame issues as general ones rather than, as they really are, concerns of particular interest to the powers that define them. Moreover, the policies that operate as international collective policies stem primarily from the leading states and reflect their interests. Often these policies are pursued by use of international organizations, but that need not obscure the clear source of the policies, which remains states.

Because of the inequality of states and their divergent interests, it is also important to engage in discussion and analysis at the level of the state and society. Each state strives for autonomy but any state's position in the international system is distinct from that of every other state. Each state engages in cooperation with others in order to fend off intrusion or to build its strength. Engagement often provides a path to development and to increased strength, which puts a state in a position to participate both more independently and more fully in the international system.

Furthermore, both of the levels of analysis, system and state, need to be considered together in assessing the consequences of joint international actions. For the most part, the greater strength of the powers leads to payoffs for them. The consequences of joint international actions for the states against whom they are directed may occasionally provide benefits but, more often, they entail costs. On the other hand, from time to time smaller units can achieve their goals against the powerful.

In any case, it remains important to hold on to the distinction between international and state levels, for the issues and interests at play in any episode or sequence of events diverge between the two levels. This becomes even clearer in the following chapters which discuss the ways in which the system is managed and then the ways in which individual states cope with the pressures that operate at that system level.

5
Hegemony: The Liberal International Political Economy

Introduction

Induced by the United States, the leading states have since 1945 created a relatively coherent order in the world that serves primarily their interests. At the same time, the arrangements provide incentives for other states to join them. In cases in which countries such as Iran, Iraq, and others resist the dominant order, coercive devices are readily available for suppressing and/or discouraging them. Because different countries, whether acquiescent in or defiant of the hegemonic order, pursue separate and often distinctive interests based upon their unequal capabilities, the order tends to be applied rather loosely to those whose power enables them to follow exceptional behavior. The least-constrained country is the predominant one, the United States.

In common usage, hegemony means that a single country holds a preponderant position over others. For the most part, this is the meaning that is employed in the following discussion, although it becomes obvious that the United States' style of leadership combines leadership of others with unilateral action when necessary (Ikenberry 2001). However, the term has been invoked by different social scientists in recent years with overtones that will reverberate in the analysis of this chapter. Kindleberger (1973, 1981) introduced the notion that a liberal political economy requires a hegemon with command over sufficient resources to maintain an order. Gilpin (1981) elaborated the notion of hegemonic stability, noting that the hegemon supplies public goods to sustain a set of governing rules in the international political economy. Such goods include fundamental security, a stable currency for exchange and reserve, and sufficient economic strength to allow the hegemon to offer trading concessions to its partners and to provide financing assistance to help some of them.

Empirical developments led observers to perceive a problem of hegemonic decline as other powers recovered from the devastation of World War II and the

71

United States appeared to lose its dominant position. Among these developments were the increased pressures on the dollar in the 1960s that led to the Nixon administration's 1971 decisions to end its linkage of the dollar with gold and to force a revaluation of other currencies, effectively devaluing the dollar. The reordering of the arrangements for producing and marketing petroleum in the early 1970s and the quintupling of oil prices in 1973 and 1974 comprised another development that seemed to represent a step in hegemonic decline. Similarly, the achievement of rough parity in nuclear weapons by the Soviet Union gave rise to the view that the United States could no longer lay claim to preponderance in the world. From the American point of view especially, the defeat in the Vietnam war and the complete withdrawal of American military forces from Southeast Asia seemed to portend a significant loss of power, with the consequent deprivation of ability to shape the world.

Although this interpretation of events overlooked the underlying maintenance of the position of the United States in the international system (Nye 1990), it gave rise to some new thinking about what came to be called hegemonic stability theory. Keohane (1984) argued that, in addition to the material resources that underlay the hegemon's influence in shaping cooperative regimes in the international political economy, ideas played an important role. Specifically, Keohane used Gramsci's view to assert that hegemony consisted of both power and ideology. Thus, even in the face of the decline of power of the hegemon, regimes might persist because their participants are persuaded that their interests are served by extant principles and practices.

All of these views of hegemony have focused on the post-World War II period and have tried to measure the position of the United States after the early 1970s against its overwhelmingly preponderant standing in the mid- to late-1940s. However, the western hemispheric giant evolved its characteristics and style from a more distant base; so a longer-term view seems warranted. Such a perspective needs to take into account the characteristics of the country that have been projected abroad and the features of its leadership style as they have been manifested in a relatively consistent manner through history. In the absence of defeat in war and occupation by any major adversary, the United States has followed a trajectory of leadership that traced a relatively undisturbed path, allowing observers to see patterns of behavioral style.

As the power of the United States grew (at least in part because of its own internal political, social, and economic characteristics) in the last half of the nineteenth century, it projected its dynamic power across the world and promoted its preferred manner of doing things. From its inception, the United States was dedicated to a democratic political order while, at the same time, it tolerated the contradictory practice of suppressing a large segment of its own population in slavery and engaged in the forcible transfer of certain indigenous populations to small reserved territories. Economically, the United States stressed individual entrepreneurship, ownership of property, free enterprise, inventiveness, labor flexibility, and free trade and access to overseas markets. These principles have been applied in many different places and historical eras and, although consistency of application has not always prevailed, the United States has clung to them over the course of more than two centuries. As its power increased, the country remained—with the partial exception of the interwar period—vigorous in spreading the practice of its doctrines abroad.

Traces of American practice are found before the Civil War, for example, in exploitation of Britain's victory in the Opium War with China from 1839 to 1842 and the pressured opening of Japan by Admiral Perry in 1853 to 1854. The paradigmatic American style of hegemonic leadership first emerged in the latter part of the nineteenth century in the western hemisphere. From the early years of that century, the United States had consolidated its hold on its own territory by excluding the European powers, and that exclusion was extended to the hemisphere under the guidance of the Monroe Doctrine.

As its power increased, the United States was able to compel France and then Spain and Britain to withdraw from the Western Hemisphere. Simultaneous with the exclusion of the European powers, the United States sought to gain the cooperation of other western hemisphere countries through the mechanism of multilateral conferences, beginning with the first pan-American meeting in Washington in 1889. That the point of the exercise was to provide a mechanism for American use, in contrast to building an institution for the sake of establishing a rule-governed common regime, was evidenced by the Olney manifesto that "the United States is practically sovereign on this continent" [South America] and by the Roosevelt "corollary" to the Monroe Doctrine that gave rhetorical underpinning to policing practices by the United States in the circum-Caribbean region.

When convenient or necessary for the United States, the country's leadership employed such multilateral mechanisms as it had helped to create. On the other hand, Washington never demurred from acting unilaterally to achieve its objectives, as it did in going to war with Spain over Cuba, in supporting Panama's fight for independence from Colombia, in building the Panama Canal, or in intervening militarily in Nicaragua and Mexico and other countries around the rim of the Caribbean.

In initiating war with Spain, the United States exhibited several other traits that would recur in its foreign policy behavior over the course of the next century. First, although appearing to grow out of diplomacy, the action followed essentially a classic pattern of presenting an ultimatum followed by military attack. Spain had demonstrated its willingness to capitulate to American demands, but Washington ordered the military intervention despite that. Second, the United States entered into an action with a crusading spirit that carried the country beyond the initial aims of its policy. Added to the achievement of Cuba's detachment from Spain were the acquisition of Puerto Rico and the Philippines, the latter especially being an afterthought to the initial operation. Third, in dictating the terms of Cuban independence, the United States retained through the Platt Amendment the prerogative of intervening in Cuban affairs for several decades. An added aspect of the style included the formulation of a legal rule to offer legitimate cover to the arbitrary tutelage. These triumphs paved the way for repeated unilateral military interventions in the Caribbean area that have continued to this day, interrupted only first by World War I and then by the necessity to exclude from the western hemisphere, respectively, Germany in World War II and the Soviet Union during the Cold War.

Beginning in the Hoover administration and continued by the "good neighbor" policy under Roosevelt, the United States sought friendlier relations with Latin America by withdrawing its small military occupation force from Nicaragua in 1933. With war clouds accumulating in Europe, Washington found many ways of collaborating with regimes in the Latin American countries in the lead-up to and conduct of the war against fascism. Other techniques that became rather common in the post-war period included collaborative activities with other governments to suppress elements in the populations, substantial propaganda undertakings, military training of other countries' armed forces, economic subsidies, and shouldering of such burdens as incarcerating in the United States German citizens picked up by Latin American governments.

With the failed League of Nations, the dysfunctional "beggar-thy-neighbor" economic policy of the Great Depression, and the tremendous destruction of World War II as background, the United States led the victors in constructing post-war arrangements that aimed at avoiding the recent past. In exercising strong leadership, the Americans did not dictate, except to the vanquished, but they did forcefully present their views to their allies and they backed up their arguments with the impressive fund of resources at their disposal. Apart from the details of the order put into place at the end of the war, the overall vision and conceptualization embraced a very broad view of security and a global ambition with regard to economic and political arrangements. Many events have transpired since the post-war arrangements were first created, and both institutions and practices have experienced considerable change. Still, many of the broad outlines remain even half a century later, and the consistency of American goals and aspirations has carried forward the hegemonic project.

Although the hegemonic order of the post-World War II period enjoys a coherence and underlying consistency, it may be described as a set of regimes dealing, respectively, with security, trade, finance, and development. In addition, the United States and its allies have also faced problems not falling neatly into these categories. I examine those under the broader and more vague headings of management and coping. Despite the analytical convenience of dividing the discussion by regime, in reality all of the activities remain related. For example, security provides the foundation for trade and finance, but these in turn often reinforce security. On the other hand, such reciprocal effects sometimes work against each other, as would be the case in which, for example, the trading gains by a partner are converted into enhanced military capacity threatening to a secure order.

Security Regime

As World War II drew to a close, the American and Soviet armies stood above all others in a distribution of power not seen since the time of Rome and Carthage.

Enriched and enhanced by the tremendous productive power unleashed by the war, its home territory unscathed, armed with the most advanced weapon of all, the United States surpassed the Soviet Union in power by a wide margin, despite the latter's edge in military land forces. Less than fifty years later, without the necessity of reproducing the Roman victory over Carthage, the United States stood alone following the Soviet Union's decline, withdrawal from the superpower competition, and disintegration. In addition to the dominant position that the United States occupied in 1945, the Soviet Union's striving to compete and catch up spurred American policy makers and people to greater efforts than they might otherwise have exerted. These efforts resulted in the phenomenal successes of production, increases in power, and spread of influence that placed the United States in the privileged position that it held at the beginning of the twenty-first century.

At Yalta, the wartime allies forged security arrangements in Europe that were intended to be temporary but turned out to prove long-lasting; and at San Francisco, they established an organization, the United Nations, designed to maintain international peace and security as well and to serve other functions, that was designed for the long term but functioned poorly in the short run. The two related developments of freezing of the divisions of Europe at the end of the war and the failure to make the United Nations work led to the forging by the United States and its allies of the North Atlantic Treaty Organization which linked North American and Western European security against the Soviet Union, whose forces extended to Central Europe. NATO provided the institutional mechanism to solidify American involvement in European affairs, but it culminated rather than inaugurated the United States' permanent connection with Europe.

War against Germany and Italy demanded such a heavy expenditure of blood and treasure that the United States faced in 1945 the challenge of constructing an order that would ensure that the catastrophe just ended would not soon be repeated. Most immediately, the occupation of Germany ensured a temporary presence, and shortly the failure of the major allies to agree on a German peace treaty or on a broad restoration of Europe as a set of independent states led to the United States-Soviet competition that required a continued American presence at the center of the European divide. Soviet consolidation in Eastern Europe, in Poland beginning in 1944 and sealed with the Czechoslovak coup in 1948, evoked a fear among both Western Europeans and Americans that commanded the American presence.

Additional fears stoked by the elections in Italy and France in 1948 further promoted American interventions, and the stand-off of consolidation of the western allies' zones of occupation in Germany, exacerbated by the reaction of the blockading of Berlin by the Soviets and the counteraction of the American and British airlift further stiffened the resolve of Washington to stand firm in Central Europe. Meanwhile, initiation of the European Recovery Program, or Marshall Plan, pushed forward the integration process that has resulted in the European Union (Milward 1984). Integration also characterized NATO. The two expressions of multilateral coordination within institutional arrangements both emanated from United States' initiatives and stemmed initially from American power and resources, but they represent two distinct tracks.

European integration, which had been prompted by the insistence of the United States on coordination of Marshall Plan expenditures by the European governments participating in the scheme, has been carried forward under the leadership of France and West Germany whose interests have run parallel throughout the entire post-World War II period. France wanted to control Germany, and Germans aspired to acceptance and influence within the international community, coincidental motivations that have remained as the central dynamic moving European cooperation forward.

Coordinated planning and command within NATO, in contrast, occurred under the leadership of the United States, with the other allies remaining dependent for their security on the superpower leader of the alliance. Despite doubts and anxieties that led France to its own nuclear weapons program and withdrawal from NATO's integrated command system, and the prodding of allies by the United States for greater burden-sharing, the United States has remained not just at the forefront of the alliance but so predominant that the Europeans cannot perform essential military functions such as airlifting forces to forward battle zones and retaining battlefield management capabilities, not to speak of possessing and employing superpower-level nuclear weapons capabilities.

As the Cold War ended and Europe became a less dangerous place, NATO's assumption of the new role of policing the Balkans demonstrated the essential features of the security arrangements in Europe: European dependence on American leadership, command, and technology. Added to these very obvious features have been the incorporation of united Germany, including the East that had existed under Soviet domination during the Cold War, and of the three added members of the alliance: Poland, Hungary, and the Czech Republic. Other countries in Eastern Europe, former Soviet allies, stand in line to join NATO.

This American predominance in European security forms but one leg of a three-legged stool of security, the others planted in the western hemisphere and at the western edge of the Pacific. Altogether, they comprise the security underpinning of globalization that is based on the foundation of United States military control of its own hemisphere flanked by two oceans and encompassing the mighty fortresses of Western Europe and Japan. The capacity for that military control stems from and is bolstered by what some call the G-3, the industrial giants of the United States, European Union, and Japan. The center of this system lies in the fortress provided by the United States itself. The terrorist attacks in 2001 comprised a serious hit but did not significantly weaken the fortress.

With the exception of a defiant Cuba, the western hemisphere remains under the protection of the United States. Resistance to American domination has emerged from various quarters and in many forms, but the United States has crushed it or found other methods for bringing recalcitrant partners in its Americas enterprise back into the fold. Throughout the twentieth century, the United States intervened militarily in the circum-Caribbean region in every period except the 1930s and 1940s. Often, such interventions took the form of direct invasion, as in Mexico in 1914, in Nicaragua in 1926, in the Dominican Republic in 1965, Grenada in 1983, Panama in 1989, and Haiti in 1994. On other occasions, the United States employed surrogates, with minimal support from covert American actions, as in Guatemala in 1954, Chile from 1970 to 1973, and Nicaragua throughout the 1980s. Often, Washington supported governments and armed forces in suppressing rebellions as it did in the 1960s in the counterguerrilla activities that accompanied the Alliance for Progress, in El Salvador from 1981 to 1992, and in the late 1990s and early 2000s in Colombia.

At the same time, the United States offered support and encouragement to groups and governments willing to join its liberal project of alliance and trade. Reversing its damaging protectionist policies of the 1930s, the United States extended wartime measures of economic support to Latin American countries during World War II. After the war, Washington promoted free trade and investment in the region; in later periods new programs such as the Alliance for Progress, the neoliberal project of the 1980s, and the promotion of export-oriented development in the 1990s were promulgated. All rested upon the foundation of western hemisphere security.

The northern border of the United States was secured both by a legacy of peaceful relations and by Canada's membership in the North Atlantic Treaty Organization. In 1947, the Rio Treaty was forged as a mechanism for security coordination in the western hemisphere excepting Canada and the then British colonies in the Caribbean. That mechanism provided the means for other countries to follow American initiatives such as imposing diplomatic and economic sanctions on Cuba, intervening militarily in the Dominican Republic, and running a pacification operation in Haiti.

Security was served also by diplomatic actions aimed at mollifying partners' grievances. For example, the Panama Canal treaties of 1979 led to withdrawal at the end of 1999 of the United States from continuous military control of a zone of Panamanian territory, while at the same time allowing access in the event of any major threat to the security of the Canal.

In the Pacific theater, the United States at the end of World War II extended its territorial domain by acquiring the islands north of the equator that Japan had acquired from Germany at the end of World War I and held under mandate from the League of Nations. These so-called strategic trust territories have remained as important bases, especially after the Philippines and the United States proved unable to agree on the continued American use of military bases in the former colony. In addition, the United States first occupied and then later negotiated base rights in Okinawa and other places in Japan. Following the occupation of Japan, the alliance between these two countries in which Japan remains exceptionally dependent on United States military protection has remained in force. Although less obeisant than Japan, South Korea also remains dependent on American protection, and it provides the United States with its last continental base in East Asia. For purposes of commerce and the pursuit of wealth, security in the Pacific is assured, for no other power challenges American military domination of the world's largest ocean.

Perhaps the most impressive feature of this security regime may be seen in its foundation on official United States policy. Determination to exclude outside powers from the western hemisphere has formed an important component of

American government policy for well over a century. As the competition with the Soviet Union emerged out of the breakup of the World War II Grand Alliance, the United States committed itself to the defense of Western Europe, and that has remained a touchstone of American policy since. Upon that touchstone has been built a further commitment to remain involved in European security in the time after the end of the Cold War. Similarly in East Asia, the occupation of Japan and the Korean war, shaped in the context of the Soviet challenge, led to a continued resolve to secure the western edge of the ocean; and China's recapture of its independence as well as its effective pursuit of wealth and prestige perpetuate that determination.

Should the United States decide to pull back from its forward defense positions and lose interest in an expansive role in the world, others would be constrained to look out for their own security. Similarly, should others strong enough to do so tire of their dependence upon the North American giant, they might also forge new policies to take care of their own security, and that would modify the arrangements that have been put into place. Nevertheless, it is the fortitude of the United States that sustains the security order underlying globalization, and it is largely the forbearance of the United States that assures cooperative partners sufficiently to dissuade them from resenting too much their dependence on the superpower.

Aside from the safety that the American policy of broad-based defense and security provides, prosperity and well-being provide props to allied support for the neoliberal order. Pursuit of wealth offers an instrumental incentive to partners. Thus another prop of globalization depends very much on the economic engines of the prosperous industrialized countries. Should that incentive collapse as a result of a deep depression, all countries would be likely to cast about for alternative solutions to the problems of their national lives. Whether a collective solution might be found would only be seen as events unfolded.

Meanwhile, dissatisfied and/or fearful rulers and groups seek greater freedom of action by pursuing policies to weaken the security order or to prepare for assaults on it. These include weak terrorist groups that mount hurtful but primarily symbolic attacks on facilities of the major powers. For example, the bombings presumably by the Osama Bin Laden group Al Qaeda against poorly secured American embassies in Dar es Salaam and Nairobi in 1998 caused considerable property damage of the sites themselves and many deaths, a stark toll. On the other hand, they had a barely perceptible impact on the power and prestige of the United States. Similarly, the attacks on the United States itself in 2001 did significant property damage and took 3000 lives. At the same time, the dramatic nature and devastation of the attacks provoked considerable fear in Americans and led the government both to engage in suppressive action in Afghanistan and to engage in a significant domestic security effort and a radical reorganization of the government. Nevertheless, the United States demonstrated its military prowess and far-reaching political influence. In addition, the American imperial reach extended for the first time to the former Soviet Central Asian republics, and the United States reentered South Asia as an influential power. By its 2003 invasion and conquest of Iraq, it secured, if it can retain its influence there, a base for operations in the Middle East.

With considerably more portent, several countries that are not major powers have been acquiring modern military capabilities, and these could prove challenging to the United States and its allies in a future attempt at suppressing the activities of one or more of these states (Bracken 2000). Even with such capabilities that might impede a superpower victory, it is difficult to foresee the rise of a challenging power or coalition that would be in a position effectively to overturn the United States-dominated security order. Thus, as long as the United States sustains its policy to uphold the security regime, the resulting order provides the essential underpinning for the economic regimes dealing, respectively, with trade, money, and finance.

International Economic Management: Trade, Monetary, Finance, and Development Regimes

To a large extent because of European conflicts, the Washington administration was able to secure American territorial integrity, to consolidate the national government, redeem the new country's debts, and to establish commercial relations with other nations. In his 1796 Farewell Address Washington stated the guideline that would provide a beacon for American policy for centuries: "The great rule of conduct for us, in regard to foreign nations, is in extending our commercial relations, to have with them as little *political* connection as possible" (Washington 1796). Since that time, the United States has followed "the great rule" fairly consistently, although the details of application vary considerably.

Even when not capable of enforcing them, the United States has steadfastly insisted on neutral rights for shipping and trading. Commodore Perry's "black ships" sailed into Edo harbor in 1853 to open Japan to trading, and Secretary of State Hay's "open door" notes in 1898 advocated nonpolitical commerce with China. At the end of World War II, American designs on Eastern Europe did not aim at political domination but simply commercial access to markets and free flow of people. Thus, in constructing arrangements for the post-war period, United States' aims remained largely those of liberal commerce, although they necessarily were shaped in the context of the political structure of the world at the time. By the end of the Cold War, the economic management regimes were broadened to encompass new participants, new matters such as agriculture and services, and new mechanisms and altered institutions.

International economics cannot be separated from domestic affairs, for the two have reciprocal effects on each other. In particular, the stage of development of the domestic economy of the dominant power shapes the arrangements of the international regimes, and pressures tend to be generated by international arrangements that have impacts on domestic economies. Thus, in the first half of the nineteenth century when it was growing its industry, the United States followed protectionist policies; yet, as its industries became world leaders, Washington tended to press other countries to adopt open, liberal economic systems that would force unprotected industries to compete against its own.

Interests, especially American ones, have provided the driving force for global economic management. In promoting those state interests, institutions have proven to be effective instruments, but institutions largely result from causes lying within states and seldom engender any dynamism of their own. A brief review of the unfolding of institutional creation, development, and modification in the post-World War II period illustrates this general point succinctly.

The economic management arrangements agreed to at Bretton Woods in 1944 consisted of these fundamental components: (1) a gold standard, with the dollar linked to gold; (2) the International Trade Organization, to promote free trade; (3) the International Monetary Fund, designed to assist countries with balance of payments difficulties; (4) the International Bank for Reconstruction and Development (the World Bank), dedicated to promoting economic recovery and development through technical assistance and lending; and (5) protected domestic economies, in what Ruggie (1982) called "embedded liberalism," or free international trade combined with welfare state protections. As Eichengreen and Kenen (1994, p. 4) note, "the postwar institutional order was not just sturdy but remarkably flexible." That flexibility has been reflected in the changed arrangements that stemmed from American interests.

Although transactions in the international economy continue to be denominated in dollars more than a half-century after Bretton Woods, such dramatic changes have occurred as to belie any institutional continuity. Not only was the currency regime undermined as the devastated countries recovered from the war and the United States spent vast sums of dollars abroad, which led to the August 1971 unilateral decision by the Nixon administration to end the gold standard. But also the new currency regime brought in a few other countries to manage exchange rates, as they did in the Plaza Accord in 1985; in addition, within the context of state-determined, G-7 framework agreements and crisis interventions by the United States, private capital has been given rein to manage financial flows. Originally, under the Bretton Woods arrangements, the IMF and the World Bank were thought to comprise institutions for international management, but they have lost this function and "are now primarily institutions to police the developing world" (Ul Haq 1994).

Substantial modification of the regime in trade occurred much more quickly, for the United States Senate proved unwilling to give its consent to the ITO. Despite that, put into place was a set of rules known as the General Agreement on Tariffs and Trade (GATT) that embodied the principle of reciprocity and the most-favored-nation principle. In the absence of an organization for doing so, the world's nations promoted trade through adherence to the principles and by engaging in a series of multilateral negotiations that led to increasingly free and voluminous trade. Only in the Uruguay Round of 1987–1994 negotiations did the participants agree to establish the World Trade Organization. Moreover, developing countries for the first time joined in the negotiations in a significant way, and both agricultural products and services were brought to the agenda, as was the issue of intellectual property rights.

Neither did it take long after World War II for the functions of assisting recovery and development in Europe to be shifted from the World Bank to the

United States under the Marshall Plan. This step entailed not just an institutional modification but also gave the United States scope for promoting European integration and insisting on agreements by the European countries to follow American prescriptions on monetary and fiscal policy and to grant entry to American administrators to foster domestic free markets and liberal principles (Eichengreen and Kenen 1994, p. 16).

Furthermore, the success of the post-war agenda in promoting economic recovery of the damaged countries and freeing trade led to erosion of the embedded liberalism bargain, for two reasons. The opening of national economies "made it more difficult for governments to reconcile their international obligations with their domestic objectives" and revealed domestic barriers to international trade and investment (Eichengreen and Kenen 1994, pp. 7–8). In addition, concessions made by the United States to its trading partners had been motivated by the American quest for their recovery; once that recovery had been accomplished, the partners became economic competitors no longer entitled to special privileges. This led American governments to demand "level playing fields," which meant that they insisted on domestic reforms, just as the United States had under the Marshall Plan. By implication, such demands became attacks on the welfare state, Americans calling upon other governments to give up the traditional function of protecting their citizens from the buffetings of the world economy.

These demands for affording a more privileged place for the market led, during the debt crisis of the 1980s, to a change in the roles of the IMF and the World Bank. They became instruments of imposing domestic reforms on developing countries through structural adjustment programs. "In the process…there was a very large transfer of risk from private creditors to official institutions…." (Eichengreen and Kenen 1994, p. 46). Following the end of the Cold War, the United States and its allies then proved unwilling to fund the transition of the Eastern European countries from centrally planned to market economies and, instead, pressed the IMF and the World Bank to engage in questionable lending practices.

Eichengreen and Kenen (1994, p. 54) argue that many of these problems "have been significantly exacerbated by the great gap in the original Bretton Woods System: the lack of a coherent approach to economic development." Quite possibly, as Keohane (1994, p. 60) points out,

> International institutions can only be understood in terms of state power and state interests. How else could we explain the underdevelopment of development institutions as opposed to the trade and financial institutions so central to the richest, most powerful countries?

One can go much further, as does Vernon (1996, p. 52), to note that, although it has used its position to foster economic cooperation among governments, the United States has not been "prepared in the end substantially to constrain its policy options…." Thus bilateral bargaining with trading partners, such as the Voluntary Export Restraints (VERs) on steel and automobiles negotiated with Japan in the 1980s, is a characteristic rather than exceptional practice. Because of its greater power, the United States exercises its freedom of action more than do its trading partners, but other countries tend to negotiate outside the principles and rules of the GATT as well. In the words of Hoekman and Kostecki (1995, p. 3), "The role of bargaining is probably the most striking dimension of the world trading system. . . ." Furthermore, despite the Uruguay Round's outlawing of VERs, American protectionism has grown since the mid-1980s through the use of antidumping and countervailing duties, so-called administered protection allowed under GATT rules. In the words of an informed observer, "Since the mid-1980s, U.S. trade policy has become increasingly aggressive and bilateral" (Krueger 1998, p. 9).

In this context, the World Trade Organization (WTO) came into existence as a rule-making and rule-enforcing institution designed to result in a global regime. However, the rules have to be negotiated in forums composed of delegates from all the member states (who have conflicting as well as overlapping interests) and enforced through dispute-resolving mechanisms with the same composition. The mechanisms include the direct confrontation of national interests in the official bodies of the WTO, as in the clash between the United States and the European Union over meat grown with added hormones. Moreover, resistance arises from within states by groups opposed to the construction by nonelected negotiations of a global regime that inevitably has consequences for them within their own economies, as demonstrated on the streets of Seattle during the WTO meeting in November 1999 and at other places and times since then.

The greater turmoil associated with the changes in the trading regime than equally profound modifications of the functions of the IMF and the World Bank may be accounted for, in the words of Vines (1998, p. 63), by the fact that the trading system is an explicit regime and that the WTO is involved in "regime construction." In contrast, the "international monetary and financial system" and the "global development policy" regimes are implicit, and the IMF and the Bank "are primarily involved in regime management."

Nonetheless, the IMF and the Bank have changed in important ways. With the end of fixed exchange rates in 1971, the IMF has served primarily as a research and surveillance institution that advises governments on macroeconomic policies, on the basis of its research, and as a lender to governments when they face balance-of-payments difficulties (Vines 1998, p. 63). By bringing together these two activities, the IMF enforces its conditionality in assisting countries and, thus, has become a very effective international organization. However, as Vines also observes (p. 65), the effectiveness of the Fund enables the richer countries "to hold back from direct bilateral political relations with the poorer countries." For Vines, this implies that the Fund maintains an international regime.

One needs to note, however, that in major crises such as those affecting Mexico in late 1994 and early 1995 and in East Asia in 1997 and 1998, the United States took the lead in bringing the assistance that enabled the affected countries to recover. Putting the matter in a somewhat different way, however effective and useful the IMF regime may be, including its utility in buffering the United States and other rich states from direct interventions in the poorer countries, the powers have not conceded sufficient resources to the international regime to enable it to manage more threatening crises. These resources remain in the hands of the rich, especially those of the United States.

Similarly, the World Bank's functions have changed from a capital-channeling agency in support of recovery from the Second World War to a combined "lending, research, and development assistance" organization that "enables richer countries to assist with the development problems of the poorer countries without entering into direct bilateral political power relations with them" (Vines 1998, p. 68). At one time, the Bank's commitment to lending for specific projects led to the investment of supplementary private capital. However, international capital markets have become increasingly integrated, and investors operate quite independently of the Bank. This separation has also been reflected in the shift of the agenda of the World Bank, first, under Robert McNamara's leadership, to giving emphasis to basic needs and then, under James Wolfensohn's aegis, to stressing poverty reduction.

These movements of the major powers away from bilateral political relations with poorer countries represent a shift of capital flows to the multilateral organizations and to firms operating in a market system. For many observers, the shift may be interpreted as an increase in the power of intergovernmental organizations and the market and a decline in the power and possibly even the form of the state. As this discussion has made clear, however, the arrangements resulted from policy decisions to insulate governments from the responsibilities of direct political relations with other states. At the same time, the powerful countries have not conceded—and it is difficult to imagine that they would concede—sufficient resources and authority to the IGOs and the market to undermine their own authority and freedom of action. The leading power has made this eminently clear by its positions on any number of initiatives, and the United States has continued to demonstrate its ability to exercise its freedom of action.

This does not suggest that intergovernmental institutions are not useful, for they contribute immensely to the management of a broad international political economy that has generated unprecedented wealth in the post-World War II period and promises to continue doing so. As the international economy developed and new problems and challenges arose, the powers responded by modifying the arrangements. Efforts continue to make changes to increase the effectiveness of the organizations and to meet new circumstances as well as to minimize the deleterious effects of inevitable crises in the future. Thus, trade in agricultural products and services, and trade-related intellectual property rights were inscribed on the agenda of the Uruguay Round negotiations. In addition, many less developed countries, bereft of any socialist alternative, engaged in the liberal free trade bargaining.

As a means of strengthening the trade regime, the World Trade Organization was created, and states engage in a continuing effort to improve the rules as well as the rule-making and enforcement procedures. Similarly, the great debate over reforming the international financial architecture that followed the East Asian crisis remains an important effort to construct an even more effective way of bolstering the stability and effectiveness of the financial and development regimes. These efforts are sustained by the powerful countries whose interest in stability, security, wealth, and well-being undergird the international effort.

Apart from making these institutions serve their interests more effectively, the powers face two other challenges with respect to them. First, the expansion of the liberal market, as the negotiators at Bretton Woods were aware, entails consequences for domestic groups. To attend to this problem, the Bretton Woods bargain included both free trade internationally and welfare statism domestically. As the international political economy has taken on an increasingly neoliberal cast and the powers aspire to intrude inside their partners' domestic economic structures and practices, governments need ways to protect their own citizens from the depredations of the market. In the WTO context, this problem is formulated as the need for governments to possess "mechanisms for managing domestic pressures for protection" (Finger and Winters 1998, p. 373) and is addressed through "pressure-valve provisions." According to Finger and Winters (1998, p. 380), these pressure valves make neither economic nor political sense and, "[w]orse, the GATT's pressure valves empower the bad guys."

In relationship to the international financial institutions as well as the WTO, labor and other groups do not have a seat at the negotiating table and they appear not to have found effective channels for making their views felt through their national political processes. Thus they have tended to resort to direct action by such street actions as the trashing of a McDonald's restaurant in France and of a significant portion of downtown Seattle in 1999. Increased representation of all affected groups and thus a certain democratization of the international financial institutions have a strong advocate in the former chief economic advisor to the World Bank, Joseph Stiglitz (2002). Rodrik (2000, pp. 348–356) would go even further in urging a reconstruction of the embedded liberalism compromise. In the short term he advocates combining "international rules and standards with built-in opt-out schemes;" in the long term he would aim for "a world of global federalism, with the mixed economy reconstructed on a global level."

The second challenge to the powers relates to development, for increased reliance on markets tends to result in more inequality not just within national economies but in the world at large, particularly between those countries that successfully negotiate transitions to high-growth economies and those that fail to do so. Actually, such failures need to be characterized in much broader terms, for effective governments and dynamic societies form, together with growing economies, an interlocked set of developments shaping states in the international system that enjoy the capacity to cope with the pressures and challenges of other states. In the absence of such developments, societies risk turmoil, civil wars, and the chaos that accompany so-called failed states. For the powers, such situations demand palliative interventions for relief and humanitarian assistance, but they usually rely upon underfunded and undersupported intergovernmental and nongovernmental agencies to administer the aid. Because such situations tend to contain great misery, they are not likely to pose any threat of serious disruption of the strong wealthy countries. On the other hand, their continued existence and occasional dramatic flarings present a moral embarrassment to sensitive observers within the rich parts of the world.

A long-run alternative to dealing with increasing inequality and recurrent political failure might be the promotion of development as a broad coherent enterprise that includes concerns with strengthening governments and societies as well as economies, that remains as dedicated to state formation and the advancement of skills and citizen education as it is to market strengthening. At bottom, such an enterprise rests upon the efforts and dedication of the respective people of different nations, but their late development can be aided by the leading powers and other rich countries.

Such assistance will probably not take the form of foreign capital flows, which the World Bank projects to be small (World Bank 1990, p. 78). Each country that succeeds in development will install an efficient financial system, including both private but regulated institutions and effective legal and supervisory arrangements. To effect such financial systems that collect and allocate savings, provide credit, and collect and manage debt requires that savings be extracted from the economy. Unless governments create the stability and institutions that instill trust in their populations, it is unlikely that savings can be extracted except by forced means. Advice, technical assistance, training, and so forth comprise the components that rich countries can offer in the absence of transfer of financial resources.

Such activities would aim at the strengthening of effective states. The characteristics and components of developmental states, and the essential functions that they perform, comprise the subject matter of a subsequent chapter. Before taking up that topic, I examine how power is managed in the contemporary world.

Conclusion

In the early years of the twenty-first century, a reasonably stable and fairly clear hegemonic coalition has laid down and effectively enforces a set of rules for the international political economy. With the United States spearheading those arrangements, its history and style offer many clues to the antecedents of the coalition rules. The United States has throughout its history adhered to a view of expanding commerce with others on terms favorable to itself and to cooperating when convenient but retaining its freedom of action to act alone when necessary.

In the post-World War II period a set of international regimes has been constructed in the areas of security, trade, finance, and development. As conditions have changed, these regimes have been modified, but the underlying continuity seems remarkable. With the end of the Cold War, with its immense relative gains for the United States, the traditions and style of American society and policy have emerged even more apparently than they seemed during the Cold War.

The following chapter treats the manner in which management of the international system occurs and the problems that attend that management.

6

Management in the Contemporary World

Introduction

The dominant discourse concerning global capitalism (Gilpin 2000; Penttinen 2000) and that examining broader globalization (Axford 1995; Held et al. 1999) present a rich picture of contemporary trends. Nevertheless, dominant discourses tend to submerge or obscure other layers of debate and struggle. Indeed, because language is so powerful, particularly as it is manifested first in rhetoric and then in settled narrative, the shaping of a debate by those assuming a position of dominance proves an effective tool for structuring power relations. In keeping with capitalism's renown for its propensity to destroy as well as create (Schumpeter 1950; Thurow 1999), its proponents in this period of immense economic change advance a neoliberal ideological agenda aimed at driving out politics from public life and establishing the predominance of the market, the private, and the individual, representing them as societal and universal interests.

Beneath the surface, voices articulate aspirations for restructuring politics and governance arrangements so as to serve the variety of purposes voiced by different groups. These include enhanced employment of international intergovernmental institutions in global governance (Finkelstein 1995), development of an international civil society (Darcy de Oliveira and Tandon 1994; Korten 1998), and championing new standards and regimes of human rights (Donnelly 1998, 2000). In addition to these somewhat submerged debates, direct resistance against the onslaught of global capitalism has been mounted from several quarters (Mittelman 1996, 2000; Panitch and Leys 1997). Although not entirely neglected, the state is usually given little consideration in these debates, and some of them contain a large dose of opposition to the state.

This chapter clarifies a number of issues in current debates about power, authority, governance, rights, and so forth. I explicitly examine debates about the nature of capitalism, the conditions of human freedom, the promotion of democracy, the construction of civil society, the meaning of citizenship, and sources of authority as well as rights and responsibilities in contemporary international security and economic structure.

Within the context of these debates, the thesis that permeates this book—that the state remains central to contemporary politics—is reiterated. Furthermore, I argue that the state forms the essential means for achieving the values sought even by protesters against globalization and advocates of institutional reform. Struggles for power can emanate from many quarters, but management can come only from authoritative political direction, and authority in the contemporary world remains lodged in states and the international organizations that they control.

Foundations and Conditions

Following the Soviet Union's withdrawal from competition in 1989 and its disintegration in 1991, the hegemonic coalition led by the United States has demonstrated in several military, economic, diplomatic means actions its determination to set down the rules that guide the international system. In 1990 to 1991, a short but intense war against Iraq, which had invaded neighboring Kuwait, drove Iraq back within its territorial boundaries. Following that military victory, the coalition mounted economic sanctions against the Iraqi regime of Saddam Hussein with the effect of wiping out the Iraqi middle class and degrading the national economy. In addition, beginning in December 1998 the United States and Britain conducted a low-keyed but steady bombing campaign against northern Iraq.

After issuing an ultimatum to the Yugoslav government of Slobodan Milosevic demanding North Atlantic Treaty Organization (NATO) access to the entire country and having it rejected, the United States and other NATO countries bombarded two of the country's provinces, Serbia and Kosovo, contributing to the creation of approximately 800,000 refugees from the province of Kosovo. Many of the refugees returned under the protection of coalition forces who remain in the province under an agreement with the Yugoslav government signed in June 1999.

Following the hijacked airliner attacks on the World Trade Center and the Pentagon in 2001, the United States spearheaded a suppressive action against Al Qaeda and the Taliban regime in Afghanistan, preparing the way for the formation of a new government in that country. In addition, the United States forged new ties with Pakistan, Russia, and Kygyristan and Uzbekistan and strengthened its intelligence and counterterrorist cooperation with traditional allies.

The Bush administration, with only Britain as a substantial ally, portrayed Iraq as a supporter of Al Qaeda and as an imminent threat armed with massive weapons, using these arguments, which turned out later to appear insubstantial, to justify an invasion and occupation of that country in 2003. In this case, the liberal coalition was at least temporarily fractured, as allies sought alternative ways of dealing with the regime of Saddam Hussein and refused to follow the course set out by a unilateralist United States.

Spearheaded again by the United States, the coalition intervened in two serious economic crises, in Mexico in 1994–1995 and in East Asia in 1997–1998, to avoid damage to the overall international financial system. Although no crisis led to it, the coalition and other countries also strengthened the international trading system with the successful conclusion of the Uruguay Round and the establishment of the World Trade Organization. Following a series of bilateral negotiations with China, that country was finally admitted to the World Trade Organization. Negotiations with North Korea aim to bring this challenging and recalcitrant state into the coalition's institutionalized arrangements.

Particularly by demonstrating its determination by these military, economic and diplomatic means to maintain hegemonic rule, the liberal coalition has consolidated its position of domination in the international system and proved its will and capacity to direct the world.

These demonstrations have evidenced three essential conditions for continued maintenance of this structure: American policy; United States military prowess; and the liberal state, with its strong capitalist economic component. Not only has the liberal state formed the basis of the coalition, but also its accomplishments have led to imitation by the formerly socialist states, including Russia, China, and India.

Stemming from the nature of the political systems within its member states, the liberal coalition promotes international arrangements based upon the ideas of economic efficiency, political democracy, and individual freedom. When the principles emanating from these ideas prove inconvenient, particularly to the coalition leader, they are sometimes put aside to serve the superpower's interests or convenience. Nevertheless, international institutions and practices more often than not further those principles.

The economic and financial institutions—the World Bank, the International Monetary Fund, and the World Trade Organization—all promote state policies necessary to and consistent with the development of market economies. On occasion, the powers intervene in such places as East Timor and Sierra Leone to reduce instability and to satisfy the consciences of their own publics. More frequently, the powers seek to avoid interventions in nonstrategic areas by substituting privately contracted services for their own discharge of humanitarian and stabilizing functions (Lentner 2000b).

Beneath these dominant characteristics and discourses, there is a variety of debates about both the nature of specific components of contemporary international relations and the normative choices to be made about future directions in the world. These issues concern capitalism, human freedom, democracy, citizenship, civil society, and sources of authority.

Nature of Capitalism

As summarized by Gilpin (1987, p. 15), Marx and Engels defined the "characteristics of capitalism" as "the private ownership of the means of production, the existence of free or wage labor, the profit motive, and the drive to amass capital." Ehrenberg (1999, p. 138) stresses Marx's (1857(1858, 35, p. 8) view that the "mode of production" was central to understanding any society and that it is the "commodity form [that] stands at the center of capitalism as a productive system."

There are many derivative characteristics of capitalism, such as its tendency to distribute products unevenly with a resulting inequality. Many have commented on the dynamic nature of capitalism produced by the intense competition stimulated by its essential characteristics.

Moreover, capitalism has manifested itself in many variants. In the broadest terms, variation ranges from free-wheeling American individualism to European corporatism to Japanese partnership between business and government. In narrower terms, this economic system ranges from the tendency to concentrate ownership in the hands of the very few, which was characteristic in the United States at the end of the nineteenth century, to the spread of stock ownership to half the population, as was the case in the same country a century later.

Different behaviors occur in separate capitalist economic systems. Some nations exhibit very high savings rates whereas others borrow others' savings for their own investment and consumption. Other manifestations of profligacy and frugality are demonstrated across capitalist societies.

Furthermore, there are divergent ideologies associated with capitalism. These include a stress on guidance of economic decisions by government acting in partnership with business; Keynesian insistence on the need to assure sufficient consumption, by governmental deficit spending if necessary; social democratic emphasis on protecting the interests of workers, a variant on Keynesianism; neoliberal views which prefer nearly complete reliance on private market mechanisms that are held to be self-correcting; and preference for the rich, as evidenced in the tax policies of the George W. Bush administration. In neoliberal ideology, the state interferes with and distorts free markets; thus, it should be minimized and relegated to defense and policing. In the other ideologies, the state forms an important component of the society that regulates and corrects market distortions and imbalances. All of these political economy ideologies treat the state only in its civil society dimensions, not its more fundamental but also wider aspects. It is in these larger measures that one finds not only critical functions of the state but also the essential foundations of the economic system.

Despite an obvious reciprocal relationship between politics and economics, between the state and the market (Gilpin 1987), the origins of the capitalist mode of production are found in the political decision by the state to protect private property (North and Thomas 1973). All the other aspects of capitalism derive from that foundation. In circumstances in which the state withdraws protection of private property, the capitalist system of production must necessarily begin to crumble. Furthermore, it is within the political system that contention over such fundamental issues occurs and in which the choice to uphold or change the system of production is made. Also, important modifications of the system of production, shifting of public production to the private sector, for example, remain political decisions that have to be made within the authoritative structure of the state. All of these kinds of decisions lie beyond the scope of the civil society, or economy, in a public sphere.

On the other hand, the economic system may work its effects so as to erode the social solidarity and political support for redistributive policies and the welfare state

(Offe 1996, pp. 172–177). Given its essentially particularistic interests, civil society foments groups seeking narrow goals that serve discrete constituencies, even individual interests, but who articulate these interests as public (Seligman 1992). Still, there are those who advocate a solidaristic civil society to promote larger public interests (Cohen and Arato 1992; Fullinwider 1999). Whether the very conception of a cohesive civil society forms a realistic vision seems problematical, for the nature of civil society identifies the idea as the realm of needs (Hegel 1952). Given the insatiability of needs, the only arena in which a common good can be achieved is the state.

Thus capitalism is a system of production chosen by states because of its effectiveness in producing goods and services. Effectiveness emanates not from ideology but from demonstrated superiority to other economic arrangements. Despite various attempts at constructing alternative systems of production— plantation economies based on slave labor and centrally planned socialist economies being the most notable in the modern period—the capitalist mode of production has proved its tremendous capacity to produce goods and services.

Two mechanisms contribute to keeping such systems of production running. The system of competition and the profit motive within capitalism itself lead to the striving, destroying, and creating that promote innovation, efficiency, and prices that tend to clear markets. In addition, governments perform a variety of functions that maintain the dynamism of the economic system. Most obviously, they regulate markets in order to uphold the foundational rule of law upon which markets are based, including the enforcement of contracts, and they regulate and manage competition to ensure that the system works approximately as it should to remain effective. More fundamentally, states provide peace and order as well as the rule of law upon which regulation rests. Other functions include investments in education (what economists call human capital formation), infrastructure, and research and development that contribute to competitiveness and to technological innovation. Furthermore, governments issue and manage money, and they follow macroeconomic policies to maintain conditions under which private enterprise can flourish. Other functions include redistribution of products for the sake of the smooth running of the market but also for such larger state reasons as equity, a political rather than an economic consideration; and negotiating with other states and with foreign firms in order to maintain an equilibrium between the national economy and international pressures.

Other aspects of capitalism such as mass consumption, high standards of living, spread of ownership, and commodification of products and spaces as well as persons derive from the fundamental system of production. It would be entirely consistent with capitalism to reallocate consumption to emphasize savings and investment or to dedicate the economy to wartime production. Restrictions could be placed on the takeover of public spaces by private firms and donors. Living standards could be modest. In all of these circumstances the capitalist system of production could flourish. On the other hand, basic modifications of the production system would engender changes in the derivative aspects of capitalism.

Conditions of Human Freedom

Despite liberalism's invocation of individual freedom and freedom of opportunity, the preeminent liberal view from Locke to Rawls stresses the satisfaction of individuals' needs almost to the exclusion of shared or social purposes and ideas. In liberal theory the state exists simply to protect the life, liberty, and property of individuals; thus it does not offer any social or political reason for the obligations of citizens to defend anything that they might have in common (Smith 1989). Yet the members of a state do share an existence that transcends their mere economic interdependence and mutual exploitation. Despite Marx's argument that the state interest is merely one particular interest against other private interests (Ehrenberg 1999, p. 133), Hegel's most important legacy, the idea of common good, remains. In Smith's (1989, p. 233) words,

> Hegel's chief accomplishment has been to show that the state and community are not just a precondition for, but a dimension of, freedom. The state is … a locus of shared understandings. A state … is a wider network of shared ethical ideas and beliefs. A state is ultimately a meeting of minds, since it depends on a common cultural history and a sense of civic identity.

Although difficult to pin down with precision, the idea of common or community good can be contrasted with the liberal view of nearly unconstrained acquisitiveness and indulgence of unlimited and insatiable needs.

Without the fundamental recognition of others that occurs within a state and the development of common purposes, freedom can mean nothing other than the pursuit of selfish interests. Each person seeks to satisfy his or her needs which, once satisfied, become redefined in an endless process of need satisfaction. Without the restraining hand of the state and of shared ethical ideas, competition to satisfy needs would become the sole quest of individuals. The only concern with others would stem from instrumental needs to damp down dissatisfaction and social unrest. In the absence of common concerns and the apparatus of the state to uphold them, violence and coercion would very likely become the rule in the competition that ensued. In contrast to the situation that prevails in well-ordered advanced industrial societies today, circumstances more nearly resembling those in Russia during the 1990s would prevail. Indeed, the circumstances would probably exceed those in Russia, for, after all, Russia does retain a legacy of a proud common past and sense of national accomplishment, no matter how forlorn the situation in the 1990s may have been.

To accomplish important objectives, incentives matter a great deal. Within liberal thinking, properly structuring incentives remains key to the efficient functioning of the market. However, without any incentives other than the particular interests of each member or group within a society there are insufficient grounds for defending the overall order that makes the free pursuit of those interests possible. Hegel thought that only war brought about the conditions in which individual freedom and the shared pursuit of an ethical idea came together to enable individuals to rise above the pursuit of their merely selfish, particular interests.

Given the contemporary world situation in which the leading powers enjoy the relative comfort of a stable peace without any immediate and serious threat of war, citizens of those countries confront the puzzle of finding incentives to defend their states. The solution to that puzzle is not apparent; but reliance on neoliberal incentive structures alone would likely lead to the destruction of the ordered arrangements that make capitalism work. As Smith (1989, p. 160) notes, Hegel thought that the creation of "stable political institutions and sentiments" would take the place of force in maintaining an effective state, and this view has entered modern discourse through Gramsci's notion of hegemony, which expresses a similar thought (Bobbio 1988). These institutions and sentiments include at least several dimensions that fall outside the market and capitalism; they require the inclusion of politics and thus stand against the neoliberal thrust that aims to exclude politics from society.

Democracy

Politics can take many forms and be expressed by a wide variety of sentiments and institutions. Despite the firm and extensive presence of democracy in the contemporary world, forms today range from autocracies and dictatorships such as that in North Korea under Kim Jong Il and Syria under Bashar al-Assad, to mixed oligarchical-civic systems such as those in China and Malaysia, to democracies such as those in Norway and France. For the most part, democracy describes political arrangements in which leaders are chosen through free elections, with the necessary attendant liberties of free speech and association as well as competing parties. Contentious issues with regard to the practice and strengthening of democracy are treated below in the section on civil society.

In the contemporary world, the dominant coalition of leading states promotes democracy as a technique of managing power and in service of a conception of a liberal or democratic peace (Bueno de Mesquita et al. 1999; Doyle 1983; Gowa 1999; Huntley 1996; Layne 1994; Maoz and Russett 1993; Russett 1995; Spiro 1994). Foremost in the thinking of those who advocate the democratic peace thesis are the views of Kant (1957) and his modern follower Doyle (1983). According to the Kant-Doyle view, liberal states are less likely to go to war with one another because, first, both citizens who must bear the burdens of blood and treasure and leaders who are constrained by electoral considerations tend to be cautious in the face of incurring personal, economic, and political costs. Second, liberal democratic states maintain respect for one another, and this may be reflected in international law. Third, citizens and officials in liberal democracies adhere to a cosmopolitan law that affords hospitality to citizens and traders from other liberal democracies (Doyle 1983). Kant (1957) envisioned a separate peace among republics through the creation of a parliament of republics. Doyle (1983) extends the claim by pointing to a separate liberal peace that has already been established. Thus, although it does not provide a plan for enlarging the number of liberal democracies, this thesis implies that international peace spreads as the number of liberal states increases. In this logic, if all the world's states were liberal democracies, international peace would reign across the globe. On the basis of this logic, United States National

Security Advisor Lake (1993) articulated the policy of democratic enlargement followed by the Clinton administration.

A less visible but nonetheless important strand of liberal democratic peace thinking derives from a different tradition, expressed eloquently by American President Woodrow Wilson. This view holds that, because wars tend to be caused by nonliberal-democratic regimes, liberal states are justified in intervening to promote liberal democratic ideas and institutions. With this logic as justification, the United States with the assistance of allies has in the last few years intervened in Haiti, Bosnia, Yugoslavia, and Iraq to rid those states of thugs and evil leaders. In the larger arena of policy on a worldwide scale, this outlook holds that wars are caused by bad or "rogue" states. That logic has led to the widespread use of sanctions against such "evil" leaders as Fidel Castro, Saddam Hussein, and others who are regarded as the source of international violence.

Aside from failing to bring down such leaders, the policies that follow from this logic led to ongoing bombing campaigns against Iraq from December 1998 to March 2003, an intense air war in Serbia and Kosovo in Spring 1999, and the imposition of economic sanctions that have brought immense suffering and hardship to the broad civilian populations in the countries affected. These policies almost inevitably fail, for they tend to destroy the middle classes that might form the backbone of liberal democracy in the affected countries. A crucial aspect of thinking with regard to the promotion of democracy entails the concept of civil society.

Civil Society

Despite a fairly wide spectrum of views on civil society, there coheres in thinking about democracy that some basis for social and political participation independent of the state facilitates democracy. From Eastern Europe comes a conception of civil society that is opposed to and is capable of replacing the state (Tismaneanu 1992), and this coincides both with an anti-state view from Latin America (MacDonald 1997) and the ascendancy of neoliberalism in the United States and Britain in the 1980s (Ehrenberg 1999). In addition to these views, advocates of democratization such as Diamond (1997) regard civil society not only as autonomous but also as coherent and whole. In sharp disagreement, Markovitz (2000) makes a strong case that civil society interests not only remain particularistic but that they are often privileged and acquire powerful societal positions because they are supported by states. Although sharing the view that civil society may develop as an independent category, Cohen and Arato (1992) think that civil society is sufficiently diverse to include protesters and perpetrators of acts of civil disobedience and that it functions as a device to monitor not just the state but also the economy. Writing on civil society also includes a weaker form that mostly is interested in promoting interpersonal trust among citizens as a foundation for democracy (Bellah et al. 1985; Putnam 1993, 1995; Tocqueville 1945).

From the point of view of managing power in the contemporary world, the stronger version of civil society that runs from Hegel through Gramsci to Cohen

(1999) offers a template within which to analyze current struggles. Although Hegel included in civil society the policing and regulating mechanisms of the state that, in Giddens' terms, exercise surveillance over the realm of the particular, he stressed that civil society remained not only a realm of needs but also of contestation. Even though civil society comprises mostly economic competition and group struggle, among the elements that are subject to contest are issues of ethical values and privileged positions in struggles for domination.

Gramsci regarded civil society as the realm in which hegemony, that is, dominant ideas, arose and the state as the realm of power and coercion (Bobbio 1988, pp. 82–88); they nevertheless worked together. Building on these views, Cohen (1999, p. 59) presents a strong defense of the public sphere in which policies and claims "can be contested and discursively redeemed." She cites Claus Offe in noting that "critical discourse in the public sphere (secured by rights) ... is crucial to maintaining trust—belief in legitimacy—in constitutional democracies." And she goes on to "defend an even stronger claim: the deliberative genesis and justification of public policy in political and civil public spaces respectively are *constitutive* of the modern form of democracy."

There are certain aspects of this larger view of civil society that are particularly germane to the struggle for domination of the liberal coalition by advocates of strong democracy in opposition to proponents of neoliberalism. First, contestation and open struggle over what values the polity is to be governed by and what policies it will pursue need to be preserved if there is to be democracy. This assertion challenges the neoliberal view that only private interests are to be served by the polity. Second, in order to ensure that an arena and opportunities for contests of ideas, values, and policies are preserved, a strong state must exist to guarantee the rights of citizens to participate. This claim opposes the neoliberal notion that private enterprise can perform every function more efficiently and effectively than can political institutions.

In those societies in which neoliberalism has risen to ascendancy, a proliferation of private mechanisms for delivering public services has occurred. Simultaneously, commerce and its values have triumphed over other activities to the extent, for example, that working hours have expanded to the disadvantage of family and leisure time, and advertising and brand labeling of public spaces diminishes the concept of the public and the sense of common life. In addition, the privatization bias of neoliberalism has had very significant effects in international politics.

In the recent past, in particular, governments have expanded their contracting to nongovernmental organizations (NGOs). According to one estimate approximately half of United States foreign aid in 2000 was expected to be channeled through NGOs (Gordenker and Weiss 1996, p. 25). To a large extent, this privatization substitutes private for state responsibility, but it has much wider implications.

In humanitarian relief situations, for example, private organizations and intergovernmental international organizations lack the political will and coercive apparatus of states that would enable them to impose an order within which they could operate legitimately to carry out their tasks. As a result, such order as exists is created by local political forces. Although many examples are available, some of the most appalling occurred in Srebrenica in Bosnia in 1995 when Dutch forces assigned to United Nations duty failed to present any obstacle to Serbian military forces intent on a massacre, the setting up of a ruling order in the refugee camps in Zaire in 1994 and following years by the Hutu Power forces that had perpetrated a genocide in Rwanda, and the taking of United Nations forces hostages in Sierra Leone in 2000. These failures of leading states to carry out their responsibilities because they had handed them off to private agencies and international organizations that lacked political capacities to establish fundamental political orders resulted in extensive suffering and death.

For the most part, those concerned with civil society place themselves within the discourse promoting democracy. Frequently nongovernmental groups do act on behalf of or serve disenfranchised groups. However, they tend to do so without any sort of accountability, either to a base constituency or to clients. Their activities are not subject to voter surveillance, to elections, or to removal from office. To the extent that NGOs are accountable, it happens indirectly through the governments that contract with them for delivery of services. Even in this minimal rendering of democratic accountability, however, the governments that carry the ultimate responsibility are able to evade accountability by the very process of privatization.

All in all, then, activities like those discussed here not only do not serve democracy; they actually render democracy problematical. An added disadvantage of the privatization of international services is that intellectual confusion obscures the basic fact that civil society emanates from liberal states. Without strong liberal states, there is no scope for NGOs to conduct their activities. Yet many advocates fail to recognize this and actually think that democracy's fate can be assured in the absence of the order and the realm of freedom that can be produced only by states.

Citizenship

In his effective critique of neoliberal thinking on citizenship, Gaffaney (1999) points to the new right's attempt to define freedom in a positive sense of "economic independence of the state" and notes that contemporary discourse in the United States is shaped almost entirely by a market vocabulary. He goes on to point out that these writers (Hayek 1960, 1979; Nozick 1974; Murray 1984; Novak 1979; Novak et al. 1987; Gilder 1981) have, in addition, argued that citizenship derives from paid employment, and he criticizes their project as an attempt to define "citizens as client-consumers." In this way, neoliberals regard politics and public life as existing only to serve the privileged private spheres. Thus the neoliberal conception of freedom is exactly opposed to the Hegelian view that only in the state do citizens gain both the recognition that affords them the rights and duties of citizenship, and the ability to transcend their needs.

Seligman (1992, pp. 126–134) identifies the roots of the contemporary puzzle of citizenship in the American tradition of individualism and its extension to the universalizing of rights, which has the attendant effect of undermining social solidarity and a traditional notion of citizenship based upon mutual recognition.

He also mentions that the privatization and particularization within both the neoliberal and universal-rights discourses have their parallel in the post-modern distrust of reason.

As a response to the dilemmas of modern thinking about citizenship, Habermas (1990) presents his idea of "discourse ethics" as a basis for moral argumentation. This approach to the problem has been taken up by Cohen and Arato (1992) in their quest for a strong democracy within a robust civil society. Although grounded in a conception of politics that is missing from the neoliberal view, the discourse ethics approach to public life lacks an ethical center and may be characterized as a procedural formalism. At the very least, though, it does involve lively participation in a public sphere in a quest for an ethical dimension. At least part of the debate in that public sphere should include Kelly's (1979) view that citizenship involves loyalty to a normative state. In that sense, public discourse must include consideration of the attributes of a common life that the participants prefer.

Furthermore, there must be an insistence on regarding fellow citizens not as isolated individuals but as members of a community. Instead of grounding discussions in terms of abstract rights or of economic exchange, debates should include notions of citizens' rights and duties within a community. In times of war, national communities do summon their citizens in such broader terms, and the sort of appeals that neoliberals make for an exclusively particularistic and private life is regarded, in its true light, as selfish and unpatriotic. In the absence of war, it may be more difficult to summon such conceptions. It is nevertheless important to do so; for capitulation to the exclusively private views that come from both left and right of the political spectrum, a refusal or inability to recognize the underlying power and legitimacy realities may lead to the destruction of the edifice upon which private activities are pursued.

Sources of Authority

Mao Zedong's aphorism that power grows out of the barrel of a gun put the matter more crudely than most, but it contained the fundamentally accurate observation that the control of violence underlies power. Control of violence is not sufficient to rule, for some order or what Gramsci called hegemony needs to be put into place to convince followers to obey and to participate contentedly in a particular political order. In much of the contemporary debate in international politics, shaped by the contention between neo-utilitarians and constructivists (Katzenstein et al. 1998), the issue is often put forward as the relative precedence and strength of ideas or material forces. The fact is that both operate in politics all of the time.

In the contemporary liberal world, authority grows from the stability produced by American military domination in the world at large and from the stable liberal states that comprise the dominant liberal coalition. Firms, nongovernmental organizations, and international organizations all derive their ability to act from these sources of authority. Individuals carry passports that gain recognition because of the authority of the issuing states. Firms are incorporated under the laws of their respective states, and they are able to enter into contracts knowing that they will be enforced in the countries in which they operate. Trade is conducted under the terms of agreements negotiated and implemented by states. Nongovernmental organizations operate either as lobbyists attempting to influence states that possess the authority to enter into international agreements or as private contractors conveying goods and services as substitutes for governmental activity. International intergovernmental organizations are founded on covenants negotiated and authorized by member states, and all of their resources are provided by those same member states. In all of these actions stemming from state authorizations it remains difficult to separate ideas and material forces, for they go together in a hegemonic international order.

On the other hand, either ideas or power can discretely erode and undermine that order. On the power side, one can envisage certain potential damaging forces. First, should the United States decide to withdraw from active participation in upholding the order, other countries would inevitably be forced to respond by putting into place other power arrangements. Second, should a challenger rise up to offer an alternative way of organizing the world order and the hegemonic coalition, or at least a saving remnant, choose to defend the existing order, a war would likely ensue to decide that contest (Gilpin 1981). At the present time, neither of those possibilities seems likely. Instead, the threat to the order may stem from ideas. From the right come such neoliberal concepts as nearly exclusive reliance on private enterprise for regulation and self-correction and even going so far, as indicated above, as to base citizenship on economic considerations. From the left emerges the movement for universal rights in the absence of citizenship and of community within which those rights could be anchored. Such private claims are erected into quests for endorsement and enforcement by centers of power, but claimants make their assertions without recognizing that any community or social interests may be at stake that would provide an occasion for democratic debate about the matters. Both positions refuse politics.

Yet politics forever remains the basis upon which social action proceeds. Structures of power exist to promote certain sentiments and institutions. In the contemporary period, liberalism is in the saddle, but the arrangements could be wrecked. One of the sources of potential wreckage is a fundamental misunderstanding that leads to dismantling of states and other public power structures that embody hegemonic ideas. Polanyi (1944) argued that the attempt to drive out politics and society and to rely entirely on the market lay at the root of the causes of the disasters of the middle of the twentieth century.

Therefore, however inadequate they may be, it is imperative that the advocates of a large conception of civil society and strong democracy sustain their advocacy on behalf of vigorous public debate in public arenas. At the very least, these supporters draw attention to the political realm of public, shared values and respect for fellow citizens. As Habermas (1990, p. 99 ff.) notes, even a skeptic who wants to remain silent has regularly to give his assent to or refusal of ongoing dialogue.

Should anti-politics prevail, the day will come when existing structures of authority will crumble, and in their place will arise contention among particularistic interests, with the result that violence rather than being controlled will be used by those interests. Such interests include predatory firms, private armies, drug traffickers, and arms dealers. Liberal optimists tend to think in terms of only the more benign components of civil society such as humanitarian agencies, civic-minded corporations, human rights activists, environmentalists, and so forth. Without the protection of state power and authority, however, even the good elements of civil society would find themselves in a position of adopting the means of the malign actors. Such a scenario offers a nightmare, not a vision.

Conclusion

Managing power in the contemporary world appears relatively easy, for no fundamental ideological position linked to a formidable power base challenges the hegemonic liberal coalition of states. By some measures democracy thrives, and certainly capitalism rides high, spreading technology and production as well as engendering immense wealth.

Broad gaps between rich and poor continue to plague the comfort levels of the complacent rich, and unconstrained violence breaks out frequently enough in all regions of the world to remind people that frightening menaces continue to use unauthorized force. A certain indifference and complacency in the United States was shattered on a bright, late summer day in 2001 when hijacked planes were crashed into tall buildings in New York City and into the fortresslike Pentagon in Northern Virginia. Still, despite the ability of some to inflict significant costs, few of these threats pose any vital danger to the centers of the liberal coalition.

Neither is there any serious ideological cleavage within the countries forming that coalition that presents any immediate threat to their domination by material force and continued ideological coherence. As in all modern complex societies, many policy matters come up for debate among people with different understandings and alternative proposals. In democratic societies those debates are usually vigorous.

Nevertheless, should the dominant discourse of neoliberalism prove altogether triumphant, the result would likely be an erosion and undermining of the political foundations upon which capitalist economies are built. And without those foundations, the world would likely face increased conflict that would further injure the economic prosperity and political stability that exists not in the whole world but in a significant part of it.

We live in a time in which the ethical foundations for states are no longer taken for granted. In that context, it is only vigorous democratic debate that offers hope for continuing to build societal bonds and community understandings that are the strength of the states that underpin the world order. Politics always remains contentious, for it involves struggles for domination of groups and ideas through institutions that settle matters at least for a time. Anti-politics may seem appealing to many; but a retreat into the private means, first, the domination by the privileged and, second, increased violence and instability when that domination is challenged. Only by recognizing the fundamental importance of the political base upon which societal activities occur can one be certain that political choices will remain available.

Such recognition can be more effectively sustained by employing a vocabulary of politics, power, state, community, and ethical life, together with concepts of citizenship with obligations as well as rights. Living in a democratic state means that one gives recognition to other citizens and acknowledges their right to participate in debates over the most profound issues that members of one's society face together. To preclude the idea of public purpose from discourse, insisting on the exclusiveness of the private and the individual without regard to others, is to prepare the way for undermining the very order that assures individuals the ability to pursue their interests.

7

Developmental States and Global Pressures

Introduction

Besides the hegemony of the liberal coalition, the other indispensable element in the liberal project is the maintenance and spread of developmental states. Evolving globalization and growing states have coincided. Developmental states remain critical to order, democracy, and prosperity. And secure and prosperous states form the backbone of international cooperation.

This chapter examines the place of developmental states in globalization, first by defining the concept and showing that such institutions have accompanied the processes of globalization. Then the chapter presents an argument that critically examines a number of other, more dominant views in conceptual and policy discourses related to globalization, specifically neoliberalism. Turning to the requisites for development and the many risks, opportunities, and policy choices faced by developmental states in the international political economy, the chapter describes and analyzes both the economic and noneconomic functions of states. This analysis draws attention to a set of conflicting policy imperatives, and the chapter concludes with a discussion of the trade-offs among those conflicts.

Globalization and Developmental States

Globalization has become such a buzzword in contemporary political and economic discourse that the term's essential meanings get lost in complex debates covering all manner of issues. Recall the definition given in Chapter Two: globalization means increasing connections across the world. In my conception, globalization may be dated from the mid-nineteenth century and regarded as a set of processes that, with the exception of some interruption between 1914 and 1945, have been largely continuous. Thus globalization is neither an ancient nor a very recent phenomenon nor a new period of history after the Cold War (Friedman 1999). Globalization expresses developments in a modern international system (Hirst and Thompson 1996), in contrast to a global one.

Many of the connections that result from the declining costs of transportation and communications have proved advantageous for economic growth, the spread of wealth and knowledge, and the dissemination of culture. In the face of exceptional population growth that multiplied the number of people on earth by six between 1830 and the end of the twentieth century, the average income, level of health and education, and other enhancements of life have increased. From 1945 until 2000 the world has witnessed unprecedented economic growth. To cite one upbeat assessment from a sober institution, "In the past 50 years poverty has fallen more than in the previous 500. And it has been reduced in some respects in almost all countries" (*Human Development Report* 1997, p. 2).

On the other hand, as made apparent by visible protests against the World Trade Organization and the international financial institutions, costs of change have been incurred by some and a measure of resistance to globalization has been expressed. Moreover, as in other eras of human history, criminals and rogues can and do make illicit use of technology and channels of commerce to enrich themselves or to advance their schemes. In the context of prosperity and well-being, modern communications magnify differences in wealth and condition and highlight phenomena like rampant disease and political turmoil.

Although globalization includes both advantages and disadvantages and comprises a variety of processes, I examine mainly the dominant optimistic ideas associated with official policies and present a view of developmental states and their requisites. In the following section, I present a critical assessment of neoliberal thinking about international relations. Before turning to that task, however, I define developmental states.

Developmental states are institutions that embody and render effective the public purposes of their communities. They provide the order protecting citizens from one another, the security protecting the state from other states and other external threats, and the laws and mechanisms for their enforcement that afford grounding for civil society to operate. A developmental state monitors and regulates the economy, and it extracts the resources from economic activities that enable it to build and maintain infrastructure to support the economy and to contribute to the sustenance of the economy. A state sustains an economy by investing in a variety of ways, especially in research and development and education, by interfering with the predatory activities of some economic actors, and by redistributing products in order to maintain standards of living but also to ensure the continuity of the community's sense of justice about itself. In addition, a developmental state performs a number of other economic functions, such as providing a currency, enforcing contracts, and adopting macroeconomic policies designed to stabilize and enhance the economy in the context of pressures of competition in the world economy.

Developmental states do not simply support the economy, however important that function may be, but they also serve other purposes. They provide a focus for identity of a citizenry; they embody the public purposes of their communities; they ensure security; and they contribute to the well-being of their citizens. Although developmental states form part of civil society by underpinning and regulating economic and other particularistic endeavors, they additionally and more fundamentally afford the means for rising above the pursuit of needs by embodying a realm of freedom that is not driven by needs (Hegel 1952; Ehrenberg 1999). They do this by maintaining a realm of public good, an arena of public space in which citizens can debate common problems and attempt to achieve a common good. However a state may be of service to an economy, without that realm of public good and freedom that transcends private necessities it cannot be a developmental state. This is what distinguishes it from states with centrally planned economies, colonized states, rentier states, and predatory states.

Although the centrally planned economy of the Soviet Union proved an effective industrial model in the 1930s and 1940s, its extensive mode of production in the end did not possess sufficient flexibility to allow it to shift to a more intensive mode with enhanced productivity (Campbell 1988; Bialer 1988). But the greater weakness of the Soviet model lay in the political system in which broad debate about the common good and the direction of the polity were largely absent (Mandelbaum 1996b). Instead, an elite claiming to possess a grasp of historical inevitability ruled in the name of the working class, a claim that was finally given up in the late 1980s. After the collapse of the Soviet Union at the end of 1991, the Russian state became colonized by holders of private power. Whether a developmental state can be built under President Vladimir Putin and his successors remains to be seen.

Iran under the shah offers an example of a rentier state (Abrahamian 1982; Boroujerdi 1996), in which a myth of a 2500-year-old dynasty was substituted for modern nationalism that might have connected the population with the state. State revenues were derived entirely from the sale of oil, further weakening the ties between citizens and the state. However burdensome taxes may appear to some, they represent a crucial connection between citizens and state. Furthermore, like the Soviet rulers and other dictators, the shah used secret police, torture, and other forms of repression to maintain his rule. As indicated in these cases as well as many others, a state that represses its inhabitants fails to enable and capacitate them as citizens and lacks a broad sense of the common good with which citizens can identify. Instead, such a state expects that citizens will simply serve exogenous ends in whose selection they did not participate.

Predatory states are those in which an elite employs the apparatus of the state for its own enrichment. Again, there are numerous examples in the world, but Mobutu Sese Seko's Zaire offers perhaps the clearest example. During his reign, the already inadequate infrastructure of the country deteriorated; the citizens were not educated; government services proved inadequate or disappeared altogether; and no evidence of pursuit of a common or public good became apparent. At the same time, Mobutu and a small coterie around him accumulated immense wealth which supplied them with great luxury.

Advantageous globalization—in which investment, trade, finance, and other benefits flow—does not penetrate into those areas without developmental states. Where command economy states, rentier states, and predatory states abound, there only fragments of worldwide connections penetrate. Wealth, well-being, and human development are payoffs from globalization only in those places in which autonomous developmental states can draw on the opportunities available in the remainder of the world to provide new sources of wealth and new ways of thinking for their populations.

This claim, that developmental states furnish one of the two essential pillars of advantageous globalization, stands in contrast to dominant neoliberal ideology that prefers enhanced markets and diminished states. But neoliberal economic ideology forms only one part of dominant contemporary conceptions about how to think about the world and how to work toward a future. Based as it is on an optimistic view of human nature and placing the individual at the core of its values, liberalism has penetrated thinking about many matters of public policy in the sphere of international relations. To elucidate this wide-ranging liberal thinking today I now turn to a critical examination of its varieties.

Liberal Thought about International Relations

Neoliberal discourse most obviously prefers markets to states, and writers perceive privatization of governing functions, advocate basing citizenship on employment, and take other positions directly opposing states. But liberal views, which are based upon individualism rather than community, extend considerably further, for in liberalism there is also a utopian or transformational outlook that includes even advocates who are not very friendly toward business and markets but who are largely anti-state. These include exponents of universal human rights, champions of an international community, supporters of humanitarian interventions, and supporters of rights divorced from citizenship. Many of these liberals also intend to give pride of place in international relations to nongovernmental organizations.

But the discourse has also shaped the programs of international institutions and practices. For example, in the programs of the World Bank poverty reduction has come to form the priority within development (World Bank 2000), and such programs are designed to strengthen public and private international agencies rather than states and indigenous institutions in countries receiving assistance. Even authorities of the leading powers seek to avoid responsibility for managing the world in which they exist by turning over important functions such as the suppression of conflict (peacekeeping) and relief for refugees to international organizations and nongovernmental organizations. Thus contemporary liberal thinking contains three prongs in a weapon that seeks to diminish the state, redefine citizenship, and substitute private for public and individual for community activity.

The first involves neoliberal ideology, which prefers markets over states, values individual needs while not recognizing a community universal, and aims to derive citizenship from employment. This ideology denies a distinct realm of politics and of public good, claiming that the common good emerges from the unrestrained pursuit of selfish interests. Another prong entails contemporary manifestations of utopianism: the assertion of an international community; the promotion of humanitarian intervention; and claims put forward on behalf of rights that are divorced from citizenship. Finally, liberal ideas are institutionalized in the practices of both public and private international agencies in which poverty reduction has come to replace development on the foreign assistance agenda, and policies aim at bolstering international organizations and nongovernmental groups rather than strengthening state and indigenous institutions. Another aspect of liberal thinking—the pennant on the weapon, perhaps—comprises ideas about the relationship of democracy to peace, but that debate does not bear directly on the matters treated here and is analyzed in Chapter 9 below.

In a long-running academic debate with John Maynard Keynes, Friedrich Hayek argued on behalf of freedom for individuals and claimed that government intervention in the economy amounted to a "road to serfdom" (Hayek 1944). His views were followed by those of Milton Friedman (1982), who argued that market capitalism is capable of self-regulation and, further, that interference in the market by government not only distorted prices but also diminished freedom. These views triumphed in the political arena with the election, respectively, of Ronald Reagan in the United States and Margaret Thatcher in Britain. Together with voices out of Eastern Europe as communism was collapsing who posited a civil society that stood in opposition to the state and that could substitute for the state (Tismaneanu 1992), the voice of unfettered market freedom proved sufficiently triumphant to form the dominant neoliberal discourse of the 1980s. With regard to international relations, it culminated with the formation of the so-called Washington consensus (Williamson 1990) which guided the policies of the leading states and the international financial institutions that they controlled. That concordance maintained that governmental economic enterprises should be sold to private interests, that government payrolls should be trimmed, and that markets should be allowed to operate without government interference in order to "get the prices right." Based on the experience of the East Asian countries, that consensus was substantially modified in the 1990s, as the powers and their institutions recognized that states contributed to economic growth (World Bank 1993, 1997). Then, in the wake of the 1997–1998 East Asian economic crisis, the makers of the dominant discourse acknowledged that unfettered markets can do immense damage and there needs to be a proper sequencing in which banking systems and regulatory regimes need to be put into place before unleashing market forces.

Despite these modifications in thinking about the proper roles, respectively, of governments and markets, neoliberal views retain considerable power in shaping thought and policy. At bottom, neoliberal ideology remains hostile to states and acknowledges only that governments need to take minimal actions to ensure that markets can operate. Some advocates perceive a permanent decline of states and increase in the effective power and influence of firms and other actors in the market (Strange 1996; Cerny 2000). Some of these views contain the further implication that debate about societal goals should not touch the activities of private enterprise, for the operation of a firm should lie within the control only of the owners and managers and, thus, not be subject to public debate. Except for defense against external enemies, maintenance of internal order, and provision of infrastructure, neoliberal ideology does not recognize societal functions comprising common, or universal, life. The viewpoint remains confined to the pursuit of individual needs, the insatiable human appetite for goods and services.

As Hayek and Friedman have clearly articulated, there is a quest for freedom, but the meaning they attribute to freedom lies in the reduced sense that each individual should be able to do what he or she wants, subject only to minimal restrictions. Thus the neoliberal conception of freedom offers a pale imitation of the grand concept that Hegel (1952) articulated in which a community, through the state, can rise above the compulsions of necessity and make choices that represent universal values, not just individual preferences and desires.

Thinking within the neoliberal camp that claims citizenship should stem from economic position, rather than from membership in a state, not only tends to exclude large classes of people (such as homemakers, handicapped persons, retirees, and so forth) but also erodes any claim for transfer payments within a polity. Neither does such a view acknowledge a concept of equity that exists separate from market efficiency.

In addition to the basic ideology that promotes freedom as the pursuit of individual needs and desires, liberalism also contains an optimistic outlook that expresses the enlightenment view that there is human progress. Contemporary manifestations of this utopianism include the notion of an international community, the concept of an international civil society, an impulse for humanitarian intervention, and advocacy on behalf of individual rights that are divorced from citizenship.

After the end of the Cold War, it became commonplace in the rhetoric of political leaders to employ the term "international community" in the context of promoting policies that they favored. Indeed, once the world ceased to be divided by the antagonism between the United States and the Soviet Union something like a concert of powers developed in which the leading states coordinated their policies in addressing challenges that they took up. In large part, this concert was led by the United States, but the exceptions proved revealing of continuing fissures and divergences of interests among the states involved.

Under the leadership of the United States, an impressive military coalition was put together in 1990–1991 to oust Iraq from Kuwait. Following that success, a system of economic sanctions and an arms control regime were put together to continue to suppress Iraq. A number of things have occurred that reveal how rickety the structure is: wrangling among the powers over the economic sanctions was recurrent and these divisions were reproduced in the debate over Security Council authorization of an invasion of Iraq in early 2003; weapons inspectors were expelled in 1998 and regained access to Iraqi facilities only for a short time in 2002–2003; and a bombing campaign, conducted only by the United States and Britain, continued for several years, and this was followed by an invasion by the same two. Continued divisions among the powers expressed themselves over the years as Yugoslavia disintegrated: while its European allies sent ground troops to Bosnia in 1992, the United States dawdled until 1995; and in 1999 NATO issued an ultimatum and conducted a bombing campaign against Serbia and Kosovo while the Soviet Union and China objected. Other events during the past decade or so further illustrate that, in the context of asymmetrical power, the United States is often able to cobble together a group of countries with which to coordinate its policy but that separate countries follow their own interests.

Although an agreement on the principles of market capitalism and political democracy provide a basis for the concert, policies vary among the participants, and no recognizable, coherent community has a continuous existence. Given some shared understanding of liberal ideology among the leading industrial countries, their leaders are able, with some justification, to articulate a set of values. These are the values of the powerful, however, and do not represent a wider international community. A more accurate articulation might be the concert, or the coalition of the powerful. But, of course, to claim that the concert makes a demand carries much less rhetorical force than a demand put forward by the international community.

Some advocate the creation of an international civil society, and many invoke the proliferation of myriad nongovernmental groups that participate in debates and some activities in international relations. One school of thought claims that the creation of such a civil society, networks of individuals and groups that coalesce across international boundaries, will form the basis for a worldwide community. On the basis of that hope, some claim that new norms are emerging and that a new set of universal principles is in the process of being put into place, thus transcending states.

Certain achievements, such as environmental agreements, an anti-personnel land mines treaty, and an agreement to establish an international criminal tribunal, are cited as evidence of the emergence of a new international community that will displace states. The fundamental flaw in this argument is that each of the agreements had to have been signed and ratified by states, and to make them effective, states remain the instruments for implementation. No other agency has emerged. Furthermore, it is well to remember that in prior eras agreements fell apart when challenged by dissenting states. It seems unlikely that a new epoch has dawned in which states will not pursue their interests as each determines, even to the extent of breaking or withdrawing from treaties. Even the leading state had been moving for many years in the direction away from the main stabilizing treaty of the Cold War period, the Anti-Ballistic Missile Treaty, and actually did withdraw from it in 2002.

Despite the continued strength of states, liberal utopianism has also put forth the view that the international community must intervene in weak countries for humanitarian reasons. Although quite selective in choosing which situations to intervene in, there have been some occasions for such intrusion. On the whole after the Somalia intervention in the early 1990s, the powers showed reluctance to intervene directly. Neither have they been willing to appropriate adequate resources to complete the actions authorized. The most common mode of intervention employs smaller countries and nongovernmental organizations operating under auspices of the United Nations. This modality shows that the major powers are unwilling to shoulder responsibility for taking such actions, and the inadequacy of the tools indicates that they are unwilling to hand control of important political situations over to agencies that they do not directly command. In addition, the situation demonstrates once again that authority resides in states, not in international organizations or in a global community. This dimension was underscored in the attacks on and conquest of Afghanistan in 2001 and Iraq in 2003.

As the last manifestation of liberal utopianism in the world today, contributors to a campaign for rights divorced from citizenship come from many quarters. Some promote universal human rights, others champion reproductive rights, and still others lobby for animal rights. All fall within the liberal philosophy that ignores community, acknowledging individuals as the only source of aspiration and demand. Each of these campaigns stems from a view that individual preferences should be treated as public rights. Such a position, however, relies wholly on the power held by liberal opinion. It does not rest on the conviction that a public or common good is served by a supporting policy.

The third prong of contemporary liberalism consists of the policies that have been adopted by the institutions, both national and international, dealing with development. Instead of aiming to strengthen states and whole societies through a complex strategy of economic and political development through robust institutions, agencies such as the World Bank have redone their policy goals to make poverty reduction the main priority. In doing so, the individual becomes the unit to be addressed and to be given assistance. The individual in this equation replaces institutional arrangements within the developing country that might be expected to be instrumental in wealth creation and poverty reduction. In addition to shifting the focus and goal of the policies, this reconceptualization also has the effect of strengthening international organizations and private agencies rather than states and indigenous institutions. Yet, as seen in the discussion above, it is in states that authority resides, and only states in the contemporary world have the capacity to embody a public good that transcends private needs.

If these implications were stated as policy goals—that is, the aim is to strengthen international organizations and unaccountable private agencies rather than democratic states and effective national legal orders—it is unlikely that such a view would prevail in public debate. However, the implications remain hidden in a utopian rhetoric and in the obvious liberal concern for the individual.

Individuals who live outside legal orders, outside secure communities, and outside political systems in which they can make their voices heard, however, remain subject only to the power arrangements and practices that structure their lives. Such an existence is not desirable, even for liberal individuals. To avoid it requires that something be added to the limited outlook of liberalism, and that leads us to a consideration of development and the developmental state.

Development and Developmental States

To a large extent, development has been treated conceptually in the post-World War II period as an economic problem, although in practice the political underpinnings have frequently operated. In the first major foreign assistance transfer, the European Recovery program or Marshall Plan, the United States transferred funds but it also attached political conditions and insisted on political requirements. An American, Paul Hoffmann, was placed in charge of administering the funds, but the program stipulated that European governments participating in it had to coordinate their economic planning and the disbursement of funds. In addition, the conception ran together economics and security, for a major impetus of the plan was to build the strength of Western European economies as a bulwark against communism and other threats. Moreover, the deliberate aiming at coordination and integration was designed to overcome what had been seen as one of the political causes of both the beggar-thy-neighbor economic policies of the 1930s and World War II: excessive nationalism.

Dovetailing of economics and politics in Western Europe continued as the North Atlantic Treaty Organization became the principal vehicle for the exercise of United States influence in Europe. One might note that western occupation policies in Germany prior to and following assistance programs to other states bore deeply into the political system and not simply the economy, for the United States and the other victors sought to and effectively did transform German society and politics, in the short run in West Germany but in the long run in the entire country.

Still, the conceptualization of development was largely cast in economic terms. In the first American foreign aid endeavor after European Recovery, the Point IV Program of the Truman administration, the idea was to offer technical assistance to countries that wished to develop. Ideologically, economic development formed the watchword in both the Truman and Eisenhower administrations, and both articulated the view that development should largely occur under the auspices of private enterprise. The single dimension of governmental concern, especially stressed in the Alliance for Progress of the Kennedy administration, designated planning as critical for development, and every government receiving foreign aid created a planning agency.

Even in the 1980s, the years in which neoliberal ideology triumphed, governments acted as the agents of transformation. Rhetoric was directed against states. In Ronald Reagan's words, "Government is part of the problem, not part of the solution." But only states possessed the authority to downsize their bureaucracies and to privatize state-owned enterprises. Major states took such actions as ending the linkage of the dollar to gold in 1971, managing the debt crisis of the 1980s, revaluing the strong currencies in the 1985 Plaza Accord, and saving the international financial system in the Mexican and Asian crises of 1994 to 1995 and 1997 to 1998, respectively. One needs to make this sort of argument only in the face of the fact that the neoliberal ideological position includes a substantial dose of rhetorical obscurantism.

A more realistic and sensible thread may be discerned in the discourse about economic development over the past fifty years or so. In 1955 Lewis wrote that governments can play appropriate and complex roles in development, although he also acknowledged that they can hinder growth as well. He listed nine categories of functions that governments can perform to encourage development, but he offset that list with nine ways that they can induce stagnation. But his conclusion stands opposed four-square to neoliberalism when he declares:

Governments also have an important pioneering job to do.... It is therefore a misfortune for a backward country to have a government which is committed to laissez-faire, whether from indolence or from philosophical conviction. (Lewis 1955, p. 412)

This thread can be picked up again in the work of Kuznets, who wrote, "... the spread of modern economic growth placed greater emphasis on the importance and need for organization in national sovereign units...." (Kuznets 1973, cited in Barro and Sala-I-Martin 1995, p. 5, fn. 2). A theme from Lewis, who stressed the importance of governmental will, appears in an important report by the United Nations Secretary-General forty years later: "The State must have the political will to act" (Boutros-Ghali 1995, p. 31). The World Bank in 1993 acknowledged the important role of the state in the creation of the "East Asian miracle" (World Bank 1993) and in 1997 its primary report indicated the important role of the state in development (World Bank 1997). In addition, a systematic treatment of the centrality of the developmental state in promoting economic development in the contemporary international political economy has formed the content of a number of important studies of a variety of practices in several countries (Evans 1995; Waldner 1999; Weiss 1998). Obviously, these works form one side of a debate in which the other position points to the decline of the state and to the rise of the market (Ohmae 1990, 1995; Stopford and Strange 1991; Strange 1996). The task here does not include a full treatment of this debate. Rather, it involves specifying the requisites and processes of development, an undertaking that requires societal and market as well as state resources. Emphasis is given to the functions that the state plays in development.

As Lewis and others have pointed out, there are many things that go into development and many tasks that must be done to make economic development occur. The activities and tasks are not random, however, for some are more central whereas others are derivative or ancillary. At the center of the development process is production. All other economic activities stem from extracting raw materials, making goods, and providing services. Extraction of natural resources and agricultural production remain essential in the contemporary world, but manufacturing and industrialization mark important functions in modern economies. At the most advanced level of development, services form an increasingly larger portion of modern economies, although they, as remains true of the other components, comprise a part of every economy. Before production can take place and continuing as the next essential component of development, producers need to accumulate surpluses in order to obtain the tools necessary for production. Although in the neoliberal view that ignores state boundaries foreign investors seeking opportunities for profits can bring their money to portfolio investments in emerging markets, the 1997 to 1998 Asian crisis demonstrated effectively the limitations of this view. Two important ingredients were missing from the arrangements that led to the rapid withdrawal of foreign funds from Asian markets: any national commitment that restricted the flow of funds abroad, and state capacity to monitor and regulate those funds. In such cases as Malaysia and

South Korea the banking systems in place, including both banks themselves and a state regulatory system, were quite inadequate. Among the conclusions of those assessing the crisis was that proper sequencing had not occurred, a reformulation of proper financial regulation that had been known for some time (World Bank 1990). In other words, before accepting hot money, states need to insure that they have both state capacity to regulate banking and banks that efficiently allocate savings to investments.

The third essential component of development is distribution, although it follows the other two both sequentially and logically. None of these components functions without state involvement, but there are many other activities that have become increasingly prominent in thinking about development to which states contribute. Education and technology stand out in this regard. From an economic point of view, education represents the accumulation of human capital and can contribute importantly to productivity, one of the keys to increasing wealth. Technology also advances productivity by rendering production more efficient, as it tends to lower costs.

Although the experience of the Soviet Union and other command economies has shown that central planning cannot cope with the complexities of modern production, states remain essential to the accumulation, production, and distribution processes in many ways. In the first place, political choices need to be made in selecting a development strategy. Second, states need to acquire capacities to do many other things associated with development. States need effective institutions giving them the capacity to work with civil society on behalf of transformation. At the same time, civil society needs to be constructed with capacities to produce and to contribute to state formation. Citizens' capacities require enhancement both for economic production and for the exercise of civic duties. Although never disconnected from its civil society and its citizens, the developmental state requires the autonomy to do what Lewis (1955, p. 412) called "pioneering," to create and maintain incentive structures conducive to growth, to plan and carry out schemes in collaboration with firms, and to mediate and resolve conflict, all the while subjecting itself to balance and surveillance through orderly and open processes.

Lying at the base of state functions germane to economic development is the provision of security (Ayoob 1995). Not far behind is "the maintenance of institutions that sustain the rule of law" (Barro and Sala-I-Martin 1995, p. 8). To lay out systematically the list of such functions one can begin with Adam Smith and end with such recent authors as Evans, Weiss, and Waldner.

As discussed by Sen (1999, p. 124–126 and passim), Adam Smith thought that some regulation of and intervention in the market by state authorities was sometimes warranted. Smith (1970/1776) regarded a state as essential to providing stability for the operation of the market, and he held that a political state was essential for defense against external enemies, for protecting property, enforcing contracts, and preserving liberty, and for functioning in the economy by providing and maintaining public works that are not profitable for the private sector. On the other hand, he was suspicious of governmental intervention in the market because it had a tendency to favor the rich and powerful, thus exacerbating problems of disparities between rich and poor. Smith's approach clearly embodied social elements that went beyond the boundaries of narrow economic matters, with its concern with security and equity.

Hegel placed these matters in perspective by defining civil society, including the market, as a component of the state. In part, the state forms an intrinsic piece of civil society in that it protects property, maintains order, enforces contracts, and regulates the market. However, the state embodies an ethical idea and a realm of freedom in which to pursue that idea, rising above the selfish interests of civil society. In contemporary thinking, Gramsci's ideas have brought forward Hegel's conception that the state encompasses something greater, but Gramsci regarded the state as the realm of violence and hegemony as the realm of ideas (Bobbio 1988); both thinkers regard social life as including both.

Contemporary analysts have identified another critical function for states in development, a transformative function that remains essential for developing countries to industrialize. Evans (1995) argues that developmental states play several crucial roles in promoting industrial transformation. First, states act as custodians by regulating and promoting rules governing the economy and by producing infrastructure and providing public services. Second, states enter into production in sectors that complement or compete with private producers. Third, states promote innovation and protect new private industries. Fourth, states support innovation and prod more risky ventures that promise future development. In exercising these functions, states need to embrace autonomous public goals while, at the same time, collaborating with segments of civil society, specifically private firms. Evans refers to this dual posture of the state as "embedded autonomy." State authorities must work closely with private entrepreneurs, but they must also retain sufficient distance and independence to break off old relationships and enter into new ones in order to promote the sort of rapid and deep development that will transform their economies into modern industrial ones.

Whereas Evans devoted his attention to the computer industry in the developing countries Brazil, India, and Korea, Weiss (1998) examined state transformative capacities in the advanced industrial countries Japan, Sweden, and Germany, although her treatment includes attention to the newly industrializing countries (NICs) of East Asia. Both authors place their country analyses in the context of international or global forces. Weiss (1998, p. 7) compares the abilities of the countries she studies to "coordinate industrial change to meet the changing context of international competition." In differentiating between strong states with capacities to shape their own industrial production and distribution policies and those less well institutionalized to cope effectively with global pressures, Weiss' views parallel those of Krasner (1993, p. 318) who thought that industrialized states with "more sophisticated economies and more effective bureaucratic capabilities" were in an advantageous position with respect to their ability to adjust to global pressures.

Waldner (1999) examines a different set of countries, specifically Syria, Turkey, Korea, and Taiwan, and expresses similar conclusions to those of Evans and Weiss, that state institutional capacity explains the difference between success and failure in late developing countries. His analysis goes further by arguing that elite conflicts, which determined whether popular incorporation occurred after the state building and industrial development enterprises, explain success in East Asia but failure in Turkey and Syria. Waldner argues that the most important transition is that from indirect rule through local elites to direct rule by elites in a central state. Without that direct rule—by what Waldner calls an "unmediated state," with its attendant highly capacitated institutions—development gets bogged down in political side payments to popular groups that detract from industrialization. This is an important argument that stands in sharp contrast to current international orthodoxy about incorporating NGOs and local governments in the process of poverty alleviation (World Bank 2000).

At the same time, it remains important to remember that markets tend to distribute products unevenly. Assuming that within a state there exists a conception of citizenship in which individuals gain recognition and, thus, logically assume rights and duties, there is an obligation to ensure some measure of equitable distribution. Markets stand for efficiency; states protect even inefficient citizens.

States thus stand at the juncture of promoting and regulating markets with a view to maintaining their positions in the international system but also to enhancing the wealth and well-being of their citizens, on the one hand, and engaging in orderly redistribution of the product both to earn the support of citizens for the national project but also to ensure the rights of those citizens on the basis of equity. This imperative for states seems confirmed in the experience with liberalization, which has generally resulted in a reduction in inequality between countries and an increase within (Stewart and Barry 1999).

But states also possess what Thomson and Krasner (1989) call "meta-political authority," or the ability to decide which matters belong to the political and which fall outside politics. In both the domestic and international realms, such authority remains essential to achieving relatively orderly politics. Without such authority inside countries, the only way of deciding such categorization questions would be resort to force, and international agreements as well are decided by force in cases in which no authority to conclude agreements is available. Ultimately, such authority rests upon the control of violence (Thomson 1995).

Clearly, then, states perform many tasks beyond those associated with markets, for which they remain essential. They serve their citizens by providing security, identity, and welfare (Nye 1993, p. 184). And they control the violence and hold the authority to maintain a peaceful and ordered realm within but also to conclude agreements with other states that assist in the preservation of a relatively peaceful international system. The major powers possess sufficient power over the allocation of territory and the establishment of international rules that one can argue that, in a hegemonic system or concert like that which prevails today, they even exercise a modicum of authority in the international realm.

For developing countries, participation in the global political economy carries both risks and opportunities. Weak countries have little or no influence in shaping the international rules under which they participate. For the most part, they must import the technology that assists with the increases in their productivity that enables their economies to compete effectively in world markets, and their producers for export must vie with those of other countries. As the Mundell-Fleming theorem indicates, they lose some control over management of their domestic economies. Another risk posed by participation in the world economy is the threat of crisis and disruption in cases in which capital may flow outward or in which recession in importing countries may lead to downturns in the homelands of the exporters. Furthermore, economic changes can at times prove quite disruptive, leading even to political instability.

At the same time, the opportunities offered by such participation include attracting capital and technology, broad markets in which to sell goods, and in the long run the potential for building national wealth and power. The last aspiration may be regarded in part as the ambition of state elites but it may also entail their response to the demands welling up from their societies.

Although participation in the international political economy in order to acquire assets to assist in development remains an essential task of governmental management, it takes place in the larger context of broad modernization and state formation. As indicated by Giddens (1987), state building as part of modernity includes acquisition and development of the means not only of participation but also of resistance to international pressures and of autonomy in the face of the immense dynamism engendered by the major powers and the economic forces emanating from within them. Thus a number of state capacities need to be developed in order to acquire the means to cope with modern pressures. These include organization of the society, control of information that is disseminated in society, surveillance of the population by the government and other agencies but also reciprocal surveillance of the government by the citizenry, the creation of administrative power, the promotion of institutions of social control and political mobilization, and the encouragement of citizenship. To put the matter in a somewhat different context, Giddens posits four institutional clusters of modernity: surveillance, capitalism, industrial production, and centralized control of the means of violence. Evans (1995) states the matter in a different form, arguing that the problem in developing countries is not too much governmental administrative capacity but rather too little.

Policy Imperatives and Dilemmas

The ensuing discussion is premised on the assumption that officials and citizens in every state aim to build states with effective capacities and to achieve state autonomy in the international system. In the absence of an effective and autonomous state, the society will not possess the capacity either to participate in the international political economy or to resist pressures emanating from it. Without a strong state, a country will either be neglected by the powers that might offer it opportunities, or suffer intervention and domination by the same powers which impress their own interests upon it and intrude in its internal affairs.

In some cases this assumption will prove contrary to fact, for the particular interests of individuals and groups may override that social aim. Civil society groups, legitimate business firms, drug traffickers, and others may find it advantageous to operate within a weak state. Certain officials, both to sustain their positions and to enrich themselves may prefer a colonized state to a developmental one. Nevertheless, these phenomena belong entirely to civil society and to particular interests, rather than to communitarian and shared interests. In the long run, whatever benefits accompany globalization processes will not accrue to such states, and they will remain vulnerable to the depredations of powerful actors. In certain cases, one may expect that failure to build a strong autonomous state in a country will on occasion lead both to internal turmoil and risk of forceful international intervention.

Political participants in developmental states themselves face substantial challenges presented by contradictory policy imperatives, dilemmas of choice, and trade-offs among policy choices. They face immense pressures from their own societies but also from the international system and other states. Some of the dilemmas arise from conflicting pressures of agents, but others are implicit in the logic of circumstances in which striving states find themselves.

In his interesting study of sovereignty in practice, Krasner (1999) discusses the variety of ways in which autonomy may be transgressed either by domination or by invitation of state rulers. The temptations to invite foreigners into state decision centers remain many. Among the most prominent are the international financial institutions that offer assistance in managing an economy and in instituting agencies and practices to develop a more sophisticated economy.

The temptation is especially great when the International Monetary Fund (IMF) has been monitoring an economic situation in a developing country and offering policy advice that has not been followed by the government. When the government runs into difficulties, it can gain assistance from the IMF and, at the same time, denounce the financial institution for forcing the government to make the decisions that it knew it should have made earlier. Such scapegoating proves convenient for politicians wishing to remain in office.

On the other hand, the IMF is the agent of the dominant powers. Unless the state in question can build up its own capacity, accumulate its own savings, and arrange for investments to increase the country's prosperity, the future will offer only continued inferior status in the international system and weakness against the dominant powers. At a moment of crisis, it may be unthinkable for a government to resist the temptation; but without a long-term strategy for increasing state capacity, effective resistance will always remain out of reach. In this sense, the dilemma of participating and resisting arises from state weakness. Thus the trick is to devise a means of transcending weakness and developing strength.

Formulation and implementation of a development strategy constitute the essential task for gaining strength. Although a state may draw some foreign investment, it must accumulate surpluses from its own internal production if it is to overcome weakness. Usually this entails extracting savings from the rural sector of its economy and making investments in infrastructure and productive facilities in its urban sector. Such action represents the beginning of the sort of transformative capacity to which Evans and Weiss pointed.

Even while extracting surpluses from agricultural production, state authorities need to keep agriculture open to international trade in order to increase its efficiency and its earnings. A corollary task is to advocate that the industrialized countries adhere to free trade principles in their importing policies. However, the industrial sector of the economy is quite unlikely to be able to compete with the mature industries of advanced economies. Thus developing states need to face the counterpressures from the imperative to protect infant industries and from neoliberal advocacy of free trade and unrestrained exports. Transformative capacity becomes crucial in facing this dilemma, for protection that lasts too long ensures that the country's industries will never be able to compete and will thus lose broader markets to competitors. Nevertheless, opening too soon may also condemn new industries that have not yet achieved competitive levels of production.

A fairly common means employed by developing countries to achieve industrialization, and incidentally to acquire technology, uses foreign direct investment by companies that enter into joint ventures with domestic owners. Governments face certain dilemmas in such situations. The first stems from the pull of privileged investors who collect rents from their participation in the joint ventures, and the aspiration to build a developmental state serving a common good. A second dilemma arises out of the need to retain the direct foreign capital investment versus the desire to achieve technological prowess if not autonomous innovative capacity. Neither of these dilemmas can be resolved in favor of the state without the presence of transformative capacity and an elite with a sense of public purpose. That elite must include not simply a political contingent but also needs to encompass significant elements of the private sector. In other words, a private sector imbued solely with neoliberal ideology and lacking any sense of larger societal purpose would not contribute to the communitarian enterprise of building a developmental state.

Among the messages being forcefully transmitted in the contemporary world by the international financial institutions and their leading supporters is that nongovernmental organizations and local governments need to be included in the battle to alleviate poverty. Both themes of that message, devolution to private and local entities and adoption of poverty reduction as a priority over comprehensive development, pose dilemmas for statesmen. Among the components of state capacity, the ability to mobilize and involve citizens and local communities ranks as quite important. In part, the ability of a central state to mobilize constituents through organizations and governments has to be instrumental, although the importance of ideology should not be overlooked. On the other hand, participation of broad sectors of the population leads, as Waldner (1999) pointed out, to a politics of making side payments that render very difficult the development of transformative capacity. It is not easy to see a way out of this dilemma, although greater emphasis on hegemonial ideology than on instrumental payoffs should more likely allow the state to gain in strength.

The other dilemma set up by the pressures of the international financial institutions and their backers, between broad development and poverty reduction, should lead to choices favoring a growing emphasis on development. There are several reasons for this position. First, broad development encompasses poverty reduction, at least in the long run (Dollar and Kraay 2000), and poverty reduction programs can be conceptualized as part of overall development strategies aimed at capacitating citizens as well as state institutions. Second, the unit of focus in poverty reduction is the individual, whereas the state and community form the unit in development. Although strong states provide the most effective protection and instrument for creating wealth for individuals, poverty reduction without development promises only continued dependency. And that consideration leads to the third reason for emphasizing overall development. By placing the individual at the center of policy, institutional development and state building lose out to the neoliberal agenda that promotes international organizations and nongovernmental organizations. Without resistance to that agenda, the developing countries are promised only dependency and an inability to gain the capacities that will enable them to choose to participate more effectively in the international political economy or to resist.

Another dilemma emanates from the necessity, in today's world, to adopt capitalist market principles in organizing the economy, on the one hand, and the recognition that capitalism generates inequality in the distribution of products. There are good reasons for organizing along capitalist lines, including the demonstrated productivity of that system as contrasted with alternatives. However, there are also sound reasons for developing sufficient state capacity to redistribute the product on an equitable basis. One reason flows from the nature of the state in which citizens are given recognition of one another and from that recognition flow rights and duties. Among the foremost rights is the one that makes a claim for equitable treatment, including income distribution, within the community. Another reason proves more instrumental. Without the political support of the populace, it is unlikely that governments can in the long run sustain participation in an international political economy, for the deprivations and dislocations suffered as a result of that participation are likely to engender revulsion and resistance. Governments can offset that resistance and earn the political support of their populations only by protecting citizens from the worst buffetings of the international economy.

All of these dilemmas and the need for states to face and resolve them point to the imperative need for developmental states. Moreover, states possess another capacity that markets cannot acquire: metapolitical capacity, or the ability to allocate matters to the political and to the nonpolitical. Although private capital flows to poor countries far exceed governmental foreign aid (ODA, or official development assistance) that allocation has been made by the donor countries. Governments in poor countries face immense difficulties, therefore, in exercising their metapolitical capacities against the structural choice made by the powers and the instruments that put that choice into effect, international institutions and private firms and organizations. In the long run, however, their ability to allocate will be strengthened by use.

Conclusion

From every corner dominant discourses in today's world favor free markets and democracy, and acknowledgment of the underlying role of the state in promoting those values tends to remain subdued. Such a cast in the discourse emphasizes individualism and economics, and it presents a conception of the state as a wholly subsidiary though supportive component of the market. In such a framing of social life, both general politics and the specific politics of state formation tend to be set aside.

Yet states need to be formed in order to provide one of the two fundamental pillars upon which the structure of global capitalism and democracy must be built. Among the perplexities of discourse and practice lies the puzzle of how to form and build states with the capacities required in the globalizing world. Although there exists no obvious solution to that puzzle, surely the problem needs to be discussed. At the same time, the main lines of dialogue mention states mostly as entities to be torn down or bypassed.

Once formed, states need to perform all of the functions to make the economy work and to form citizens and make political choices. The last comprises the most difficult of challenges for political leaders. At the very least, there is a need to attend to an analysis of leadership and the skills that leaders possess. In addition, some attention should be given to the valuable services that politicians perform for their societies: making judgments and decisions, finding compromises among clashing groups, offering visions of potential for their societies, and forging aggregations of people who, as communities, can strive to achieve political goals.

Foremost among the achievements that political leaders can accomplish is to clarify the choices that their states need to make and to mobilize support on behalf of the appropriate decisions. As the discussion of the many dilemmas involved in development indicated, the choices are rarely easy. Nevertheless, the overall direction of political vision for countries aspiring to development needs to be toward building their states and their political societies. Building an efficient and productive economy forms an important component of that enterprise, but it is not the end. The ultimate goal has to be an autonomous state, with effective institutions and participating citizens, able to make choices in the face of the formidable pressures and opportunities of a dynamic world.

8

State Responses to Globalizing Pressures

Introduction

Experience has demonstrated that autonomous states cooperating in a liberal international economy engender wealth and well-being as well as safety and security. In addition, the path of autarky such as that taken by Myanmar (Burma) leads to economic decline, as do choices of predatory states such as Zaire and, more recently, Zimbabwe. Similarly, colonized states such as Russia since 1991 have an overall tendency to decay while an elite may enjoy a highly privileged life yet suffer from a lack of public security and safety. Developmental states offer a model, but at the same time such states exist in the context of a globalizing system that presents them with hazards even as it offers them opportunities. Thus leaders and peoples need to employ the advantages but resist those pressures that promise to interfere with their own autonomous development.

Autonomous development includes both economic and political dimensions. Not only do an appropriate economic development strategy and other economic policies need to be devised but also a state needs to be built and formed. Although members of the society need to develop skills and other attributes forming human capital, they also need to become citizens in a state with a dimension of freedom to seek a common good with their fellow citizens. Those citizens need to be inspired and directed by leaders who themselves possess both a dedication to the polity that they serve and a sense of connection to the citizenry whom they must convince in order to gain support. At the same time, political leaders have to be given enough scope to act effectively, sometimes and temporarily without effective shackles on their freedom of action, and restrained from the practice of undue corruption and use of their offices for personal gain. Governmental structures have to be put into place that function effectively to make and implement clear decisions that achieve public purposes and monitor and regulate the private activities that underlie economic production and related activities. Such requirements contain a variety of tensions and contradictory aspirations. That is the nature of political choice and political life.

This chapter outlines a view of the political requirements involved in state building, the structure of government necessary to maintain and regulate civil society activities, and the sorts of activities and policy choices that governments will face on an ongoing basis as managers of developmental states. Second, the chapter examines the needs and choices involved in creating and maintaining a developmental state that takes advantage of the liberal international economy and, at the same time, guards against the pitfalls and hazards presented by the world as a whole or predatory parts of it. Kept in mind throughout is the recognition that autonomy needs to be increased even while pursuing wealth and power through cooperation in the wider world.

Successful Models for Development

Although each state faces the challenge of forging its own place in the world, the experiences of those that have enjoyed success offer a variety of exemplars. In addition, there are broad models that offer perspectives on the choices and the international contexts that previous state leaderships have faced; these aid in understanding the sorts of choices that may confront leaders now and in the future.

Despite the advocacy of American neoliberals who express a universal impulse by holding up the United States model as the archetype for everyone, the North American superpower offers just one of at least four contemporary successful models. In the 1990s, the United States economy demonstrated a dynamism surpassing the other mature economies in its job-creating and economic growth based on corporate restructuring. Concurrently, both the military prowess and domination of command-and-control information systems have given to the United States an inordinate measure of safety and security. Above all, the United States shows the way to others in its ability to shape its environment while also acting autonomously when snubbing constraints. For example, at the same time that the American government closes its borders to trade in certain products, sugar providing the clearest example, and lays out immense subsidies to its agricultural sector it demands that others adhere to free trade principles and end subsidies.

As developed at greater length below, the United States promoted and supported authoritarian government and militarization in Korea, among other countries, during the Cold War but in the post-Cold War period encourages democracy and human rights. During the 1950s through the early 1990s in the western hemisphere the United States allied itself and assisted governments that engaged in suppression of popular movements and in torture and extrajudicial killings, such as those in Guatemala. In the post-Cold War period, the United States encourages democracy and the protection of human rights in the same places. To a large extent, the variation in policy can be explained by changes in the historical circumstances and the constraints of the international system, but such dramatic shifts in policy can only be taken by a state with the considerable autonomy that its capabilities afford it. In considering the constraints of the international system, moreover, one needs to keep in mind the very great effects that the weight and policies of the United States have in shaping those constraints.

Although neoliberals stress the individualism and lightly regulated nature of American social and economic arrangements, the coherence and unity of the American market need also to be noted, and one would be derelict not to notice that a strong sense of nationalism and solidarity also characterizes the American people. Very firm institutions of government offer mechanisms for deliberation, but they also provide for decisive choices and the bureaucratic instruments for giving effect to decisions. These characteristics are often obscured because of the peculiarities of the system of shared and separated powers among the branches of national government and of the system of federalism. Looked at from a nearer angle, the American political system offers extensive opportunities for the debate, maneuvering, and conflict that characterize lively politics. Nonetheless, viewed from the perspective of the world as a whole, the United States is quite capable of acting with vigor, direction, and unity.

Europe provides other models. Given its security during the Cold War that was shaped by the bipolar distribution of power between the United States and the Soviet Union, Western European countries made considerable progress in economic growth through cooperative schemes. At the center were France and West Germany, whose policy choices in the context of the aftermath of World War II led them to integrate their economies. Like other countries in the region, they present a different model than the United States for organizing educational systems, structuring government, arranging labor relations into a corporatist form, providing extensive welfare support to citizens, and other social and political arrangements.

For Western European countries during the Cold War, with others added after, cooperation in a security alliance with the United States brought the fundamental benefits of safety and stability. Within this context, these countries were able to pursue economic gains with little concern that neighbors might turn those economic assets into security threats against them. Under that security protection, furthermore, the Western Europeans forged cooperative institutions and complex processes that brought their economic systems into exceptionally close cooperation.

While the international context together with the resulting schemes for cooperation dampened almost to extinction expansive manifestations of nationalism, coherent national solidarity and policy autonomy persisted. For many years, the resistance of Britain to European integration provided the most obvious manifestation of this autonomy, and that country's remaining outside the European central banking and single currency system still illustrates the autonomy. Moreover, other countries such as Norway, Denmark, and Sweden have also demonstrated national coherence and policy autonomy in rejecting participation in the European central bank scheme and the Euro as their currency. France has long insisted on a measure of autonomy both within Europe and within the North Atlantic alliance. Since the end of the Cold War Germany has begun slowly to move in the direction of displaying openly its considerable autonomy that in the Cold War context was exercised with greater discretion.

Japan and the other East Asian developmental states offer yet other exemplars of successful models for at least consideration if not imitation by developing countries. Evolving over the years from the pre-Meiji restoration period, Japan's system of governance and economic development was forged in the run-up to and conduct of World War II as the government and conglomerate businesses formed a partnership that largely provided a model for the Japanese system in the post-occupation period.

Japan faced an international environment that forced it to open to the rest of the world and that embodied the heyday of the capitalist imperialist drive of the late nineteenth century. To confront such hostile pressures, Japan industrialized and then joined in the imperialist scramble. Part of the Japanese expansionism included the colonization of Korea and Taiwan, both of which suffered during the colonial period but also benefited from the colonial legacy (Cumings 1987; Kohli 1999). Furthermore, as Johnson (Woo-Cumings 1999) has argued, both China and Japan were spurred to development by nationalism. Particularly when considering Japan and Korea, the pressure of the United States in two separate eras to open their markets proved critical to their development. In addition, both Korea and Taiwan, as well as Finland and Austria, harnessed "very real fears of war and instability toward a remarkable developmental energy, which in turn could become a binding agent for growth" (Woo-Cumings 1999, p. 23).

Nationalism figures powerfully also in the fourth major contemporary model, China. The major accomplishment during the Cold War was the gaining of political autonomy, even as China endured economic and human catastrophes in the midst of some development. Since the death of Mao Zedong and the accession of Deng Xiaoping in 1978, China has also launched a major drive for economic growth to catch up with the richer powers. In addition, the country has regained territories lost or partly detached in the past, specifically Tibet, Hong Kong, and Macao. Taiwan remains an object of a Chinese quest for territorial integrity, but the separate development of Taiwan and its protection by the United States makes the aspiration of one China an elusive and perhaps a problematical one.

The Chinese model presents the most direct challenge to the liberal view that society and the economy precede and shape the state. Regarding the Soviet case of reforming the political system before restructuring the economy as a gross error, the Chinese government has remained adamant that the Communist Party must remain in control of the state in order to provide the stability that underpins its pursuit of economic development. Furthermore, communist or not, the Chinese people remain strongly nationalist with a sense that they are involved in a broad enterprise of social solidarity to make China strong and respected in the world.

As every other country must do, China has to cope with the international context of the time. Thus the country has sought to modify its internal laws and rules to attract foreign investment and has concluded extended negotiations to join the World Trade Organization. It also faces in the early twenty-first century the prospect of an American-Japanese-South Korean alliance and the apparent aspirations of the alliance leader to develop and deploy theater and national anti-ballistic missile systems that would give it, in effect, a possibly decisive strategic advantage in any military confrontation with China. This might induce China to embark on a major program of building additional components of a strategic nuclear-armed missile system, which would in turn probably prompt India to compete with it. These concerns add to the general ambience in East Asia that has led the Chinese to work with the North Koreans to damp down tensions and to try to manage the Taiwan situation so as to provoke neither war nor independence. As is also true of other countries, China faces American and European pressures on behalf of improving human rights.

Each of these four successful models for development exists and grows within a specific set of historical circumstances and international contexts. What seem common to all are social solidarity and nationalism, stimulation provided by fear of war, aspiration to compete with others either by maintaining one's lead or by catching up with the leaders, and strong governmental commitments to development. In meeting those commitments, different states have advanced distinctive policies and methods of pursuing wealth. Certainly each of these countries offering models stands in stark contrast to the failures of predatory states, command economies, and autarkies; each also provides an exemplar of success in forging political and economic systems that advance wealth and power in the particular international circumstances in which it finds itself.

Contemporary examples are not the only source for seeking models, for history and experience offer material for thinking further about paths to development. First, industrialization has occurred over time in fairly distinct stages that can offer insight to those advancing today. Second, choices have been made in the past of distinct development strategies and of comparative advantages to hone.

Stages of Industrialization and Development Strategies

States developing today are regarded as late developers in view of the fact that industrialization has been occurring since about 1750 when the industrial revolution began with the invention of the steam engine and the use of coal as a fuel, transforming first British society and then others. Urbanization and the factory system took hold, replacing agriculture as the predominant mode of production; then the railroad sped up and reduced the costs of travel and shipping.

A second phase of industrialization began around 1860, with the United States and Germany as the leaders but also Italy and Japan following closely along, when steamships, the telegraph and telephone, chemicals, steel, petroleum, and machine tools were introduced to increase production immensely. In this second phase, heavy industry characterized the model of economic growth followed by the advanced countries, but the period also included such major inventions as electricity, the submarine, the airplane, radio and television, radar, jet engines, rockets, and atomic fission and fusion that resulted in both exceptionally powerful bombs and energy production. Toward the end of this phase the leading industrial countries also shifted from coal to petroleum as the dominant source of energy fueling their economies.

A third phase of industrialization began around 1950, first with the application of mechanical automation and robots and then the increased application of computer-based information control to production, finance, and commerce, and the growth of the service sector of the economy. In the most advanced country, the United States, tremendous airlift capacity enabled it to conduct massive military operations at great distances, and its control of information-based battle control systems allowed it to dominate battlefields. In the third phase, space became a major arena for commercial and scientific as well as intelligence activities, and it seems likely that space will eventually become an environment for military action.

Although internal developments produced both innovations and output, states and societies were often spurred by international events and contexts to accelerate innovation or to devise technological responses to others' advantages. Such competition appeared especially prominent in the second phase of industrialization, when Germany sought to meet the success of Britain, and Japan strove to become a power in order to prevent its being reduced to dependency by the Western powers. The Soviet Union explicitly sought to catch up with the United States and the Western European powers before World War II and then to gain on and surpass the United States in its aftermath.

As the mightiest innovator and producer, the United States too was spurred by its fears of being surpassed by its enemies in the Second World War and of maintaining its dominant position during the Cold War. Since then the United States has continued to strive to maintain its position not simply by invention and production but also by structuring international institutions that afford it the means of managing economic affairs in the world as a whole. In addition, the United States has continued to strive to retain its dominant position as the world's foremost military power.

It is not only the powers whose economic and military histories have been partly and importantly shaped by the international contexts they faced. Every country's life exists in international circumstances that structure choices for it, as a few examples illustrate. In the 1930s as the United States enacted the Smoot-Hawley Tariff to protect its domestic economy, the Latin American countries had little choice but to compensate for the loss of markets. Thus they devised a strategy of import substitution in which they manufactured what they had previously purchased from the more highly industrialized countries. Japan's recovery from World War II devastation was greatly aided by both the Korean and Vietnam wars, as it became a supplier of *materiél* for the United States forces fighting in those places. In Europe the Marshall Plan provided direct aid that was motivated by competition with the Soviet Union, and American security protection gave a context that enabled the economic cooperation evidenced in the European Community.

Aside from making the point that both internal developments and external circumstances shape economic development strategies and affect chances of success, I also emphasize that economic and political development need to be analyzed in specific historical terms. There certainly are broad matters that can be considered by any developing country, and there are alternative development strategy models. Nevertheless, each country has a unique background, a unique set of domestic conditions, and a unique position in the international system; its leaders and people must, therefore, devise specific policies to address their own discrete problems.

They may draw on the advice of others, and they may acquire technology to help them to industrialize, but no off-the-shelf solutions are available for their problems and circumstances.

As noted, the Latin American countries were forced by American protectionist policy to adopt an import substitution industrialization strategy (ISI) in the 1930s. By the 1970s that ISI strategy had become exhausted because the developing countries following it found themselves in the position of continuing to import the components and machinery required for the production of finished consumer goods. In addition, they tended to extend advantages to their industrial sectors while depriving agricultural sectors of foreign exchange and innovative technology; yet agricultural exports were expected to pay for the components and machinery imports critical to the development strategy. Nonetheless, one of broad questions to be considered by authorities seeking development is to what extent should import substitution be embraced.

No development strategy stands whole and alone, and the obvious limitations of import substitution need to be kept in mind. Nevertheless, some goods can economically be produced within the confines of a national or regional market without unfavorable dependency on imported licensed components and machinery. Food and beverages, clothing and shoes, furniture, handicrafts, and other products can ordinarily be supplied by businesses and workers within a national economy. In addition, many services are not exportable but rather are supplied within the context of a national economy. Both subsistence agriculture and surplus agriculture form part of the national economy. Thus it is unlikely that a development strategy can rely entirely on export-led industrialization, however advantageous that may be for particular countries. What also remains important regarding the domestic economy is that it needs to be attended to by the government both to insure its sustainability and to make it serve public ends. These include both the collection of taxes and the generation of savings for investment. Although foreign direct investment offers some funding for productive investment, a state that aims to gain autonomy has to generate its own savings and investments.

Complete reliance on import substitution industrialization is unlikely to occur except in such drastic circumstances as those evident in the Great Depression when developing countries were cut off from traditional markets or in the face of sanctions imposed by hostile countries. However, ISI remains available as a component of a broader development strategy that relies primarily on export.

The greatest advantage of an export-oriented industrialization strategy is the availability of a very large market that extends way beyond the borders of a single country or region. In particular, exports can be sold in the world's wealthiest markets. Thus, by selling products or services that are consumed by Americans, Europeans, and Japanese, smaller countries can employ the principle of comparative advantage to gain wealth considerably greater than they could by purveying such products and services only within their own borders. Some outstanding examples are offered by South Korea, which has become the world's leading shipbuilder, and Singapore, which completed the chain for twenty-four-hour global trading in financial products. Many countries have joined in the tourist trade, selling their resort and vacation services to visitors from throughout the world.

As reiterated by economists since David Ricardo first promulgated the concept, a country benefits from employing comparative advantage by specializing in the production of those goods that it produces most efficiently. In large part, a country's comparative advantage is shaped by its factor endowments, things such as a tropical climate for growing bananas and other fruits, mineral resources that can be extracted, or cheap labor to reduce costs. However, comparative advantage can also be fashioned by public policy that aims to find a world market niche and by the availability of capital and technology. Part of the strategy of the developmental states of Japan and the East Asian NICs sought to gain market shares in such industries as steel, shipbuilding, and computer components. Many countries have chosen to play host to major hotel and resort corporations seeking to invest in leisure industries in enclaves along scenic beaches in warm climates, thus combining factor endowments and available capital and technology in the choice of devising a development scheme based on comparative advantage.

Another major incentive for a developing country to encourage and accept foreign direct investment (FDI) lies in the acquisition of technology. Thus states aiming to develop insist that firms seeking to invest must also transfer technology to the host state through its co-owners, managers, and workers. In addition to the skills, organizational and production techniques, and technical knowledge that such transfers entail, the gained technological acquisitions hold the potential for forming a basis upon which the host state can build its own technological education, training, and innovation. In the long run, such a tactic can promise self-sustaining growth, increased wealth, and political autonomy within the context of the international political economy.

In addition, technology is key to intensive growth and enhanced productivity. Economic growth occurs nearly everywhere on an extensive basis by adding factors of production. For example, simply by adding additional land and labor, agricultural output is increased (Jones 1996). Or, by building another factory, installing additional machines, and hiring more workers, output in any established industry will be increased (Campbell 1988). However, significant increases in production and wealth follow from increased output by existing factors of production, and such tends to occur from additional capital investments and even more so from new technologies (Krugman 1994). For example, with robotics the output of a single worker may equal that of twenty or more workers laboring manually. For countries aiming to develop into thoroughly modern states, intensive growth remains mandatory.

To accomplish intensive growth, both effective governments and creative entrepreneurs have to contribute to the undertaking. Each of the successful models sketched—except the Soviet Union which failed to achieve intensive growth (Bialer 1988)—found ways of effectively governing while also structuring incentives to encourage the creativity and risk-taking associated with entrepreneurship. Even though the specific mixes of politics, bureaucracy, and private enterprise varied between, say, the United States and Japan, each devised arrangements that encouraged research and development, innovation and creativity, and enterprise. Even in the Soviet Union, through its educational system and research institutes, creativity and inventiveness were encouraged to enhance growth in heavy industry, the military, and space exploration. What was lacking was sufficient freedom for individuals to become fully creative, to work openly with colleagues, and to retain some of the benefits resulting from their creativity.

As has been indicated, foreign investment offers a source of savings that can be used as part of an economic development strategy. However, no state can expect to achieve a significant level of autonomy if it relies solely on foreign savings; it must generate savings from its own economy. To accomplish this in a poor country presents a formidable challenge, but it can be done through forced savings collected by taxes for pensions, public savings through a postal savings system, or private savings based on the incentive of interest paid on accumulations. In Muslim countries, where the payment of interest remains prohibited, functionally equivalent incentives can be offered. Once savings begin to mount, it is also crucial for a country to establish an effective banking system, including both agencies for recycling savings to productive investments and effective regulatory/supervisory mechanisms, to put the savings to productive use.

Even though the ultimate goal in a development strategy is autonomy and the freedom of action that it conveys, all of the activities associated with economic growth occur in an international context. Many of the activities rely upon support from other countries in the form of FDI but also in their importing the products and services exported by the country in question. Thus autonomy does not equate with isolation or autarky. What autonomy does entail is sufficient strength of capacities and independence of judgment to participate freely in a global political economy. Aspirations to gain both strength and freedom do not form part of the agenda of private entrepreneurship and individual goals; they belong to the realm of social and political life, and they are fulfilled through capacitation and building of state institutions. Through such institutional strength and freedom, nations have the ability to participate in the international political economy, but they also retain the capacity to resist involvement on terms unacceptable to them. In order to assume such a position, societies must form states.

State Formation

Economic growth remains an indispensable goal for developing countries whose leaders and people aspire to power, wealth, and autonomy, for industrial wealth forms the bedrock for national power. Without such power, no country is in a position to make choices about its future, its place in the world, and its relations with others. Furthermore, a critical component of a successful drive for economic development is a developmental state, a public apparatus with the ability to select policies conducive to economic growth and the strength to direct and regulate the economy while avoiding corrupt and uninformed choices that retard growth.

Such an institutional formation, with its "embedded autonomy" (Evans 1995), embodies the statal component of what Hegel termed civil society that is primarily shaped by the private sector pursuing particular interests. In the Lockean liberal scheme of things, this is the fundamental basis for the state, merely to serve as the referee for private interests and the guarantor of private property rights, although Locke did regard a "federative" power to conduct relations with foreign governments as another function of liberal government. Fundamentally, then, liberal government is limited government. In the modern interpretation, it is a government that gets out of the way of economic production activities but gives preference to corporate enterprises and supports those social programs that enhance capital formation, both human and financial.

Even though liberal discourse does not include allusions to larger purposes, those do function in liberal societies whose citizens are expected to inform themselves about politics, to aggregate themselves in groups and political parties that not only participate in public policy discussions but also formulate programs for governance, and to pay for and serve in armed forces on those occasions when it is required. These duties of citizens arise from the assumptions and conditions of political life in liberal societies. Among the assumptions is that each person is capable of making autonomous choices that serve his or her own interests. Among the conditions of a liberal society is that limited government and responsiveness to the citizenry entail periodic elections, continuing debates, and the provision of services.

The liberal state provides one exemplar of success in economic growth, and it affords a model of citizen involvement and benefits. In the absence of explicit consideration of broader state formation, issues of state responsibilities tend to take place as discrete policy debates on separate issues, and private groups are able to act on public matters but without any need to be accountable or subject to electoral scrutiny. Such private activities have grown in the post-Cold War period as governments have devolved functions to the private sector. This has been a particularly prominent feature of government and the economy in the United States. In addition, it has been extended to international activities, especially in the areas of humanitarian relief and foreign direct assistance.

This survey attests to the comprehensive nature of state formation. The enterprise needs to include a substantial number of matters, at a variety of levels. To summarize, state formation consists of forming effective institutions and procedures for deliberating, making decisions, and ruling. Ruling includes the provision of order and the suppression of threats to security (Ayoob 1995). To build such an order (Huntington 1968), elites need to construct institutions to surveil and police. Even more efficacious for producing stability is the provision of competent governance, which relies on institutional coherence and consistency, bureaucratic expertise and competence, and the underlying educational infrastructure for training the experts. However, bureaucratic institutions must be supervised by political leaders who both direct and manage bureaucracies and ensure their responsiveness to the citizens whom they serve by interpreting the permanent government to the nation and by pressing the nation's concerns on the bureaucracy.

These buffering functions remain prominent in promoting and regulating the economy, for government must be capacitated to perform the several functions of a developmental state, as described by Evans (1995). A dynamic economy is unlikely to emanate from a desultory state; economic growth depends as much upon the effectiveness of government as upon the initiative, cleverness, and drive of private entrepreneurs and a skilled and hard-working labor force.

In addition, government has the difficult but essential task of arranging for the distribution of products. Much of this task can be taken care of through framework legislation that allows collective bargaining between management and labor and that builds human capacities through education, health programs, and welfare, but distribution may also be channeled by subsidies and tax legislation. At the end, government must provide for those citizens whose fundamental sustenance and health are not taken care of through market and government programs aimed at production and general welfare. These matters come under the headings of poverty reduction programs, welfare schemes, housing subsidies, old age pensions and medical care, and similar activities.

Many of these matters pertaining to state formation and functioning pertain to civil society matters, that is, considerations that address the individual, group, and particular interests of citizens, associations, and private groups. For the most part, these comprise the functions of government within the ordinary discourse carried on by liberals. However, states also represent and are the mechanisms for achieving that which its citizens have in common. Although their common interests come to the fore most prominently in relations with other countries, state authorities and citizens forge links through the use of common symbols and activities that emphasize national solidarity and common purpose. Consideration of state formation, though, necessarily includes attention to external relations and security matters.

Security and Diplomacy

Although devotion to economic development remains central to the policy matters that developmental state leaders must be concerned with, concentrated attention can occur only within a secure and peaceful framework. Thus states have to be secure, a condition ordinarily stemming only from attentiveness to and effective policies in response to threats. At home that includes routine policing; abroad it entails the creation and nurturing of armed forces, acquisition of arms, and formulation and execution of security policy. Because the circumstances in which leaders need to meet these challenges vary with each state, one does not want to offer any detailed analysis of the matter. In addition to direct security concerns that involve armed forces and other paraphernalia designed to protect borders and the citizens and property within them, the conduct of relations with neighbors and other potentially menacing states contributes to security.

Furthermore, states engaged in broader interactions with the rest of the world require diplomatic policies and activities designed to promote and protect their interests in the variegated international life that characterizes contemporary international affairs. These include bilateral relations with those countries having the most direct impact on any given developing country, but they also encompass both regional and global multilateral forums. Again, the circumstances of any given country vary considerably, so broad generalizations do not seem to be warranted. On the other hand, those matters of commerce, finance, and other subjects with direct effects on economic development afford opportunities for developing countries, singly or together in coalitions, to participate in shaping international policies that affect them. Moreover, through their participation in broader matters such as peace operations and the formation of new international regimes developing countries can sometimes build up good will that may serve them in their economic aspirations.

As essential as security matters and diplomacy are for establishing a base and erecting a framework within which economic development occurs, the primary matters for developing countries lie within their borders and are shaped by their own societies. In addressing state building, however, the international environment cannot be shut out, for it forms a set of circumstances and pressures with which developmental states need to cope even as they engage in building their capacities, institutions, and practices to achieve their goals.

Building Developmental States in a Globalizing World

The East Asian countries that provide the empirical examples of developmental states were fashioned in a particular time and place, in a series of unique circumstances. States today face different constraints, and they have emerged out of different histories. Still, there are certain political and economic guidelines and warning signs that can be derived from both the economic development literature and the literature on developmental states.

Central to the concept of the developmental state is nationalism (Woo-Cumings 1999) which acts as a spur to development. Although more often than not, nationalism tends to be viewed as a mobilizing device for expansion, at bottom it means more and less than that dimension. Nationalism shapes a people's identity through which they can focus on a manageable group to live with and serve. It distinguishes the group from the outside world with which it interacts, and it offers a criterion for determining interests. The nationalism that goaded China in 1937 and Japan during World War II to develop occurred in the context of war and hostility, a specific circumstance not available to many countries in the contemporary world. Nevertheless, the nation forms the basis for making choices, organizing an economy, and interacting with the international environment.

Globalizing pressures emanating from the leading powers include the promotion of neoliberal decision rules, such as reducing subsidies and shrinking government. Nationalism in this context affords a standard against which to assess the proffered rule. State authorities, confronted with pressures from IFIs or donor governments, can decide whether the reduction of a subsidy, say, serves the interest of the nation. Because subsidies tend to be aimed at particular groups, it is quite possible to argue that a larger national interest is served by withdrawing the subsidy. On the other hand, subsidies provided so that the poorest citizens can be sustained by a minimal diet and essential services, it can be argued, underwrite the national interest of insuring minimal rights and standards for every citizen.

Whichever may be the case, the criterion lies in the hands of state authorities acting for the good of their nation, not with external powers wielding their particular ideology. As Pempel (1999) has reminded us, though, developmental states by their nature remain vulnerable to the external environment, a structural weakness characterizing them. In some cases, a country's need for external assistance may be so dire that authorities are coerced to submit to conditions with which they do not agree. On such occasions, however, they can resist the outside pressures to the best of their ability. Furthermore, nationalism should goad them to seek to avoid such coerced situations in the future by formulating national plans to enhance autonomy.

Many societies do not suffer or enjoy the circumstances of external threat to push them toward cohesion, and many are riven by ethnic, religious, class, and other divisions that inhibit or preclude nationalist identity. To some extent, the pressures of globalization exerted by international financial institutions and firms and other market forces offer a substitute for a security threat, but it is a pale one. Elites may try to shape national agendas, to some extent, by using whatever leverage they might possess to deal directly, on a bilateral basis, with a major power or another country. In that manner, they will be seen by their populations as national leaders dealing with the authorities of other nations, rather than as representatives of a weak society submitting to international civil servants and with wealthy, powerful business people. In cases in which national leaders do not possess such leverage, they can move their national agendas forward by insisting on conditions for the intrusion of international institutional personnel on the national administration. One condition would almost certainly entail a time limit. Another would require that any technical or administrative mission has to include a training dimension aimed at teaching national personnel the skills and knowledge necessary for doing the job undertaken by the international technicians.

To give themselves the political strength to take such positions, political elites also might follow two courses of action, the first indicated by Gramsci (1971), and the other by Huntington (1968). Gramsci argued that, to achieve dominance in a society, political leaders need to conquer intellectuals with a theory or way of thinking that becomes hegemonic and that they can be mightily helped in this endeavor by "organic intellectuals," or thinkers who promote the views of the political elites. Huntington's thesis is that political organization forms the basic and essential ingredient for the institutionalization of a modernizing, then modern, regime. Thus developmental state leaders need to formulate and articulate convincing ideas that will inspire and mobilize followers and to engage in organized politics, largely through political parties, to harness the energies of the variety of political participants in changing societies.

Johnson (1999) has argued that a single overriding objective such as war or a space program allows planning to work better than the market. In the case of the East Asian capitalist developmental states, economic development served each as that overriding objective. The regimes leading the states gained their legitimacy from the achievement of the project, not from their method of selection (Johnson 1999, p. 53). At the same time, dedication to achieving the developmental project mobilizes people, thus distinguishing the developmental regime from an authoritarian one because it serves the nation as a whole and from a central planning, Leninist one because, instead of excluding people who want to work for a common goal, it includes them (Johnson 1999, p. 53). Such projects are necessarily confined to the nation; the confinement makes them feasible by merging general national identity with a concrete undertaking that promises to strengthen and enhance the nation.

At the same time, as Onis (1991, p. 116) argues, the public-private cooperation necessary to carrying out the project has been engineered by state elites, whose "single-minded commitment...to growth, productivity, and international competitiveness" was stimulated by external threat. In addition, the elites were able to mount a drive for development and transformation while ignoring "considerations relating to income distribution and social welfare" because the "industrialization drive...[was] initiated from a relatively egalitarian base" (Onis 1991, pp. 116–117).

Adoption of such a single objective may prove easier to achieve in a relatively homogeneous, egalitarian society than in a fragmented one with significant class, religious, linguistic, and income differences. As Waldner (1999) has indicated, leaders may be tempted in such circumstances to make side payments to selected groups, thus undermining their efforts to forge national unity and to pursue a single-minded objective. Both ideology and political organization may help in alleviating this matter, but undoubtedly some political leaders will fail to build developmental states.

For those who do succeed, the institutionalization of a tense set of relationships between the government and the private business sector presents a particularly formidable challenge. The tension arises out of the contradictory impulses of cooperation and consensus between government and business, on the one hand, and considerable independent state monitoring and control of, and sometimes compulsion directed toward, business (Onis 1991). In Evans' (1995) conception of "embedded autonomy," governments must maintain a close association with the private firms that provide the means of economic growth while simultaneously keeping sufficient distance from them to withdraw support from specific enterprises and transfer it to others for the purpose of fomenting economic growth. In pursuing these tense functions, governments aim at transforming their economies into industrial producers in order to build a strong economy.

In addition to working cooperatively if in disinterested fashion with industry to build up the economy, states also require the creation and strengthening of state institutions that supervise, regulate, and discipline firms. For example, political elites have the task not only of promoting the establishment of an efficient banking sector in the economy but also the challenge of setting up governmental institutions that impartially supervise, regulate, and discipline the very banks comprising that sector. Similarly, other sectors of the economy need to be supervised and regulated to ensure the safety, health, and well-being of workers and citizens. Governmental institutions also need to provide currency, manage exchange rates, collect taxes, and the myriad other tasks that governments perform to sustain a vigorous economy. Contracts must be enforced by government agencies and courts. Beyond those matters, government planning agencies give overall direction to nations' economies; government must act as an agent of its industries in negotiating with other governments to ensure the terms of international contracts, such as those providing for the transfer of technology and for capping the proportion of foreign investment allowed in particular industries or enterprises.

As this discussion has indicated, the demands on political leaders prove quite extraordinary if they are to pursue the long-term goal of sustained political and economic development. The tasks involved are too many and too complex for individuals to take on by themselves; thus bureaucracies must be created in order rationally to perform all of the functions and deliver all of the services indicated. Indeed, analysts of the developmental state model (Koo 1987; Johnson 1987) stress that bureaucratic capacity and autonomy comprise critical components of that model. Capacity is evident, for well-trained and dedicated civil servants remain crucial to the operation of a modern state. The reasons for autonomy, on the other hand, are less evident, but two are central.

It is by setting up bureaucratic institutions dedicated to the performance of segmented functions that a state can effectively carry out tasks that are in tension with or inconsistent with other things that states must do. For example, states both foment banking and rational lending, and monitor and regulate the banks that comprise the financial sector of the economy. To run these tasks together would almost certainly invite corruption, favoritism, inefficiency, and so forth. On the other hand, by creating separate bureaucratic agencies to perform the discrete functions, although not ensuring complete efficiency and honesty, makes those attributes much more likely to be attained.

The second reason for establishing autonomous bureaucracies is to avoid what Waldner (1999) calls side payments to particular interest groups. In a comparative study of developing countries, he concluded that the single-minded dedication to the common good of economic development was undermined by the involvement of groups in a pluralistic political process, when leaders diverted resources to clients rather than assigning them to wholly public projects. Although from the point of view of pluralist democratic theory such politics fits better with democracy, it does so in the very limited sense that specific groups benefit. Developmental state theory, however, acknowledges the lack of attention to redistribution policy in the model, and Amsden (Onis 1991, pp. 121–122) argues that the developmental state is inherently unstable because of its undemocratic character.

At the same time, the developmental state has proven effective in "building up economic infrastructure through education, training, and research" (Onis 1991, p. 124). Furthermore, most writers on the developmental state take the position that, because of its contingency or historical specificity, the developmental state may well prove capable of evolving in a democratic direction, as South Korea and Taiwan have done. Meanwhile, the concentration of power in the hands of political and economic elites serves the entire nation.

As part of its policy framework for guiding and directing economic development, the developmental state shapes comparative advantage. Factor endowments cannot be entirely ignored. Yet, they do not limit the specific place in a global division of labor that a developing country can occupy. The state may take into account a factor endowment such as cheap labor and husband it by promoting cooperation between management and labor in the country's industries. In addition, as Japan and South Korea did, state planning agencies can determine a product or industry in which the country can specialize and seek to fill a particular niche in the world market.

Some readers might object to the analysis of those from the developmental state school of thought, for two reasons. Despite the fact that the literature largely represents empirical studies, some may think that any set of related studies eventually evolves into an orthodoxy. In addition, official policy makers from the leading states and the mass media that amplified their views reversed rhetorical course at the time of the East Asian economic crisis of 1997–1998. Whereas they had referred before then to the "East Asian miracle," they afterwards assigned to those same countries the sobriquet of "crony capitalism." Although the first reason appears spurious and the second evidences the whimsical nature of popular discourse, one can find other sources that testify to probable contributions to economic development.

In a study done for the Group of Thirty, Hughes (1985) identified a number of lessons to be derived from the empirical record of development. First, poverty alleviation appears to stem from "policies that provided rapid improvement in access to productive income earning activities," not from redistribution of assets or income (Hughes 1985, p. 5). This lesson coincides with the arguments in favor of pro-growth rather than poverty reduction policies made over the years by Bhagwati (1998). In addition, logic suggests that "[o]nly countries that grow rapidly have the means to redistribute incomes (Hughes 1985, p. 5). Even though Japan, Korea, and Taiwan, for diverse reasons, began their developmental trajectories from a relatively egalitarian base, Hughes notes that Sri Lanka did not improve upon its social conditions because of slow growth and countries such as Tanzania and Jamaica, which emphasized equity while ignoring growth, achieved neither.

Hughes (1985, p. 16) goes on to state,

> The only hypothesis that explains why some developing countries have grown rapidly, while others have not, links the adoption of a positive development philosophy with a policy framework that leads through market mechanisms to efficient resource allocation and utilization.

She also stresses that development requires a recognition of uncertainty as "normal" and "pervasive." Thus individuals have to be presented with incentives to take risks. This requires active social and political policy making by governments. Hughes (1985, p. 16) puts the matter succinctly:

> Governments have an essential role to play in establishing social and political cohesiveness and the rule of law. They must also provide a sense of direction, building social consensus around growth objectives and policies necessary to implement them. Despite the prevalence of uncertainty, individuals and enterprises have to explore options for the future. Governments have to

choose carefully among investment and policy options because resources are scarce, lead times can be long and they must avoid introducing additional uncertainty into the system by frequent policy changes.

Although the key policies remain economic, the leadership and consistent direction involved are obviously social and political. Furthermore, policies in the fields of education, health, and welfare continue to be crucial for determining not only productivity but also the distribution of income.

Conclusion

The emphasis in this chapter on states, nationalism, development strategies, autonomy, and choice points clearly and definitively to a rejection of the neoliberal advice to countries immediately to expose themselves to the global market. That advice comes from the dominant states and the international institutions that they control at a stage in history at which they have gained sufficient economic and military strength to stand on their own. They have already gone through stages of state formation, war against predatory neighbors, forging of national unity, and industrialization under the protection of tariffs and other mechanisms to promote development. Developing countries today have many tasks to perform, but they would be most unwise, if they can avoid undue coercion from the powerful, to submit to the neoliberal formula that is constantly pressed upon them.

They surely wish to take advantage of the technologies available and the markets willing to buy their goods and services, but they surely also need to do so in order to build their own strength and autonomy. They need to be in a position to make choices and to determine their own destinies, not isolated from the pressures of international life but as integral yet independent participants. The cross-pressures undoubtedly prove to be immense, but that is what political life is like. If developing states do not evolve their own capacities they will simply end up dominated, with their destinies shaped by the powerful. That would be a fate perhaps a bit removed from traditional imperialism but still subject to the mechanisms of control and domination whose levers are manipulated by the leading states.

This chapter has attempted to describe the tasks and undertakings necessary. In the following chapters, the considerations of civil society and citizenship form the subjects of analysis.

9
Civil Society and Conditions of Peace

Introduction

At the present juncture of history, the traditionally separate debates about civil society and conditions of peace are sometimes run together. This conflation occurs in a period of deep political and economic change, complicating efforts to understand what is involved. Furthermore, the idea of civil society in particular is infused with normative considerations. An additional complication stems from an erosion of what has long been considered a distinction between domestic and international spheres of action. Debates about these matters are not confined to academic halls and conferences of intellectuals; they form an important component of discourse in contemporary politics both within countries and across the international system. Thus any treatment requires attention not just to the ideas at stake but also to the context in which power is distributed and exercised in political arenas.

To elucidate and clarify these matters, this chapter treats each of the two concepts—civil society and conditions of peace—in turn, discusses the relationship between them, and offers an explanation of the underlying structural power conditions that give rise to the present situation. It examines civil society as a philosophical concept and discusses its place in contemporary practical political debates, with some added observations about the effects of dominant understandings of the idea on practice. The chapter then takes up the matter of conditions of peace in traditional political thought, with particular emphasis on liberal thinking. In the following section, the two matters are brought together through a discussion of how the prevailing ideas about civil society have affected practices involving peace and war, with brief attention to Rwanda, the wars in Bosnia and Yugoslavia, attempts to establish international criminal jurisdictions, and the campaign for a land mines treaty. Finally, the chapter offers an explanation for current conceptualizations about and practices concerning these matters, and it notes some of the problems and conundrums of the situation.

Civil Society

Although many strands are woven into the fabric of current discourse about civil society, the central debate is between proponents of social solidarity and champions of individualism and private enterprise. In the latter camp are advocates of individualism, privatization, reduction of the state, and establishment of universal norms and practices unrelated to specific societies and community institutions. They distrust government and the public arena, and they do not like vigorous debate and political contestation. On the side of the former are those who believe in democratic participation, social movements, public space and public responsibility, common good, and the efficacy of public institutions. Not every contributor to the debate fits neatly into these broad alternatives, but the dichotomies of public-private and individual-social capture the essential character of the discussion. Most contestants share a conception of civil society that is separate from the state, and they engage in an implied or explicit normative discourse.

Civil society did not form a category in ancient and medieval political thought, although Aristotle did encompass within the *polis* other differentiated layers of activities, particularly economic, that shared a dimension of a common ethical life within the polity. With the development of modernity and especially the rise of industrial society and national states, civil society was conceived as a separate sphere of activity and institutions between the individual and the family, on the one side, and the state. Closer to our own time, a new conception has arisen in which civil society forms a separate sphere that limits or opposes the state (Ehrenberg 1999).

In the contemporary world it remains impossible, despite such efforts as those of Arendt (1958, 1970), to restore a whole and coherent polity; the separation of state and civil society is here to stay. That separation began to be seen at the end of the eighteenth century in the Scottish Enlightenment (Ferguson 1995) and by Smith (1970/1776) and Kant. Smith regarded a state as essential to providing stability for the operation of the market, and he held that a political state was essential for defense against external enemies, for protecting property, enforcing contracts and preserving liberty, and for functioning in the economy by providing and maintaining public works that are not profitable for the private sector. Kant stressed that individual autonomy and a secure civil society require a law-governed state. As summarized by Ehrenberg (1999, p. 117), Kant thought, "There can be no freedom without law, no civil society without the state, and no peace without coercion."

For Hegel (1952), who clearly separated civil society from the state, the problem posed by civil society was that it generated inequality and poverty. Even though the division of labor and interdependence in modern society lead to a mutuality in which selfish individuals serve one another's needs, the unrelenting pursuit of insatiable needs remains essentially particular. Even this particularistic sphere of civil society requires state institutions for regulating it. However, the state for Hegel in addition consists of an ethical sphere of universality that is founded on freedom. In Ehrenberg's (1999, p. 128) portrayal of Hegel's thought, "Its strength rests not on force but on its ability to organize rights, freedom, and welfare into a coherent whole that serves freedom because it is not driven by interest." Thus the state does not simply serve the economy; it serves the broader purposes of its citizens' freedom, even in functioning as the protector of the whole in peace and war. As pointed out by Pelczynski (1984, p. 11), the distinction between state and civil society is not an institutional distinction; it is one of ends: "the activities in the civil sphere are aimed at particular interests or private rights of individuals and groups; those of the political sphere—at the general interests of the whole community." At its apex, in war, the interests of the individual and of civil society are merged in the ethical purpose of freedom.

Marx (Ehrenberg 1999, p. 133, citing Marx n.d.) argued against Hegel, holding that the state, rather than embodying the universal, represented the particular interests of a single class. He turned to the proletariat class to find the universal, and he regarded the state as the coercive sphere. Gramsci (Bobbio 1988, pp. 82–83) modified the Marxian conception by treating the state as coercive but civil society as the realm of ideas at the same superstructural level (Bobbio 1988, p. 82). Gramsci also regarded civil society, the hegemonic realm of ideology, as the leading element in political domination. By placing hegemonic ideology in this paramount position, Gramsci leads back to Hegel. An important component of modern thought about civil society traces its antecedents along this path, from Hegel to Gramsci and then to Parsons and Habermas.

In an early twenty-first century context, Hegel's universal that culminates in the merger with human freedom in war in which life and property are sacrificed to a common good, may to some ears sound quaint. However, as Steven Smith (1989, p. 233) argues, for Hegel

[t]he state is not simply an instrument of force and coercion but a locus of shared understandings. A state is more than an instrument for ensuring civil peace; it is a wider network of shared ethical ideas and beliefs. A state is ultimately a meeting of minds, since it depends on a common cultural history and a sense of civic identity.

This is a consideration to which it will be necessary to return after a further excursion into more recent developments in the concept of civil society and a consideration of how civil society and conditions of international peace are related.

Contemporary thinking about civil society tends to be dominated by two strands of thought, one from Eastern Europe and the other from American liberals. As Soviet support for Eastern European communist regimes weakened, there arose in Poland with Solidarity, in Czechoslovakia with Charter 77, and in Hungary with the Hungarian National Forum, a movement impelled by the conception that civil society could successfully oppose the state. Seligman (1992, p. 2) notes that Tismaneanu (1992) claimed that "civil society through such organizations ... undermined the authority of the State in Eastern Europe." Commenting on the intellectuals such as Adam Michnik who articulated the thesis, Ehrenberg (1999, p. 173) argues that their views reached beyond Eastern Europe:

[A] pervasive distrust of politics and the state had turned these analysts toward private property and the market ... But the impact of their critique was considerably broader; its antistatist core resonated in the West and has become an important part of the sustained attack on living standards and the welfare state that dominates contemporary public life.

A legacy from Tocqueville (1945) impels the more recent American effort, most prominently argued by Putnam (1993, 1995), to promote a conception of civil society that remains mostly private, in the realm of PTAs, bowling leagues, and other nonpolitical activities designed to build interpersonal trust. However, that is trust that is confined largely to the interpersonal and is likely to be devoted merely to small endeavors rather than to larger public purposes.

In the Hegelian conceptualization, the market constitutes the most prominent part of civil society. As the power of the market has grown in the post-World War II period, a major attack on the welfare state and the intellectual underpinnings of a Keynesian interventionist state has been mounted by the economists Hayek (1944, 1972) and Friedman (1969, 1982) and their followers, resulting in a convergence with the Eastern European intellectual and practical currents. In the international arena, the leading liberal powers and the international financial institutions that serve their purposes forged the so-called Washington consensus (Williamson 1990) on the broad international economic policies that they would pursue. On the whole, the ideas of the consensus stressed a neoliberal view that preferred market-friendly development policies and private rather than governmental approaches to social problems. These trends, together with the end of the Cold War, a turn to privatization, and the employment of the small notion of civil society in the promotion of democracy in the world has been met by a countering intellectual trend.

Drawing together the work of Gramsci (1971; Bobbio 1988) and Parsons (1971) to introduce a three-part formulation of state, market, and civil society, Cohen and Arato (1992) devised an approach that promotes a richer, larger, and more vigorous modern claim for civil society. They also build on Habermas' (1990b) discourse ethics in hopes of promoting a utopian goal of a universalistic dialogue through a sphere for public discourse that is not penetrated by either the state or the market. Cohen and Arato (1992, p. 91), while drawing on intellectual traditions after him, regard Hegel "as the most important theoretical forerunner of several later approaches that have preserved their potential to provide more global, intellectual orientation even in our own time."

The center of gravity of the contemporary debate about civil society, then, revolves around questions of democracy. Disputants diverge on questions of retaining autonomy of groups separate from the state versus a recognition that "[t]he legal protection of rights and the operation of official democratic forms greatly influence the formation and operation of associations within civil society, which take on the character of the larger political and legal framework" (Fullinwider 1999, p. 4). Some authors (Markovitz 2000) perceive a more integrated relationship between state and civil society in which the state mostly serves dominant interests in both. To some extent as well, there is a divergence over whether civil society is germane to small questions or remains relevant to grander themes of political debate. For some like Barber (1984, 1999), civil society as the idea of "thick democracy" forms a crucial bulwark against the totalizing tendencies of the market as well as the coercion of government.

Some activists, particularly in Latin America, propagate a version of civil society that both resists corrupt governments and, through actions, trains citizens in democracy. In Korea, which is dominated by two powerful state apparatuses, at least in South Korea vigorous civil society activity by disadvantaged groups has erupted at points when the grip of a repressive apparatus loosened and may be considered to have contributed to the strengthening of democracy (Koo 1993). Furthermore, because big business owed its rise to wealth to privileged treatment from authoritarian governments and had in turn supported those regimes, its leaders found it difficult to establish its own social and moral authority (Koo 1993, p. 9). This point has been reinforced by the revelations that transfers of wealth to North Korea had been used essentially as bribes to induce the regime to agree to aspects of President Kim Dae Jung's "sunshine policy."

Although the discourse about civil society focuses primarily on issues of democracy and state-market relations in a liberal order, the idea of civil society also has broader international dimensions, with effects on practice, especially in the post-Cold War period. To unravel the civil society debate with regard to contemporary politics, one needs to recognize the modern attack on the state from both left and right sides of the political spectrum.

From the right comes the attack not only on the welfare state but also on the public sphere as a whole and, with it, citizenship. In contemporary society, "branding" by private corporations has worked its way into public spaces including libraries, schools, and universities, as well as streets and sports arenas so extensively that individuals and groups are hard put to find public spaces that give the appearance of arenas for the consideration of common issues. Public services such as prisons, schools, trash collection, and many more have been privatized. Going even further, a political theory of the "New Right" holds that "citizenship ... depends on paid employment. Full citizenship depends on market participation as a wage-earner" (Gaffaney 1999, p. 180).

In parallel with the right's driving out public space and inserting private claims as legitimately public, different particularistic claims emanate from the left. Private values, sometimes presented as "generalized universals" (Seligman 1992), lay claim to public space. Included are such matters as human rights, animal rights, and reproductive rights. As Seligman (1992, p. 133) states, "None of these are citizen rights. They are, rather, private passions and interests projected into the public arena in terms of rights."

International dimensions of these issues have manifested themselves in debates particularly about globalization and humanitarian intervention. Those whom Held and associates (1999) term "hyperglobalizers" champion the formation of a global market and the erosion and irrelevance of nation-states. Within this category of thinkers Held and associates include both neoliberals and post-Marxists, the first of which laud the triumph of economics over politics and the latter rue the domination of the market.

From another corner of the political arena come those who advocate military and political intervention to protect and/or improve human rights, humanitarian agencies that act as the private purveyors or substitutes for government action in political emergencies, and nongovernmental organizations (NGOs) that monitor government activities and/or seek to influence governments through private activities. The last, in particular, articulate claims that there is forming a new, international civil society that transcends state boundaries and, by doing so, helps to render states obsolete (Macdonald 1997).

This brief survey of civil society has indicated that the concept covers many different understandings. In general, civil society is composed of individuals and groups that pursue private and particular interests. Many are anti-statist and opposed to broad political conceptions of deliberation through vigorous debate about large public questions of how societies should be organized, significant public policies that affect all the members of the society, and the most critical decisions of war and peace. Some regard the state in Marxist terms only as a coercive apparatus embodying particular interests. Another view is the Gramscian conception of civil society as the ideological and leading component of systems of domination. Others conceptualize civil society in Hegelian terms in which it forms a component of the state; civil society groups, then, can monitor state agencies, but they also recognize that there are broader common public purposes in the state that transcend civil society and that, to a large extent, civil society depends upon state structures and functions. Crucial to the understanding of the adherents of this view is their recognition that civil society is "historically produced" and that it is "wreckable," as Keane (1998, p. 50) notes by quoting Hegel. These divergent views of civil society affect greatly how conditions of peace are understood and approached. Before bringing these two concepts together, it is necessary to analyze the second.

Conditions of Peace

No policy activity undertaken by states surpasses the importance of war and peace. Intellectually, the causes of war and conditions of peace, together with the subsidiary problem of the nature of power, have always formed the central problematic of international politics (Holsti 1985, p. 8). This view has come under attack by modern and post-modern exponents of quite divergent views. For the most part, these critics of the traditional approaches to understanding international politics do not address the central issues of war and peace, but they do often contemplate ways of ordering the world. Among those who do explicitly concern themselves with the conditions of peace are constructivists like Ruggie (1998) and Wendt (1999), who are intent upon building a transformed world order. If their normative optimism proves justified and the world in the future becomes transformed from one shaped by the ordering principle of anarchy to one of government under a central authority, the traditional problematic will disappear.

Meanwhile, an analyst today must confront the problems of an untransformed world of states.

In his masterly analytical survey of western thought on the issue, Waltz (1959) arranged thought about the causes of war into three "images:" human nature, the internal structure of states, and the anarchical structure of the international system. In this chapter, I do not deal with the first image, human nature. I discuss the internal structure of states, especially democratic states, for this second image most directly connects with civil society discourse. I also employ the third image, the one that concerns the international system structure. Waltz' conclusion, even more forcefully put in his more recent work (Waltz 1979, 1986) is that autonomous states pursue their interests within a structure organized without authority and shaped by a distribution of power across the units. Each state pursues its own interests in the way that it chooses, and it is likely on occasion to use force because there is no way of reconciling all of the conflicts of interest that arise in a condition of anarchy (Waltz 1959, p. 258). Thus the state is not simply the ultimate instrument for the achievement of freedom that Hegel claimed (Smith 1989, p. 233); it is also the repository of force and the guarantor of autonomy within which freedom can be achieved against other states' pursuing their interests by the use of force. Thus, in explaining the conditions of peace, one must look to the state and its power in relationship to the position of other states and their power and interests.

Among ideas about war and peace, two schools of thought are most closely related to the concept of civil society. The first school embodies theories of neoliberal institutionalism (Axelrod 1984; Bull 1977; Hoffmann 1995; Katzenstein et al. 1998; Keohane 1984; Keohane 1989; Keohane and Nye 1989; Krasner 1983; Mearsheimer 1994/1995; Nye 1988; Ruggie 1983). The second treats the relationship between liberal democracy and peace (Bueno de Mesquita et al. 1999; Doyle 1983, 1986; Gowa 1999; Huntley 1996; Layne 1994; Maoz and Russett 1993; Russett 1995; Spiro 1994).

Neoliberal institutionalism is devoted to mitigating the effects of anarchy by international cooperation through international organizations, regimes, and less formal institutions. Under conditions in which security is abundant—such as those in Western Europe during the Cold War, in the post-Cold War situation of US military domination, or in an envisaged world with many powers possessing effective second-strike nuclear capabilities (Waltz 1993)—a model of complex interdependence (Keohane and Nye 1989) becomes an appropriate tool for analyzing international politics. In this model, there is a diminished distinction between domestic and international politics, and nongovernmental organizations as well as firms and international organizations can appropriately be considered as participants in the processes of international cooperation. Among those participants are included the sorts of associations that fall within the meaning of those forming civil society. By including nongovernmental actors and transnational activities, those expostulating the complex interdependence model elide second and third image explanations for international peace.

It is important to note that scope for action by civil society associations in international relations is afforded by the security established by states and politics.

As shown in the following section of this chapter, states are also in a position to authorize activities by private organizations as substitutes for actions for which states would traditionally be responsible. In those cases, sometimes security has not been established in difficult international circumstances except insofar that no major power checks or interferes with the activities of civil society groups acting in place of a leading power or a dominant coalition. In effect, those groups represent the reach of dominant states as instruments promoting order. On the other hand, such groups often are not wholly backed by those dominant states.

At the level of the second image, proponents argue that peace will result from the establishment of liberal democratic states. Two separate lines of thinking are associated with a liberal democratic peace, one associated with Immanuel Kant (1957), the other, with Woodrow Wilson (Waltz 1959, esp. Ch. 4). In the Kantian view, there are a number of reasons why liberal states are less likely to go to war with one another: involvement in decisions to go to war of citizens who must bear the costs and a political process in which leaders are constrained by electoral considerations; respect for one another which may be reflected in international law; and a cosmopolitan law that affords hospitality to citizens and traders from other liberal democracies (Doyle 1983).

Kant (1957) thought that republics might establish a separate peace by creating a parliament of republics; his contemporary disciple (Doyle 1983) extends the claim by pointing to a separate liberal peace that has already been established. Thus, without specifying the mechanism that might enlarge the number of liberal democracies, the Kantian view avers that international peace spreads as the number of liberal states increases. In this logic, if all the world's states were liberal democracies, international peace would reign across the globe. Adopting this argument, United States National Security Advisor Lake (1993) articulated the policy of democratic enlargement followed by the Clinton administration.

Enlargement of the community of liberal democratic states provided a guideline for policies directed toward Eastern Europe and Russia as well as China. But the Clinton administration also embraced a version of the Wilsonian vision of spreading liberal democracy. Although its rationale appears to be a twin of the Kantian logic, it is much more muscular, for it includes a guide to action that entails the use of force. Following the logic that wars are caused by states that are not liberal democratic ones, the Wilsonian impulse leads to intervention to promote liberal democratic ideas and institutions. Just as Wilson intervened in 1914 to get the Mexicans to elect "good men," Clinton intervened in Haiti, Bosnia, and Yugoslavia to rid those states of thugs and evil leaders. In the larger arena of policy on a worldwide scale, this outlook holds that wars are caused by bad or "rogue" states. That logic leads to the widespread use of sanctions against such evil leaders as Fidel Castro, Saddam Hussein, and others who are regarded as the source of international violence. Aside from failing to bring down such leaders, the policies that follow from this logic have led to ongoing bombing campaigns against Iraq from December 1998 to March 2003, an intense air war in Serbia and Kosovo in Spring 1999, and the imposition of economic sanctions that have brought immense suffering and hardship to the broad civilian populations in the countries affected.

Perhaps the most dramatic example of this tendency was the invasion and occupation of Iraq in 2003 by the United States under the Bush administration. An examination in the next section of the relations between civil society and conditions of peace elucidates at least some of the reasons why these policies almost inevitably fail.

Civil Society and Conditions of Peace

As Tocqueville noted in the nineteenth century, the presence and activities of a wide variety of civil associations characterized American society, and his observations were echoed in the latter part of the twentieth century by Bellah and associates (1985) and others. Moreover, the use in the United States of private contractors to provide public services has been a tradition, although the practice has increased significantly in the era of neoliberal ascendancy since the early 1980s. With a modification of government policy that led to a preference for private action, the number of civil society associations and firms designed to gain contracts and carry out the assigned functions has burgeoned.

Contracting by governments to nongovernmental organizations has extended to the international realm. Gordenker and Weiss (1996, p. 25) note that "[i]n 1994 over 10% of public development aid ($8 billion) was channeled through NGOS, surpassing the volume of the combined UN system ($6 billion) without the Washington-based financial institutions." And they add, "About 25% of US assistance is channeled through NGOS ... ," and that the figure was expected to rise to 50 percent by 2000. Apart from the magnitude, another important implication—that states have to some extent substituted nongovernmental delivery of goods and services for official assistance—should also be noted: "'The increase of donor-funded NGO relief operations and Western disengagement from poor countries are two sides of the same coin'" (Gordenker and Weiss 1996, p. 25, citing Omaar and de Waal 1994, p. 6). These developments fall into the neoliberal pattern of privatization that has marked the path followed in the last quarter of the twentieth century and continued in the twenty-first.

The neoliberal political program remains the most prominent ideological project in the world at the beginning of the twenty-first century. Nevertheless, its apogee was reached in the years following 1988 when the so-called Washington consensus prevailed. That broad agreement by the dominant powers and the international financial institutions aimed to minimize the state bureaucracy, to reduce and end government subsidies to citizens, to privatize state-owned enterprises, and to place government taxation and expenditure policies on a sound and balanced footing. Also included in the agreement was a commitment to a development strategy of export-oriented growth and to free flows of foreign direct investment, free trade, and unfettered international financial movements.

In view of the exceptional growth experience of the East Asian countries, some resistance to the neoliberal project occurred. In 1993, the World Bank published *The East Asian Miracle*, noting that states can play an important role in promoting economic development. This counterreaction to the neoliberal assault on the state gained strength with the publication of the *1997 World Development Report* (World Bank 1997), which emphasized the necessity of the state. To some extent in this debate, the 1997–1998 East Asian economic crisis placed in the hands of neoliberals a cudgel that they termed "crony capitalism" with which to bludgeon their ideological opponents. Given the recovery of most of the affected states by 2000, a climate exists for the return of the rhetorical struggle. In a recent poverty report (UNDP 2000), the United Nations Development Program stressed the role in a global strategy of national governments' devising and implementing national poverty reduction programs, rather than assigning those tasks to international organizations and nongovernmental groups.

Still, the neoliberal project promotes privatization and the delivery of goods and services through intergovernmental organizations and private agencies in international relations, particularly in poor and weak areas. To a large extent, this policy direction represents an abdication of state responsibility by the leading powers, and that leads to substantial problems, which I illustrate by briefly treating two cases: the aftermath of the Rwanda genocide in 1994 and the land mines treaty negotiations.

In the contemporary context, another substitution of state activity occurs through the campaigns to promote universal rights, to establish international criminal courts, and to prosecute former government officials elsewhere for crimes that they allegedly committed in their own countries.

The inadequacies of civil society activities as a private substitute for state responsibilities are sharply illustrated by the aftermath of the genocide that occurred in Rwanda between April and July 1994 whose repercussions continue to this day. Following the genocidal rampage promoted from the capital Kigali by a Hutu Power government, the perpetrators as well as large segments of the Hutu civilian population were driven from the country by a Rwanda Patriotic Front (RPF) army that had invaded to suppress the *Interhamwe*, the Hutu fighting forces (Gourevitch 1998). Refugees fled to neighboring countries, most notably Zaire, now known as Democratic Republic of Congo (DRCongo). Having failed to mount an effective intervention to stop the genocide, the powers authorized and supported for the refugees significant relief efforts that were carried out by United Nations agencies such as the High Commissioner for Refugees (HCR) and the United Nations Childrens Fund (UNICEF), and nongovernmental relief organizations such as the International Rescue Committee (IRC) and the International Committee of the Red Cross, which provided food, clothing, shelter, sanitary facilities, and medical care. In the camps political organization, and thus effective control over distribution of the assistance, was mounted by the Hutu Power cadres who were intent upon returning as an invasion force to Rwanda.

As pointed out by Doctors Without Borders (*Médecins sans Frontières*, MSF), the French-based medical relief organization, which withdrew from the operation because of this situation, the relief agencies had no capacity to separate fighters from civilian refugees; such a task would have to be performed by state-organized military forces. Although MSF respected the potential role that military forces could play in relief efforts (Minear and Guillot 1996), other representatives of these civil society groups rejected cooperation with military forces. As a result of this failure to address the security problem, the refugee camps formed a base for those who remained a military threat to Rwanda.

It was not until 1997 that the refugee camps were broken up by RPF forces and their Zairian allies; the action took place in the context of the overthrow of the predatory, kleptocratic Mobutu Sese Seko regime and its replacement by the regime headed by Laurent Kabila that renamed the country DRCongo. Repercussions continued into 2000 and following years as a major war, involving six countries and a number of nongovernmental groups, proceeded in that huge central African country. Thus the privatization of governmental functions in the aftermath of the Rwanda genocide that authorized civil society activities not only failed to secure peace but actually contributed to the continuation of war in the African Great Lakes region.

Not only does this case illustrate the inadequacy and inappropriateness of civil society groups for constructing the conditions for peace but also it reveals the erosion of the democracy-building function of civil society that forms its central thesis in the theoretical literature. The reason why the major powers refrained from directly intervening in the morass of refugee and post-genocide politics was an aversion to accountability to their own citizens.

However, the humanitarian agencies—intergovernmental and nongovern-mental—are not accountable either. They do not possess charters that make them accountable to any citizenry, and they do not need to face elections in any arena. In entering into local politics, they became pawns in the power relations prevailing in the refugee camps and thus supporters of killers. Instead of acting as monitors of states and markets in well-ordered societies, they scrambled to give succor to the miserable refugees, and they were not accountable to them either. Neither did the civil society organizations contribute to building a democratic community or to any sense of trust, the central aim of the advocates of the small version of civil society. In the circumstances, therefore, these agencies provided for the needs of desperate people, a generous and worthwhile function that nonetheless appears wholly unrelated to the conceptions of civil society that prevail in the contemporary academic and liberal public policy debates.

A different manifestation of the promotion of peace through the activities of civil society groups occurred in the campaign to ban land mines, often heralded as a triumph of networked interests of dedicated government officials and NGOs. The 1997 Ottawa Treaty bans all types of anti-personnel land mines; and hopes for enforcement include the view that public opinion will insure that states have to abide by its terms, even if they had not signed the treaty. Among the countries that had not signed by the end of 1999 were the United States, China, Russia, India, Pakistan, Korea, and Turkey.

As Brown (2000, p. 6) points out, however, anti-vehicle land mines which contribute importantly to the fundamental humanitarian problems associated with land mines are not banned by the treaty. Part of the reason for that is that the Austrian government "had a key role in drawing up the first working draft of the convention," and Austrian manufacturers produce anti-tank mines that are persistent. In contrast, American land mines self-destruct or neutralize themselves within a short time. Yet American mines are banned, and those produced by Austrian manufacturers or under license are allowed by the treaty. A proposal that all mines should be detectable and self-destructing was defeated at one of the meetings considering the treaty, and an American request for special treatment of the Korean security problem was also rejected. Brown (2000) details other complexities of the process involved in the land mines campaign, but his most important point is that the undertaking moved forward without regard to including the concerns of the powers that manufacture and use land mines, and the primary movers ignored the complexities that they brought to the bargaining table. In some ways, the objective was to isolate the United States. At the same time, the North Atlantic Treaty Organization's preparations for dealing with the issue of Kosovo were hindered by the fractures in the alliance over the land mines treaty, and the Slobodan Milosevic regime in Yugoslavia, unhindered, sowed the region bordering Albania with land mines.

Clearly, cheap weapons that are easily manufactured and proliferated throughout the world pose humanitarian problems of immense dimensions. No one with any feeling can help but be moved by the tales of innocent farmers and children in former war zones suffering death and maiming from these weapons that remain in the aftermath of wars. The control of these and other weapons has remained on the international agenda among states for decades, and they should form part of ongoing diplomatic negotiations. Indeed, civil society organizations can play an important role in pressing governments to attend to such matters, sometimes to giving priority to them.

On the other hand, states have much broader responsibilities than civil society organizations which remain particularistic. In the case of the land mines treaty, the specific agenda of the Ottawa Convention was signed by all the members of NATO except Turkey and the United States, leading to a crisis in the organization in 1998 that seriously hindered cooperation and planning for action with respect to Yugoslavia on the Kosovo question. In the scheme of things, a world without the stability that NATO provides as a fundamental condition of peace would be a much more dangerous one than one without an anti-personnel mines ban. There is no reason not to have both, but the negotiation of any effective arms control agreement requires the inclusion of the powers that manufacture and use the arms, and their reservations and concerns need to be taken into account in the negotiations. Single-minded civil society groups are not geared to thinking in the broad strategic terms that major states are compelled to consider.

The campaign for universal criminal law, which would substitute international for state tribunals, began in the wake of World War II with the Nuremberg Trials and the prosecution of Japanese "war criminals" (Dower 1999, esp. Ch. 15). Following the end of the Cold War and in the context of the breakup of Yugoslavia, a special war crimes tribunal for Bosnia was established to prosecute and try persons accused of committing war crimes and crimes against humanity (May 1999). As an afterthought, a parallel tribunal was established to deal with the accused in

Rwanda. More recently in 1998 a United Nations-sponsored conference in Rome adopted a treaty establishing a permanent criminal court.

Although some persons have been arrested and a few of them have been tried, the effort on the whole has not resulted in the arrest of many of the leading persons accused. Within Bosnia, NATO forces have been reluctant to arrest top leaders of the Bosnian Serbs who had ruled at the time of the Bosnian war between 1992 and 1995. The execution of the arrest warrant issued for Slobodan Milosevic of Yugoslavia required the threat of withholding funds to the successor government, which traded Milosevic for foreign economic assistance. In a not altogether unrelated case, Britain did arrest and later release former Chilean President Augusto Pinochet, although no nonstate tribunal was involved. In all of these situations, the object of creating international institutions to substitute for state ones can obviously be achieved only by states. In view of the modest accomplishments so far, the question that poses itself is: Why has so little occurred? The answer tends to be similar to the response to another question: Why has Wilsonian intervention to implant civil society largely failed? Thus I return to both questions after consideration of that topic.

Driven to some extent by the conception of civil society emanating from Eastern Europe as well as by a basic liberal optimism at the end of the Cold War, the major powers—more often working through the United Nations but outside that framework as well—have attempted to implant some version of democratic civil society in several countries by means of military and civilian intervention. Upon the request of the powers, United Nations Secretary-General Boutros Boutros-Ghali (1992) formulated guidelines for such interventions. The interventions include actions in Somalia, El Salvador, Angola, Haiti, Cambodia, Bosnia, East Timor, Kosovo, and Sierra Leone. Of these, only the intervention in El Salvador can be considered successful. Several of the interventions, including those in Somalia and Angola, ended in withdrawal in the face of hostility. An intervention force under auspices of the United Nations in Sierra Leone in 2000 faced a choice of repeating that withdrawal experience or engaging in combat to defeat a rebel armed force. Although some residual effects of the intervention in Cambodia remain, one cannot claim that the country has a democratic civil society. The effort in Haiti appears to be largely a failure; the operations in Bosnia, East Timor, and Kosovo remain in process, with substantial contingents of military and police forces preserving order and civilian operations working to establish civil societies.

Wilsonian intervention to implant democratic civil societies has proven largely a failure because there exists neither a community and institutional base nor a sufficient international threat to provide the necessary political impetus to mobilize the immense efforts that success would require. Despite contemporary rhetoric about "the international community" and "global governance," different states can at best coordinate their responses to problems that they perceive in the world.

Situations such as those in Somalia, Angola, Cambodia, and Sierra Leone touch liberal sensibilities about human suffering, but, for most people, identities and shouldering of responsibilities remain national. At low costs, most democratic citizens support humanitarian relief activities, in cases of which they are aware, in acute disasters or ongoing suffering. On the other hand, attention to situations tends to be brought through a combination of agitation by civil society groups and determinations of national interests or political advantage by political leaders. Thus wars in Sudan, Rwanda, and DRCongo draw no or very little attention, and operations ended in Somalia and Angola without protest or even very much attention. Not even in the case of Haiti, where there was a single country, the United States, that faced an embarrassing situation, the intervention ended without notice. Also missing from these cases was any substantial threat of international war that might seriously destabilize a region or disrupt the interests of a major power.

Without such motives and incentives, states are unwilling to commit the immense resources needed to do the job. A number of requirements are necessary. First, a state must be established; that is, military control of a territory has to be gained and an effective coercive and administrative apparatus has to be put in place. Second, economic enterprises run by either private firms or government agencies or both need to be founded and operated. As these foundations are being put into place, there may emerge elements of civil society free to and capable of monitoring the other components of the state. Such massive undertakings require efforts that can only be motivated by highly significant public purposes. Yet the very character of contemporary liberal thinking that carries a heavy dose of anti-government rhetoric and that has all but lost a conception of high public purpose and of public space ensures that it cannot supply the impetus.

In both the campaign for universal criminal law and Wilsonian interventions to implant democracy, then, there is an inconsistency between the aspiration to establish new conditions, on the one hand, and the opposition to strong states and other political institutions that could give effect to the objectives sought. The so-called international community consists of a coalition of states. It does not comprise a true community or possess coherent political institutions. It contains no conception of citizenship or of law or of public space. It does reflect the preoccupation with civil society at the expense of states, for international politics is a realm of particular interests without any coherence, freedom, or coercive apparatus that would be supplied by a state. In short, despite certain levels of cooperation and coordination among states and other participants, international politics remains a realm of anarchy.

Power, Peace, State, and Civil Society

Establishing the conditions of peace remains one of the most important aspects of human endeavor, and it requires a broad sense of common good that exists quite beyond the realm of civil society, which deals only with human needs. The universal, or common good, belongs in the realm of the state in which freedom transcends needs. In the Hegelian scheme, the universal is most closely approached in war. Given the current conditions of security, stability, and peace in the world, leaders and citizens face a major challenge to preserve a conception of the common good. In order to do that, it becomes necessary to understand the present condition and its causes; to motivate the quest, one needs to understand how particularistic needs have come to be projected so prominently into the public arena. Then, one needs to see what problems associated with conditions of peace are implicated in the small conception of civil society that appears most prominent in contemporary discourse.

In the contemporary world the fundamental situation is that no balancing against the United States has occurred and no major power acts as a challenger to the United States in international politics. A broad concert of liberal democratic, industrial states agrees on the general rules of management of the international order, although that agreement has been strained by unilateral United States actions in the Bush administration. That concert rests upon the firm base of the military power of the United States, but it also relies upon the policies of the United States that maintain its involvement in the Western Hemisphere, Europe, and East Asia and its support of worldwide regimes to manage security and economic affairs across the globe. It is the dominance of a liberal coalition that affords the space that enables the private actors of civil society to act. Without the underlying power and the favorable policies, civil society might lose any scope for action in international affairs and might very well be wrecked.

Thus the hyperglobalizers who believe that the state forms an obstacle to private activities lack an appreciation of the power base that protects them and enables them to operate. Anti-statist proponents of civil society fail to recognize their own dependence on both organized coercion and the broader normative implications of states that give them freedom to pursue their own agendas. Advocates of the small version of civil society simply ignore the wider and more important kinds of matters that political communities need to face. A wholly private and particularistic civil society is bound to lead to conflict and inequality that only states are able to cope with effectively and offset in larger societal and political interests.

Both the smaller and the larger versions of civil society conceptualizations have at their core a normative concern with promoting democracy. In the international arena, however, the activities of nongovernmental organizations and private corporations run into problems associated with democracy at every turn. A humanitarian organization proffering aid to refugees, for example, is neither elected by anyone nor accountable to any democratic society or process. Its relationship to its clients remains a hierarchical rather than an egalitarian one, for no ties of citizenship and mutual obligations tie the aid givers to the recipients. Agencies compete with one another for publicity, funds, and missions; they do so not in a democratic political arena but rather in field settings and in private solicitations. To the extent that they have ties to any democratic process, it is through the governments that charge them with assignments and that subsidize their activities. But the relationship even here obscures matters of democratic accountability, for the private agencies substitute for governments that are able to disclaim responsibility and thus avoid democratic accountability.

Similarly in the private economic sector, firms appropriately pursue profits, investment opportunities, market shares, and so forth. They contribute to the building of wealth, but the liberal creed largely excludes the domain of private enterprise from any democratic political process. In the contemporary world, although most firms remain implanted within national territories and are thus subject at least to governmental regulatory supervision, many corporations operate without regard to citizenship, bonds of mutual obligation within a society, and clearly defined lines of accountability.

Thus development of an international civil society in the absence of a well-established peace underwritten by military power and a dominant coalition remains an illusion. The causal path between civil society and conditions of peace runs from the latter to the former, not the other way around. That does not mean that civil society properly understood cannot make a contribution to maintaining conditions of peace.

Conclusion

The large view of civil society recognizes a sphere of activity in which private nongovernmental groups monitor the activities of the state, helping to insure that states neither become oppressive nor shirk their responsibilities. In the version of civil society that places it outside the realm of the market as well as the state, groups may also perform the function of monitoring the predatory tendencies and the unequal effects of capitalist economic practices, demanding a governmental rein on the former and governmental redistributive policies to offset the latter. Even in the version that incorporates market actors within civil society, there is an important role in insuring that the public good is fulfilled by the state.

Finally, the large view of civil society requires that all citizens and groups insist on retaining a concept of the common good, a public sphere in which the large issues facing any polity can be debated, and the government, while avoiding tyranny, maintains both the strength and the dedication to bring together all citizens in the enterprise of achieving freedom and the concentration of power necessary to preserving the state's autonomy against others who might threaten that freedom. In this sense, civil society can make a contribution to achieving conditions of peace by promoting democratic debate within public space on large issues and by defending the state even while monitoring it.

10
Citizenship and Public Space in Globalization

Introduction

An increasingly common observation holds that social solidarity has weakened and continues breaking down in the contemporary globalized, privatized, and individualistic world. Furthermore, some argue that in the process of globalization power has become divorced from politics, the result of the diffusion of power away from political institutions, specifically the state (Bauman 1998; Strange 1996). The solidarity afforded by nationalism has come under attack by the capitalist logic of unfettered investment and commerce that ignores borders and insists on market efficiency. To this attack have been added direct political and military interventions, as occurred in Bosnia over the years since 1995, to suppress nationalism, the twentieth century's paradigm of social solidarity. Sustained denigration and erosion of the welfare state give additional credence to the theme of societal breakdown.

Some respond by calling for the formation of a global civil society (Darcy de Oliveira and Tandon 1994; Korten 1998) or, as Greider (1997) does, for an ideology of "global humanism." We witness contemporary manifestations of an even more serious cosmopolitanism in the work of Nussbaum (2000) and others. Concerns such as these represent symptoms of the changes that are occurring in the world around us, but no consensus has formed about the nature of the problem. Absent a clearly defined problem, of course, no agreement has been formed about a solution. This chapter discusses the contemporary unease and uncertainty, defines the problem and its difficulties, and offers a means of thinking about a solution.

After noting the sense of inevitability contained in most of the writing and rhetoric about globalization, I describe the situation in substantially different terms. Even though symptoms of social solidarity's erosion are evident, the cure offered most prominently by advocates of civil society and proponents of nongovernmental groups actually reflect the assumptions of dominant modes of thought. These overlook the continued fundamental underpinnings of contemporary power arrangements in which states provide the foundations for global developments, thus conceding too much in the normative struggle over arrangements in the future.

To address the contemporary situation, I invoke a number of basic premises. First, politics is fundamental to the processes of change occurring in the world. As in most change, the dynamics stem from the most powerful centers and are shaped by the politics of those metropoles (Waltz 1979, 1986). Second, politics involves both material power and normative preferences, which tend to be closely linked (Carr 1964/1939; Gilpin 1981, 1987). Third, power does not simply involve the use of violence and domination of one group by another but also entails constitutive, or intransitive, power in which members of groups gain empowerment through their interactions, using symbols, in public space, and by forging institutions (Goehler 2000).

In the next section I describe and analyze critically the dominant discourses about globalization. These dialogues do not simply describe developments in the world but also present facts within ideological frameworks based on assumptions about trends in the world. Both right and left positions assume that fundamental changes are in progress and that these entail the weakening or demise of the state and the nation as basic institutional means for organizing politics and public life. A third strand in the debates emphasizes strong democracy and a large concept of civil society that assumes the existence of a state that serves broader public purposes. The following section discusses the requisites for continued globalization and notes, in light of these requirements, that the right ideological position remains untenable in the long run and that the left approach would have to be built on a foundation of strong states, a stipulation unlikely to be accepted by advocates of new international identities. In the last major section of the chapter, I discuss a possible path to the recapture of notions of public space and common good within the context of the states that remain requisite to further globalization. Guideposts on this path are provided by the works of Hegel and Arendt and the American founding fathers. The chapter closes with a brief conclusion.

Globalization Discourses/Ideologies

In the contemporary world very powerful pressures exert themselves against traditional societal bonds, and individuals are left isolated, reliant on their own devices to succeed in both private and public spheres (Bauman 2001). The pressures extend across many dimensions: national loyalties get undermined by economic, cultural, and political activities; political parties, once powerful institutions, have often become merely convenient vehicles in which to carry the ambitions of individual leaders; labor unions have weakened, and the bonds between workers and firms have loosened in the face of restructuring, downsizing, and so forth.

In the wake of the Cold War, class identities have diminished; in their place have arisen, partly under color of the Internet, new forms of international cooperation among individuals and NGOs (Arts 2000; Green et al. 2000; Holmes and Grieco 2000; Scholte 2000). These developments have led many to believe that as national and state bonds dissolve they will be replaced by new identities that will, in turn, give rise to new forms of global solidarity (Ruggie 1998; Wendt 1999). Despite the promise held out, these views remain aspirations and do not reflect solid achievements. Nevertheless, the activities of individuals and NGOs, both those that promote causes such as environmental protection and those such as drug traffickers, have proven prodigious. In the case of activists on behalf of publicly conceived causes such as health care and nutrition for deprived populations, the activities include a conception of a public good. Nevertheless, without any clear institutional forum in which to debate public policy issues and to conclude those debates with authoritative decisions, the idea of common good has been diminished from the prior conception that prevailed within states.

Other activists lack even that diminished conception of public good, for the usual thrust of nongovernmental groups in the contemporary world entails the promotion of private preferences as public issues. Seligman (1992, pp. 128–140) has illuminated this in the case of advocates of human rights and animal rights. In the case of drug traffickers, money launderers, and so forth, the public element is completely lost, for these activities are undertaken entirely for private gain.

Added developments further erode public space and any conception of public good. Intrusion of private corporate symbols into public spaces—increasingly prominent as sports arenas, libraries, universities, and other public gathering places are labeled with corporate logos and named for corporate and individual donors—reduces not just public space but the conception of a separate sphere in which to consider the public's business. Privatization of what had been public services, from education to trash collection to policing to prisons, further erodes the idea of a common good.

All of these developments together have a cumulative effect of deanchoring citizenship from membership in a state. International pressures to rationalize production on a global basis and responses that aim at reshaping identities on a similar plane combine with unrelenting private pressures within states to undermine traditional conceptions of citizenship that include rights and duties. The tendency is for individuals to be regarded as isolated actors, responsible for their own successes and failures, without obligations to others (Bauman 2001). At the same time, nothing stands in the way of such individuals' demanding recognition of their individual preferences under the banner of individual or human rights. Such a stance departs significantly from traditional conceptions of citizenship.

In the past, individuals acquired citizenship within states through their recognition by others. Such recognition is extended upon the basis that citizens undertake duties toward their fellows, and the corollary of those duties is a set of rights. In contemporary globalization discourses, duties have fallen by the wayside, and only rights are left. But those rights are not those derived from citizenship. Instead they are claims upon others but without any set of reciprocal duties. How rights become recognized and fulfilled falls within a haphazard politics involving NGOs, international organizations, and states, with the last retaining the authority to sign and ratify treaties and the power to implement or disregard them.

Another development that has contributed to the deanchoring of citizenship from the state was the civil society movement within several Eastern European countries in the end stage of the Cold War. As conceived within this strand of the debate, civil society was thought of as separate from, antithetical to, and a substitute for the state. It was a radical conception that departed from the traditional Hegelian notion of civil society that formed a component of the state. Moreover, the movement dovetailed with neoliberal views that sought to diminish the state. Together they gave impetus to the outlook that states presented obstacles rather than instruments to freedom and enterprise.

In sum, globalization discourses and other contemporary pressures have the tendency to deanchor citizenship from the state, to diminish public space, and to expunge the idea of common good. This tendency is further reinforced by casting globalization and other prominent discourses in terms of inevitability. Frequently observers detect a pressure or a trend and pronounce it irresistible, as though no human agency had any control over the course of events. Such observations tend to a large extent in today's world to be cast in terms of neoliberal ideology, the most prominent contemporaneous framework for considering world developments.

Neoliberal ideology stresses competition among individuals and does not contain a conception of common purposes. Through a division of labor, markets spontaneously arise to furnish the needs and desires of consumers, thus avoiding the necessity of formulating any conceptualization of interests held in common by communities. Thus governments are largely regarded as obstacles rather than instruments to the achievement of material prosperity. Given the world that neoliberals found, they positively opposed governmental production enterprises, redistribution of wealth, and the provision of publicly supported welfare programs. Instead, they advocated privatization and the ending of subsidies and governmental protection of its citizens from the buffetings of the market. Additionally, they encourage the adoption of liberal market principles for everyone without regard to institutional preparation for competition in international markets. Neoliberals also argue on behalf of nondiscriminatory treatment of all economic activities irrespective of national origin.

These pressures emanate not from a disembodied discourse or an inevitable force called globalization; rather, they come from a United States-led liberal coalition that structures the international political economy. That hegemonic coalition forms one pillar upon which the success of globalization processes rests. The other pillar is the spread and consolidation of effective states. As one surveys the world, one can see that modern economies and cultures have penetrated those areas in which effective states provide appropriate conditions and have not entered areas of weak states, political turmoil, and so forth.

Confronting current conditions of the deanchoring of citizenship and the disappearance of public space, some participants in the globalization discourses have offered answers to the collapse of traditional ways of thinking about such matters.

Contemporary Citizenship Discourses

In response to the pressures and uncertainties of current conditions, observers have offered three distinct alternative viewpoints on the place of citizenship in the contemporary world. From the left, groups promote the idea of a global civil society designed to surpass state boundaries as well as to project private preferences as public issues (Darcy de Oliveira 1994; Korten 1998; Seligman 1992; Warkentin and Mingst 2000). From the right, advocates foment a property- and employment-based citizenship, an unfettered freedom for corporate activities, and a preference for privatization of public services (Friedman 1969, 1982; Gaffaney 1999; Hayek 1944, 1972). Both of these positions demonstrate an anti-statist attitude coinciding with the dominant discourses of globalization, and both regard the state as little more than a mechanism serving the market. A third perspective promotes strong democracy and a larger concept of civil society derived from Hegel and his followers (Barber 1984; Cohen and Arato 1992; Fullinwider 1999; Hann and Dunn 1996). This school of thought offers a vision of common good and regards the state as an entity that serves broader public purposes than the mere servicing of the market.

Empirical support for the leftist view that a global civil society is forming has been provided by the proliferation of international NGOs in the post-Cold War period. On the other hand, this literature largely neglects any consideration of the conditions that have led to NGO proliferation. In fact, the immense growth of private activities in the public sphere has sprung from the nature of the powerful coalition that underpins the contemporary hegemony. That liberal coalition is founded on the principle that individuals and groups should be provided with scope for active participation in public affairs. Implemented traditionally within the liberal democratic countries, the principle has naturally been extended to international affairs as liberalism has triumphed in the world system with the ending of the Cold War.

Thus the immense growth of NGO activities in international politics, although certainly given a great deal of dynamism by the energy and resources of the individuals and organizations themselves, results from political decisions and a framework that has been put into place by the leading powers. All of the resources dispensed by the intergovernmental organizations and many of those spent by NGOs are supplied by governments, and authorization to undertake tasks must be given by governments. In those cases in which NGOs such as Human Rights Watch remain independent, their effectiveness lies in their ability to affect governments' decisions and behaviors. To understand and interpret these activities, therefore, one needs to incorporate a grasp of the political context in which seemingly autonomous organizations exist and operate.

The right's agenda has been achieved empirically in the adoption of extensive programs of privatization as well as liberal market principles in both advanced and developing countries. In addition, corporate and other monied interests have secured an increasingly influential role in the politics of liberal democratic countries as well as such developmental states as Japan and the East Asian tigers (Gomez and Jomo 1997; Johnson 1982). These victories have been achieved because political decisions have been made to promote economic growth through private enterprise as well as the succumbing of politicians to the reciprocal effects of money in election campaigns and lobbying efforts.

Contrary to the view that the broad adoption of liberal market principles and the shift of production from public agencies to private enterprise results from a shift of power to firms and away from states (Strange 1996), I believe that these phenomena emanated from state use of meta-political power. Meta-political power, which only states possess, is the authority to decide what falls into the public sphere and what, private (Offe 1996; Thomson 1995). On the other hand, having benefited from the increased resources available from their activities, firms and other wealthy actors enjoy reciprocal influence on the political process. Moreover, states remain the effective instruments for addressing market failures and economic crises.

However impoverished and without political assets, citizens have nevertheless not been subject anywhere to the imposition of the new right's version of employment-based citizenship. In order to reach that profound change, it would be necessary for states to adopt such principles. As long as democratic citizens exercise due vigilance and their voting and speaking rights, it seems unlikely that such a view would be adopted. This seems particularly to remain the case as long as the third—strong democracy and large civil society—view persists articulately and actively.

This larger conceptualization of civil society, which was set out by Cohen and Arato (1992), introduces a three-part formulation of state, market, and civil society by drawing on the work of Gramsci (1971; Bobbio 1988) and Parsons (1971). They also build on Habermas' (1990) discourse ethics in order to promote a sphere for public discourse separate from both state and market. Despite their homage to Hegel (Cohen and Arato 1992, p. 91), these advocates' argument has flaws. First, it is difficult to separate concepts of state, market, and civil society in practice. In the Hegelian scheme of things, state regulatory institutions formed part of civil society, the most important constituent of which was what we today call the market and which Hegel (1952) termed corporations. Furthermore, the same persons who have particular interests also have universal interests. Hegel thought that civil society was thus a "moment" in the state. As Hann (Hann and Dunn 1996, p. 9) has argued in a different context, "The assumption of an overriding antagonism between state and society is futile. If these terms can serve at all, the task must be to investigate their complex and continuous interactions."

The second difficulty with the larger conception of an independent civil society is that too frequently the term is regarded as referring to a coherent unified entity. In reality, civil society can at most consist of multifarious groups, each pursuing its particular interests. To the extent that coherent political positions based upon shared understandings and symbols can be achieved, that is state activity. In Hegelian terms civil society forms a component of the state; civil society groups can monitor state agencies, but there are broader common purposes in the state that transcend civil society; and civil society depends upon state structures and functions. Additionally, it is important to recognize, according to the Hegelian viewpoint, that civil society is "historically produced" and that it is, as Keane (1998, p. 50) notes, "wreckable."

Whatever criticisms one has of the large conception of civil society, nevertheless, one must acknowledge its contribution to sustaining a public discourse that occurs in public space about important political issues. In giving further consideration to our problem of protecting citizenship and public space, the remainder of this chapter describes the requisites and conditions for preserving a notion of common good and the public space in which to deliberate. In approaching those matters, the first order of business is to consider the situation of globalization, in order to determine whether this quest remains merely utopian or falls under the rubric of achievable aspirations. That is, do present conditions dictate that individuals are to become increasingly isolated from each other and that social solidarity is unlikely to be reinforced, restored, and/or rebuilt? Or, do current circumstances hold out the potential for maintaining social bonds and notions of civic responsibility as well as providing opportunities for renewed citizenship participation within a context of considering the common good? I argue on behalf of the latter.

Present Conditions of Global Order

A broad global order requires that the states comprising its leadership must be secure, rich, and strong. In addition to providing a continuing basis for operation of the international political economy (Lentner 2000b; Wolf 2001), strong states remain essential for international cooperation. Effective international bargains cannot be forged by weak states, and no other groups or entities possess the legitimacy to enter into and enforce contractual arrangements that establish rules to govern international relations. On occasion, states may authorize private entities to lay down rules in restricted areas, say, accounting, but the determination of such allocations of authority fall under the rubric of meta-politics, an exclusively state function.

In the contemporary world, both the material power and the policy commitment of the United States form the foundation upon which the liberal order rests. Other states comprising a concert or coalition also prove important for the maintenance of the order; for, should they defect, they would do so to balance against the United States, checking it rather than supporting its order. Such recent activities as the 1991 Gulf War against Iraq and the US-led resolution of the Mexican and Asian financial crises of 1994–1995 and 1997–1998, respectively, demonstrated in an overt and clear way how material resources, leadership, and policy commitment can be brought to bear to preserve or restore the stability that underlies the international order. These activities could not have been undertaken by weak states.

From the perspective of citizenship and public space, the other pillar underpinning globalization, developmental states, seems more centrally instrumental. It is clear that stable, well-ordered, law-based states form prerequisites for capitalist economies. Even most standard arguments about globalization that are entirely market-oriented and assume the weakening of states concede this service function of the state. However, it is impossible to construct a state that is limited to such narrow functions. States also provide identity for citizens who assume as members responsibilities and rights, and they provide the security and order that their citizens require to pursue their lives. States also include the mechanisms for achieving social and political purposes as well as the organs of deliberation and decision making that allow for the definition of those purposes. States also protect their citizens from the security threats and economic pressures that emanate from abroad.

These are matters crying out for attention, but the present condition includes the anomaly of cultural and political discourses that largely leave aside concerns about the material and organizational requisites for the reproduction of such desired ends as ensuring prosperity, alleviating poverty, and sustaining community. Yet it is hard to imagine how these matters could be achieved without strong states.

To recapture the notions of public space, common good, and duties and rights of citizenship, we need to go beyond the discourses of neoliberalism and even those of civil society. To address the central matters, I turn to three sources that seldom enter into the globalization dialogue: Hegel, Arendt, and the American founding fathers.

Citizenship and Public Space in the Contemporary World

In the liberal scheme of things, individuals and their corporate parallels form the central entities, with the state as a coercive apparatus existing simply as a limited mechanism for registering demands emanating from self-interested entities. This view, in which whatever public good that may develop stems merely from the unintended clash of individualistic desires, has become even more unable to deal with political concerns such as citizenship and common good under modern doctrines of neoliberalism. Increasingly, as was noted above, modern discourse isolates individuals from their societies and states and renders private demands as claims for public rights (Seligman 1992, p. 133). Furthermore, in this view the state is regarded merely as the enforcer of individual and corporate rights (Smith 1989).

We can do better by turning to Hegel (1952) who concerned himself with the problem of a common ethical life, which he found in the state. He distinguished between state and civil society, the latter essentially including the market and the realm of pursuit of particular interests. In one sense, the economic division of labor in capitalist society and the interdependence it produces inadvertently leads to a mutuality in which selfish individuals serve one another's needs. Nevertheless, such mutuality does not produce any political concerns with a common good. Human needs and desires are insatiable, so that the unceasing pursuit of them tends to generate inequality and poverty, even though civil society includes a state regulatory apparatus. However, the state consists of much more than a mechanism for supporting the market. For Hegel, the state in addition consists of an ethical sphere of universality that is founded on freedom. Thus the state does not simply serve the economy; it serves the broader purposes of its citizens' freedom, even in functioning as the protector of the whole in peace and war. As pointed out by Pelczynski (1984, p. 11), the distinction between state and civil society is not an institutional distinction; it is one of ends: "the activities in the civil sphere are aimed at particular interests or private rights of individuals and groups; those of the political sphere—at the general interests of the whole community." At its apex, in war, the interests of the individual and the state are merged in the ethical purpose of freedom.

In an early twenty-first century context in which the social and political realms, in Arendt's (1959, p. 31) words, "constantly flow into each other," the distinction often gets lost. Hegel's universal that culminates in the merger with human freedom in war in which life and property are sacrificed to a common good, does not resonate in modern ears. Yet a full understanding of contemporary politics needs to include the distinction between common good and particular needs and interests.

Furthermore,

> The central feature of Hegel's theory of the state is its respect for rights, crucially including the right to recognition (*Annerkenung*).... What Hegel calls the institutions of ethical life, or *Sittlichkeit*, are there to preserve and enhance our right to mutual recognition and esteem. (Smith 1989, pp. x–xi)

It is only in the realm of shared values rather than merely material interests for which a common life becomes worth sacrificing and fighting. Thus the state is above all an ethical community, not an instrument for the achievement of material interests, although the achievement of those may provide the capabilities for defending the shared ethical life. More significant than the violence involved in expressing the common good transcending particularistic interests is the building of sound institutions that can preserve the common ethical life and the sentiments and shared values that underlie it (Smith 1989, p. 160).

This conception of the state, which goes a distance beyond the liberal conception of civil society, entails a confrontation with matters of common good and citizenship. In view of the fact that in modern life no authority hands down what those matters shall consist of, it becomes incumbent upon us to find ways of acting that can create such states.

It is difficult to see how these matters can be approached from a liberal point of view that excludes them. Similarly, matters like these can hardly be handled on a worldwide basis, for it appears impractical for the communication and structuring of symbols that are necessary to state formation to occur on such a scale. After all, the formation of institutions that embody mutual recognition of citizens and a coherent ethical idea uniting them has necessarily to occur on a scale that allows individuals to act politically. This constraint becomes clear as we consider how it can come about, an inquiry that takes us to Hannah Arendt.

Arendt drew a clear distinction between power and violence. Power was constituted through public action in which individuals gained empowerment by speech to forge communities. In her words,

> Power is what keeps the public realm, the potential space of appearance between acting and speaking men, in existence.... Power is always ... a power potential and not an unchangeable, measurable and reliable entity like force or strength. While strength is the natural quality of an individual seen in isolation, power springs up between men when they act together and vanishes the moment they disperse. Because of this peculiarity, ... power is to an astonishing degree independent of material factors.

> The only indispensable material factor in the generation of power is the living together of people. Only where men live so close together that the

potentialities of action are always present can power remain with them.... (Arendt 1959, p. 179–180).

She understood the creation of political community as taking place in two stages, actions by a set of founders that set up a public space and the actions of others who can exercise their speech in that space (Fuss 1979).

Building on Arendt's conceptualization of power, Goehler (2000) has demonstrated the link between a Weberian understanding of power as domination and violence, on the one hand, and Arendt's insight that power must be constituted through human action. Goehler calls these distinct manifestations transitive and intransitive power. He thus calls attention to the intrinsically normative content of power relations, whether violent or constitutive; that is to say, power always is linked to purpose. Moreover, Goehler points out, the realm of constituting power through public speech in concert with others also entails the employment of symbols that provide evidence of the common values of communities. At the same time that they constitute communities, however, citizens acting in concert organized around symbols also confer authority on those acting on their behalf through the state. In turn, authorities then exercise coercive power on their citizens, although they do so legitimately because they have been authorized to act transitively by the intransitive undertakings of their constituents.

In the process of acting in concert, citizens confer upon one another recognition as participants in the fundamental community undertaking of state formation and reproduction. That recognition confers upon citizens responsibilities for participating and reproducing the polity but also the right to engage in further speech to continue to shape the common life. Once formed, a state acquires institutional structures that maintain a legal order and the means for running the society. Clearly, such an order includes space for civil society's particularistic activities. But this conceptualization also indicates that much more is involved, for the very foundations of a common good and a citizenship that transcend the realm of civil society have been established. The legitimacy of authority arises from the constitutive aspects of citizen activity. Thus, any concerted, successful attempt to diminish the common ethical life, say, by repudiating the obligations of the state toward its citizens to a neoliberal conception, would produce a crisis of legitimacy for the state. In that case, a revolutionary situation would be created in which either violence would lead to the domination of one group that would impose its regime on the population, or the occasion would produce a new constitutive dialogue leading to the formation of a state based upon different principles from those of the previous regime (Arendt 1965). Obviously these are matters of the first order, fundamental to politics.

Politics consists, above all, of practical endeavors. Thus little theory and few generalizations can guide leaders who undertake to engage in state formation, revolution, or reform. Every set of participants faces a practical situation that is constrained by traditions, by available ideas, and by material circumstances. Yet models of action are provided by history, and some are relevant in light of politics as elucidated by Hegel and Arendt. Others may have their own exemplars, but mine is the politics of the American founding fathers, a set of talented political leaders who, in a crisis of legitimacy of their early republic under the Articles of Confederation, forged a new constitutional arrangement that has lasted well over two centuries. Their actions reflected eighteenth-century ideas and a practical situation that has not been and will not be duplicated. Much of what they did remains irrelevant to other situations, and some of their actions such as the compromise that counted slaves for purposes of representation and direct taxation as three-fifths persons, although practical at their time cannot be held up for imitation.

In his insightful essay about them, Roche (1961) describes the founding fathers as reformers and democratic politicians. Although representatives of the respective states in which they resided, they brought to bear a national outlook that led to their concern about protecting the international position of the United States. They were also democratic politicians, willing to lead and maneuver against opponents but nonetheless convinced that their efforts required popular approval. On the whole, the Constitution was the result of political bargaining that included avoiding some issues, using ambiguity on others, and overlooking a number of matters. The American founding fathers were neither gods nor philosophers but rather practical men of affairs. In Roche's view (1961, p. 33):

> To conclude, the Constitution was neither a victory for abstract theory nor a great practical success. Well over half a million men had to die on the battlefields of the Civil War before certain constitutional principles could be defined. . . . The Constitution was, however, a vivid demonstration of effective democratic political action which literally persuaded its countrymen to hoist themselves by their own boot straps.

Neither the philosophers Locke and Montesquieu, upon whom the Americans drew, nor the arrangements that resulted in federalism, separation of powers, and other particulars of the US system need to be translated into other vernaculars or built into other political systems. What Roche argued, and what can be applied, are the effective use of democratic leadership and its endorsement by the citizenry. Although he did not invoke them, Roche's analysis illustrates a case in which Arendt's conception of power was given effect: leaders and citizens engaged in serious talk.

Furthermore, the mechanism of practical political leadership and popular endorsement set the stage for the fulfillment of citizenship duties and the exercise of citizenship rights following the building of the state. As Roche noted, the definition of the state and its reproduction required not just politics but also violence. Going beyond him, one notes that certain aspects of the ongoing process of state building required actions outside the constitutional boundaries, such as street demonstrations, civil disobedience, and nonviolent confrontations with law-enforcement authorities in the women's, labor unions', and civil rights' movements. Even these actions, nevertheless, involved conceptions of common good and political action in public spaces. Certainly, none of this politics is embraced by the neoliberal view, for the case on behalf of vigorous politics articulates an endorsement for moving beyond the parlous stage of contemporary life in which an impoverished conception of public opinion has substituted for informed, substantive public debate (Habermas 1989). Such a vigorous politics as I am advocating entails a much more expansive conception of the state and political action, not to speak of the notions promoted in this chapter of common good and citizenship.

Although not transferable to other countries, the broad and practical aspects of the US experience can resonate with other polities. Others face different practical circumstances and are constrained by other traditions and inspired by different ideas. Still, the ideas of common good, of leaders acting in public space to forge reforms, and of their maintaining connections with populations from whom they seek endorsement are relevant to varied situations. Moreover, these conceptions occur within the framework of maintaining the positions of states within the international system. They do not offer merely formulas for either capitulating to hegemonic forces in the international arena or simply offering resistance to those forces. Rather, they argue on behalf of forging autonomous states, with strong citizen bases, and imaginative leaderships that can build developmental states that will be in a position to make discrete decisions about cooperation and resistance. Finally, these views offer a means of overcoming the globalization-induced deanchoring of citizenship and disappearance of public space and the idea of common good. They provide not a formula but a guideline to empowerment as a political process that can lead to strength in the face of stronger powers and their international organizational instruments. They respond to the conventional view but not inevitable occurrence of the breakdown of social solidarity in the face of global pressures.

Conclusion

Prevailing discourses frequently regard globalization as a single, onrushing, inevitable force. But present circumstances are not driven by disembodied and inevitable historical developments. Instead, the thrust toward cultural transfers, worldwide rationalization of production, and a liberal international economy is given its dynamic by a political agenda promoted and sustained by a liberal international coalition of states and built upon US military power and policy commitments. In addition, the main elements of the continued growth of the liberal international economy rest upon the existence and spread of strong developmental states. However, states cannot be constructed merely as elements designed to serve as support for private enterprise and a neoliberal agenda that diminishes public space and the idea of common good and that deanchors citizenship from its traditional locus in the state and erodes social solidarity from its nationalistic base. For the very conception of a state includes broader aspects of duties and rights of citizenship and an ethical realm that unites citizens in freedom beyond their pursuit of selfish interests.

Prominent efforts to confront the pressures against traditional citizenship and social solidarity promise failure, for several reasons. The left response, which aims at an international civil society, seems doomed because the scope is too broad for effective political action leading to the constitution of power. On the other hand, the right or neoliberal attempt to base citizenship on employment is too narrow. Should the neoliberal program be implemented, it would undermine political support for its own agenda. The large conception of civil society seems not to appreciate the incoherence of the very notion and does not address the broader question of state formation and reproduction.

Because globalization is built on a foundation of violence and politics, those are the realms in which to seek responses. I have argued that Hegel provides the broad conception of the state, that Arendt gives us the theoretical model for action that leads to empowerment, and that the American founding fathers offer a model of practical politics that gives a way of forming and reproducing a state.

Thus, rather than fading away in the contemporary world, the state remains an essential mechanism for the choice of whether and under what circumstances to cooperate with or resist the very powerful states promoting the neoliberal agenda. Effective states acting with and on behalf of their citizens and societies can benefit from certain of the globalization trends, but they can also oppose unwanted and undesirable pressures. In doing so, they will not only protect their citizens but will also strengthen their own abilities to participate effectively as autonomous units in the international system.

In politics there are always choices. Because others make different choices politics also always involves struggle. There is nothing inevitable about globalization. Social solidarity need not be eroded away and can even be strengthened. It is likely to do so, however, only if choices are made on behalf of building strong effective states through imaginative leadership and public practices that involve endorsement of leadership initiatives by a vibrant citizenry cognizant of its duties as well as its rights. And such cognizance can only occur if citizens maintain a conception of a shared ethical realm that surpasses their individual and group particular interests.

11
Malaysia and Southeast Asia in Globalization

Introduction

Although globalization applies to the entire world, it is useful to focus on a single country and region to detail and to highlight the many aspects and complexities of globalization processes that have been described and analyzed in previous chapters. To that end, this chapter concentrates on Malaysia, a Southeast Asian country that has enjoyed some of the advantages of globalization and suffered some of its unwanted consequences. Malaysia offers examples of both insertion in and cooperation with the international political economy and resistance to unwelcome pressures. The country has demonstrated how politics drives economic activity as well as how the reciprocal effects of economics on politics shape national life.

Malaysia's fate has been linked to its region and to wider influences for many centuries, so an overview of its history helps to establish what is continuous and what is novel about contemporary global trends and Malaysia's relationship to them. The region of Southeast Asia in which Malaysia is located includes the giant neighbor Indonesia and the small island nation Singapore as well as the other seven members of the Association of Southeast Asian Nations (ASEAN). In the early fifteenth century the lands comprising the Malay peninsula and the Indonesian archipelago were converted, through trade and missionaries rather than conquest, to Islam. The indigenous Malay populations of insular Southeast Asia had been connected through trade and travel not only among themselves but also with China and India even earlier. Portuguese and Spanish explorers arrived in the sixteenth century, only to be replaced by the other European countries, the Netherlands and Britain, which imposed imperial rule, respectively, on Indonesia and on Malaya and Singapore. For a time during World War II Japan ruled the entire region. When the war ended, the United States and Britain reclaimed their former colonial possessions and both the Netherlands and France fought wars to reimpose their colonial rule, the former until 1949, the latter until 1954. The Netherlands' departure left a single country, Indonesia, that, despite its composition of some 3000 islands, was ruled by a single coherent government with wide popular support.

France's effort to regain control over its Southeast Asian colonies proved very costly and ended in defeat. Upon the French departure from the region in 1954, three countries remained, one of them, Vietnam, divided into two separate states ruled, respectively, by different, ideologically distinct governments. It was not long after that the United States became involved in supporting several South Vietnamese regimes and then brought to bear its considerable military power in Vietnam in an action that lasted from 1962 to 1973. Following its cessation of direct military action in 1973, the United States remained a presence in South Vietnam until that part of the country was conquered by a northern army in 1975, when the Americans withdrew even their diplomatic personnel.

After the Second World War the British returned to rule their colonial territories in Southeast Asia. Following a lengthy guerrilla war, Britain in 1957 granted independence to the Federation of Malaya, led by Malay elites who had been groomed for leadership during the colonial period. The new federation included the Malay states as well as the former colonies of Penang, Malacca, and Singapore. In 1963 the federation expanded to include the Borneo territories of Sabah and Sarawak and it assumed the name Malaysia. Racial tensions between the indigenous Malay populations and the immigrant Chinese and Indians increased in severity until 1965, when Singapore, with an overwhelming non-Malay population, was expelled from the federation.

In the basic meaning of connectedness with other parts of the world, globalization thus was affecting Malaysia and the Southeast Asian region long before contemporary concerns and vocabulary made their appearance. In recent times, new pressures as well as new aspirations have emerged, but these novel features of the political, social, and economic landscape remain connected to and influenced by earlier experiences and the patterns that have been left by them. Thus the approach to analyzing Malaysia must be concrete and historical, even though broader categories are employed in order to deal with the themes set forth in the book as a whole.

Global Pressures Then and Now

Lying at the southeast extremity of the Asian continent astride important waterways forming trade routes and close to the Indonesian archipelago, the Malay peninsula has figured in the ambitions of many different civilizations and has been affected for centuries by pressures stemming from around the world. Near the beginning of the Christian or common era traders from India visited the area, and subsequently Buddhist and Brahmin missionaries, as well as Hindu colonists entered the region. Aspects of Indian culture were adapted into Southeast Asian cultures, although there was very little Chinese and Indian immigration to the area. Incursions from Sumatra occurred in the eighth century, and the Cholas from India invaded in the eleventh century. The thirteenth and fourteenth centuries saw a military contest for the peninsula between Java and Siam. Finally, in the early fifteenth century Malacca established itself as a Malay-dominated state, whose rulers were converted by Gujarati traders to Islam, which later spread throughout the Malay peninsula and south through the Indonesian archipelago. Malacca rose to become one of the most important trading ports in the world, in part protected by China, which had sent out envoys in the first few decades of the fifteenth century looking for tributaries, against the ambitions of Thai rulers. The Portuguese captured Malacca in 1511, but it was wrested from them by the Dutch in 1641. It was during the Napoleonic wars that Holland asked Britain to administer Malacca for it, and then formally turned over control to the British in 1824. Except for the Japanese occupation, the British did not leave until 1957.

Both Malacca and Singapore formed ports located on trade routes, and this led to openness of their economies. An international division of labor and export production had been established in Malaya before the arrival of European colonial power in the nineteenth century (Drabble 2000, p. 5). Then, revolutionary changes in Singapore resulted from "two developments in the international economy...: the inauguration of the Suez Canal in 1869" and the advent of steamships later in the nineteenth century, from which point Singapore became the main port for Malayan trade (Huff 1994, p. 8). In the following century, Singapore experienced "a commercial explosion" (Huff 1994, p. 11). Its trade increased more than sixfold between 1871/1873 and 1900/1902 to reach an annual average of S(ingapore)$431 in the latter period and then leaped again between 1910 and 1927, reaching S$1832 for a pre-Second World War high. This economic growth relied upon tin, rubber, and petroleum, all staple products from the Malayan region (Huff 1994, p. 14).

Drabble argues that a turning point from extensive to intensive growth occurred in Malaya with the advent of rubber cultivation in the first two decades of the twentieth century. This development occurred under the colonial regime which brought some infrastructure, foreign capital, and a policy of bringing in immigrant workers. At the same time growth was driven by the response of indigenous farmers to export crops.

Although extractive and agricultural industries grew in Malaya proper, Singapore developed a number of economic characteristics that distinguished it as a staple port. These included

> five main, related characteristics: the performance of entrepreneurial, investment, management and mercantile functions connected with the production of the staple; the provision of financial services; processing of the staple commodity; marketing services including the role of the port as the region's main market for the staple; and the close involvement of business interests in the port with hinterland production. (Huff 1994, p. 16)

In this tradition, Singapore also developed processing industries for tin and rubber. By the 1970s Singapore firms "began to manufacture oil exploration equipment" (Huff 1994, p. 22). Then, a world market center grew as "Singapore established itself as the world's greatest market for rubber and tin."

Although economic growth burgeoned, laying a foundation for even greater expansion of wealth after independence, the pattern of development rendered Malaya dependent on a few commodities and exposed the country "to the vicissitudes of the international economy" (Drabble 2000, p. 48). Exposure particularly to the American economy meant that Malaya suffered immense losses in the Great Depression, with its export earnings falling seventy-three percent from 1929 to 1932 (Drabble 2000, p. 125).

In the post-World War II period, straddling the pre- and post-independence periods, Cold War pressures bore on Malaysia in the form of an internal communist insurgency and the regional violence attendant upon the French and American wars against the countries of Indochina. Additionally, Malaysia faced the hostility of Indonesia during the mid-1960s when for three years it pursued a "confrontation" policy toward the Malaysian federation. Following independence, both Malaysia and Singapore took advantage of favorable international economic developments by industrializing with the assistance of foreign investors. Particularly after the 1985 Plaza Accord which effectively led to the devaluation of the Japanese yen and then to Japan's decision to place its manufacturing investments overseas, Malaysia and Singapore gained substantial FDI. For example, Japanese direct investment in Malaysia increased forty-nine percent from 1981 to 1987, from 2545 to 3802 million ringgit (United Nations 1992, Table 9). As the world became increasingly connected electronically, Singapore found a niche in services (Huff 1994, p. 38).

Perhaps the dominant pressure of the post-Cold War period emanated from the triumph of neoliberal ideology, which not only trumpeted the virtues of market economics and privatization but also fostered the notion that a broad new liberal and democratic world order was being put into place. That notion presented not just a vision of a world dominated by the powerful liberal democracies but also claims for adherence to liberal norms and for contributions to peacekeeping and other tasks devised by the leading powers.

Neoliberal ideology pressed for countries to open themselves not only to foreign trade and foreign direct investment but also to the many new financial devices that were allowing capital to move virtually without restriction throughout the global economy, without consideration for national borders. Amsden (2001, pp. 268, 256) characterizes this as "the major threat [of] *denationalization* at the firm level," which stemmed from the adoption of "an offensive rather than a defensive strategy" by the United States and Britain to pry "open markets of weaker economies." It became apparent in 1997 that the free flow of financial resources that had grown since the early 1970s carried not just benefits but also considerable risks, as the Asian financial crisis caused substantial damage to Malaysia's economy, and even more to the economies of its neighbors Thailand and Indonesia (Athukorala 1998a). Malaysia also drew substantial numbers of illegal immigrants from neighboring countries to its relatively prosperous economy.

One also needs to note that ownership and immigration patterns not only characterized the economy but also shaped political and state formation arrangements. Ownership was spread between indigenous and foreign capital, with the former segmented by race. Singapore has relied on immigration from China and India, and thus does not resemble the racial makeup of its hinterland. The

Malaysian hinterland also contains Chinese and Indian components, but the majority, sixty percent, of the population is Malay. Especially in Malaysia racial politics has proved central to domestic political and social stability, state formation matters, and economic development strategy.

Malaysia's contemporary encounter with globalization processes has included a variety of pressures comprising challenges as well as opportunities. As is true of any state, Malaysia is neither altogether invulnerable nor completely lacking autonomy. The following analysis illustrates the general themes of this book as manifested in a single country.

Security

In his narrative of Singapore's development following independence, Lee Kuan Yew begins with security, emphasizing that "without it there would be no investments" (Lee 2000, p. 41), jobs, and exports. Other social and economic basics also had to be put into place for the country to develop, but security formed, as it does in other countries, the essential bedrock upon which other activities are built. Both Malaysia and Singapore have been made aware of the fundamental quality of security and defense by their experience in World War II and the aftermath.

Although Britain had prepared for the defense of Malaya by fortifying Singapore against an attack from the sea, it failed to withstand a fairly easy takeover by the Japanese in 1942. Meeting little resistance, the Japanese army entered Malaya from the north and its soldiers traversed the country on bicycles, taking Singapore from the peninsula side. Apart from military dimensions, British policy had structured a purely economic society. In an assessment of the British defeat by Japan in Malaya, Thompson concluded that "[t]he root of the evil lay in the purely economic form of imperialism which developed, and which failed to weld the peoples of the country into a Malayan nation" (Thompson 1943, p. 314). Others attribute the defeat to the weakened state of the British army as well as its lack of training for the type of warfare faced in Malaya and to the superior strength of the Japanese armed forces.

In order to preserve themselves, Malay rulers decided to cooperate with the Japanese, and the Malays were dealt with in a less rough manner than the Chinese, who were treated particularly harshly during the occupation. Indians were treated worse than Malays although not as roughly as the Chinese, in part because the Japanese sought to promote Indian nationalism.

Shortly after the end of World War II, in 1948 communist revolts broke out in several Asian countries, including Malaya where a predominantly Chinese insurgency operated. For a number of years Malaya lived under an "emergency" in which counterguerrilla tactics included relocation of large numbers of rural Chinese people into fortified, government-organized compounds. It was during this time that the notorious Internal Security Act, which remains in effect, was first instituted and used as a tool for suppression of militants. Although the emergency ended in the late 1950s, it was not until 1989 that the communists finally acceded to an agreement formally to end their insurgency. Even during the emergency,

Malayans pressed toward independence from Britain, and they finally gained it in 1957.

The security difficulty faced by both Malaysia and Singapore in their early years of independence stemmed from the uncertainty of British intentions. Although the British promised in 1966 to protect Singapore, it was only two years later that the Wilson government decided to withdraw from the Asian mainland in 1971. With the pullout, a Five-Power Defense Arrangement was established that provided for consultation among the parties (Australia, Britain, Malaysia, Singapore, and New Zealand) should Malaysia or Singapore be attacked. In short, both countries had to build up their own armed forces although they retained allies who might assist them. Over time, British responsibility has diminished while that of Australia and New Zealand has grown, but primary responsibility for their defense has come to be lodged in Singapore and Malaysia themselves (Chin 1983).

When in 1963 Singapore, Sabah, and Sarawak were added to the federation of Malaya, the country faced an undeclared war from Indonesia, which Sukarno referred to as a confrontation (*konfrontasi*). Following Sukarno's downfall in 1965, that security threat not only receded, but the security environment improved greatly with the formation of the Association of Southeast Asian nations (ASEAN) whose members (Brunei, Indonesia, Malaysia, Philippines, Singapore, and Thailand) sought to cooperate with one another.

As a country besieged by an internal communist threat, Malaysia benefited from US policy in Vietnam and in the Cold War in general. In the words of Nathan (1998, p. 531), "Essentially, Malaysia's security needs were well provided for within the broad framework of Anglo-American defense cooperation in the first two decades of the Cold War. . . ." Nonetheless, since the end of the Cold War Malaysia has been in the forefront of ASEAN expansion, which has grown to ten members, to include Vietnam and Myanmar. Overall, the post-Cold War security environment has remained stable, allowing both Malaysia and Singapore to develop confidence and to pursue largely unencumbered economic activity. Such a benign situation, however, has not led to neglect of security concerns. As put by a Malaysian minister of defense, "it is axiomatic that both the domestic and regional security environment have to be stable and peaceful in order for us to sustain growth" (Baginda and Mahmood 1995, Foreword).

Contemporary Malaysian thinking about security is layered, dealing with military protection of the country and with problems in its vicinity, maintaining ties with the Five Power Defence Arrangement and bilateral military ties with ASEAN partners as well as security contacts with major powers, and taking part in broad international peacekeeping operations.

With the formal ending of the internal war in 1989, the government of Malaysia began to reorient and transform its armed forces toward a conventionally structured, externally oriented military organization. Specifically, the size of the army has been reduced and the naval and air forces have enjoyed a buildup (Interview, 3/11/98). Some have expressed the ambition to develop self-sufficiency in defense industries (Baginda and Mahmood 1995, p. 8). Meanwhile, Malaysia has made extensive purchases of new arms in order to modernize. The country's strategic interests concern its core territory, the Straits of Malacca and Singapore, and sea lanes, although any threat to one of the original five countries of ASEAN amounts to a contingent threat to Malaysia.

The Seven Power Defence Association continues to serve training and exercise functions; in addition, the SPDA remains prepared to assist in the defense of Malaysia and Singapore. Furthermore, Malaysia and Singapore participate in the ASEAN Regional Forum, which links the countries of the region in a periodic dialogue with the major powers including especially Japan, the United States, and China, but the European powers as well.

In 2004 Malaysia does not face a direct security threat. Its overall approach is to embrace regional and broader forums and to engage with countries that have interests in its region. Thus, in anticipation that China's interests will grow, the government engages China in a variety of governmental and nongovernmental forums, and there is an anticipation that China's navy will one day ply Southeast Asian waters even as the United States Navy maintains its presence (Interview, 3/17/98).

Two potential threats wait in the wings. Although it has been set aside for some years, a claim by the Philippines to Sabah lurks as a potential territorial dispute. Then, given the instability of Indonesia since the 1997–1998 economic crisis, the possibility for a significant breakdown in that country and a consequent flight by large numbers of people to Malaysia prompts thought about internal security problems emerging from a massive and destabilizing influx of refugees. Another security concern, although not an imminent threat to the government, stems from the worldwide networks of Islamic-based, anti-western terrorist organizations, some of which appear to have used Malaysia as a meeting ground if not as a base.

For the most part, though, Malaysia's security concerns are not pressing. The government pursues an active policy of participating in cooperative security activities in order to help sustain an orderly and peaceful international environment.

State Formation and Politics

The Malaysian state and the central political matters involved in its formation and operations have been shaped by the confrontation of the local population and its elites with many influences from the outside world as well as by processes that take place within the structure of power relations within the country. As noted above, immigration patterns and trade from the distant past had given the region its dominant Muslim religion and its ethnic character of Malay predominance mixed with a variety of other groups, including the aboriginal *Asli Orang*, the most important of which are Chinese and largely Tamil Indian. European, specifically British, colonialism appeared in the nineteenth century, and Japanese imperialism prevailed for a few years in the 1940s. Like other colonial peoples, Malayans developed nationalist sentiments in the twentieth century. In doing so, they built specific institutions that reflected solutions to the varied clashing interests and groups that characterize the country.

Malaysia became independent in the midst of the emergency in which the colonial government had spawned a good deal of repressive legislation that the new state inherited. Like other countries gaining their independence in the post-World War II period, Malaysia adopted democratic forms, but these have been accompanied by authoritarian characteristics that have increased over time. Specifically, authoritarian measures were adopted on the occasion of a riot following elections in May 1969, and the political system has been shaped importantly in an authoritarian direction by Mahathir Mohammed who became prime minister in 1981 and served in that capacity until the end of October 2003 (Milne and Mauzy 1999; Perlez 2003). With political parties and contested elections, the government tends to be responsive to certain political pressures, but the scope for politics is also severely constrained by forbidding the discussion of some fundamental issues, by restricting the mass media, by emasculating the courts, and by ruthless intimidation and sometimes incarceration of political opponents.

Central to the Malaysian state and politics is race—the distribution of ethnicity among Malays, Chinese, and Indians—which shapes the society's consciousness and guides government policy. At independence, the elite agreement provided for political dominance by Malays, while the economic position of non-Malays would not be disturbed. It was understood that the economic position of Malays would be brought up and that national identity was to be established on the basis of the Malay language (Crouch 1996, pp. 20–21). Yet race, the most important characteristic of Malaysian society, has lain for the last thirty years outside the realm of legally acceptable discourse about policy and the future direction of the country.

Formally, a parliament is elected on a regular basis, but the ruling party has never been defeated at the national level. Still, that party forms the core of an alliance of parties based upon ethnic identification, called *Barisan Nasional,* an arrangement that facilitates elite accommodation on important matters. At the same time, the system is based upon a recognition of Malay dominance with subordination of the Chinese and Indian groups. These modern governing arrangements exist side by side with an older political authority based upon a traditional ruling aristocracy.

As is the case with other countries, any attempt to understand the contemporary state requires some examination of history to grasp how the present system came into existence and evolved. Current practices and policies continue to be affected by the strong currents of race and often contradictory, unresolved attempts to reconcile different aspirations over the twentieth century.

Prior to British rule, there had existed unrestricted back-and-forth movement of people between the Malay peninsula and the Indonesian archipelago. Toward the end of the nineteenth century, however, significant numbers of Indonesians settled in Malaya and others took up residence as part of their pilgrimage to Mecca (Roff 1967, pp. 35–36). This decrease in geographical mobility may be attributed to British rule which pursued contradictory aims. First, the colonial power aimed to build political stability and a bureaucratic government as a condition for economic exploitation of Malaya's natural resources. Second, the rulers justified those aims by "an expressed concern for the welfare and advancement of the Malay people within the framework of traditional Malay society" (Roff 1967, p. 12). Following this "schizoid" policy, English schools in the late nineteenth century educated mostly Chinese and Eurasians. In order to save money, at the end of the century the British turned over education to missionaries who, forbidden to proselytize and faced with resistance by Islamic parents to alien influences, educated mostly non-Malays (Roff 1967, p. 29).

From the middle of the nineteenth century forward, a variety of Malay sources gave expression to the linguistic and cultural struggle as the new influences and practices from Europe and China presented the challenge of new fashions, customs, and terms. Although often enough English terms were imported directly into *Bahasa Malaya,* the new urban intelligensia felt more comfortable with Arabic terms as they increasingly identified themselves as part of the Islamic world which, of course, remained culturally centered in the Arab region of Southwest Asia and North Africa (Roff 1967, pp. 46–48). At the turn of the century, thoughtful Malays came to recognize the backwardness of rural Malays, especially in contrast to prosperous urban Chinese communities in Penang and Singapore, and they continued to try to find solutions to the problems presented by an impoverished and uneducated class (Roff 1967, pp. 54–55).

The evolution of Malaysian nationalism took the form not of advocating social and political change but rather a turn toward religion. In promoting Islam, advocates championed the traditional Islamic concept of *shari'a* in which political and social concerns are encompassed in life organized according to the precepts of the Koran. Intellectuals read news from the Middle East, especially Turkey, and Japan. The periodical, *Al-Imam,* introduced modern reformist ideas from Egypt. Thus, in lieu of political nationalism, Malayan longing for a wider unity was expressed in terms of religion and the experience of colonial rule (Roff 1967, pp. 56–65).

At the same time, the British in the twentieth century only tentatively provided education and advancement for the Malay aristocracy and admitted some educated Malays into the civil service. These formed a new leadership group that was influenced by Western ideas. Meanwhile, most of the lower-level workers in government were Chinese and Indian. The bulk of the Malay population remained in the traditional economy, largely untouched by modern economic and social influences (Roff 1967, pp. 109–124).

During the 1910s, 1920s, and 1930s voluntary associations of Malays proliferated, tending to build a consciousness of the larger whole Malay community. Even though members of these associations and their leaders envisioned the possibility of national independence, the culmination of aspirations for independence had to await the end of the Japanese occupation and winding down of the British empire. When independence did arrive, it took "such a form as to leave intact the sultans and their states, the final and enduring symbol of Malay political authority and cultural identity" (Roff 1967, p. 256), and that form remains nearly a half-century later.

In parallel with Roff's analysis, Tunku Abdul (1984, pp. 5–6) encapsulates the growth of Malayan nationalism in several streams: first, that "influenced by the Islamic renaissance in the Middle East in the late nineteenth century;" second, "English-educated aristocratic administrators;" and third, "Malay-educated teachers and journalists attracted by the concept of a 'Greater Malaysia' or 'Greater Indonesia.'"

However Malay nationalism might have evolved, it was reshaped by the Japanese occupation, which had several effects on the politics of the country. Local Malay administrators, whom the Japanese used to rule, suffered losses of jobs and reductions in standards of living, which "brought about a certain amount of social leveling," and brought elites and masses into a closer relationship (Halinah 1975, pp. 136–141). In effects on race, the Chinese redirected their political attention from China to Malaya, and scarcity forced many Chinese to settle in Malay rural reserves, where some Malays entered the labor market as small traders, a segment of the economy that had previously been monopolized by Chinese. Malay interests were thus pitted against Chinese, departing from the separation and isolation that had prevailed under British rule. Armed resistance to Japanese rule came largely from the Chinese community; as the resistance became a political force, its aims deviated substantially from the Islam-oriented Malay outlook. At the end of the war in 1945 and 1946, a good deal of racial tension and violence spread throughout much of the peninsula. After the war, left-wing nationalist aspirations for independence in which race played no part challenged Malay assumptions and led to a concern for survival of the Malays among not only elites but also rural masses. Elites had long been vexed about Malay endurance; for example, in the 1931 census Chinese were shown to have outnumbered Malays in what the latter considered "their own country" (Tunku Abdul 1984, p. 5).

Coinciding with the racial divide, clashing visions about citizenship shaped the road to independence and persisted afterward. The Chinese sought to implant the idea of a single Malayan citizenship, whereas the Malays aspired to an ethnically based state in which Malays dominated. With the British administration as a participant, Malayans pursued their quest for independence around the issue of race (Ongkili 1985), although the leading Malay party, UMNO, remained clearly dedicated to a plural form of citizenship. A different view has consistently been presented by the Islamic party, *Parti Islam Se-Malaysia* (PAS). PAS aims to create a theocratic state in which *Bahasa Malaya* would assume the position of an exclusive national language and education would be reoriented to produce a Malay nationality in which different new requirements of citizenship from now-existing ones would be imposed on non-Malays. Substantial ideological and financial support for PAS comes from Egypt, Libya, Iran, and Saudi Arabia (Alias 1991).

The issue of race, as Milner (1998, pp. 163–169) pointedly contends, is a distinctive one that has been constructed out of many strands, some of which are noted above, but at its core lies the fact that Malays define themselves partly in opposition to characteristics of Chinese. The Malayan commitment to race has become even clearer in the post-independence period, especially in the Mahathir era with the prime minister's especially poignant views about race. Mahathir draws a parallel between Malays and North American Indians, and he expresses the fear that, without race-conscious policies, Malays, who regard themselves as indigenous to the territory, will be confined to reservations, with the country's future placed in the hands of the more recent immigrants (Mahathir 1970).

When the colonial power attempted to foment a constitution, it faced an impossible task of satisfying all groups. Indeed, upon their return to the area after the end of the war the British had abandoned their pre-war policy of favoring the Malays. It was in opposition to the British plan that the Malays mobilized against British designs (Tunku Abdul 1984). In the end, the constitution embedded a Malay privileged position by including "the adoption of Malay as the national language; a special position for Malays in recruitment to public services, in the granting of state scholarships and in the granting of commercial licenses; and the reservation of land for Malays … " (Ongkili 1985, p. 68).

It was during the lead-up to independence that the United Malays National Organization (UMNO) was born; this organization founded to promote the idea that Malaya was for the Malays has persisted as the core political organization in Malaysian politics. At the same time in the late 1940s the Malayan Chinese Association (MCA) and the Malayan Indian Congress (MIC) were founded. Most of the important political deals of the post-independence period have been shaped through negotiations and electoral cooperation of these three parties in their coalition called the Alliance (later termed *Barisan Nasional*).

Nonetheless, the period of constitution writing and lead-up to independence took place in the context of the emergency that lasted until about 1960. In the context of a British commitment to bring the country to independence, the military proved an effective instrument for suppressing the rebellion. Most important to the success of the operation were, first, the implementation of cooperation and coordination on a national basis; second, separation by resettlement of the Chinese base from the fighters, who took to the jungle; and, third, effective prosecution of the military action. Through propaganda, police efficiency, and other actions, the British managed to gain the support of the population (Mackay 1997).

In the negotiations for national independence, special Malay rights were retained. These included preservation of the traditional rulers and even strengthening the position of the one who serves on a rotating basis as king (*Yang di-Pertuan Agong*). Malayan land reservations were also retained. As a peculiar case in the context of post-1945 newly independent states, Malaya adopted Islam as the state religion, although the practice of other religions is tolerated.

Leadership aspirations to achieve a more integrated nation led to the incorporation of Singapore, Sarawak, and Sabah in 1963 even while strengthening the dominance of Malays and other indigenous people, a group that has come to be know as *Bumiputera* (sons of the soil). The elaboration of this larger Malaysia, however, provoked the informal war of confrontation by Indonesia. In addition, the Philippines asserted a claim to Sabah. Before long, in 1965 under pressure, Singapore separated to establish itself as an independent state. In the judgment of some (Ongkili 1985, p. 231), the separation was designed "to forestall a possible outbreak of communal violence." Despite a postponement, however, communal violence did break out in May 1969, an occurrence that led to the suspension of democratic institutions and to the establishment of an authoritarian regime. That regime, in turn, launched the country on a path designed to raise up the economic position of the Malays and to ensure their continued dominant position in Malaysian politics.

State and Politics After 1969

The Malaysian state has demonstrated its capacity for effective governance and economic development, and it has held its own in maintaining position in the international system. Its characteristics are those that combine contested elections—albeit held in highly unequal electoral units with very divergent constituencies—with the means available for strong executive action. Quite draconian measures remain at the ready to ensure order. Conceptions of basic rights differ substantially from the liberal model of governance and the value of individualism. In recent years, evidence and arguments have appeared to raise seriously the question of tendencies toward a predatory state; that question is bound up with development strategy and the pressures of neoliberalism as well as of corruption and cronyism within Malaysia.

Regular contested elections form one of the central institutions in Malaysia, for even though opposition parties have almost no chance to accumulate enough power to win, their participation in campaigning pressures the ruling BN coalition to debate the issues (Crouch 1996, p. 75). At the same time, the government has in its hands a variety of political controls that can be used not only to maintain order but also to obstruct the opposition. These controls include: emergency powers given by the constitution; detention without trial allowed by the Internal Security Act; the Sedition Act, which is used to "inhibit discussion of some of the country's most controversial political issues" (Crouch 1996, p. 83); the Official Secrets Act, which disallows publication of government documentation; licensing of newspapers; and other mechanisms to control labor unions, middle-class organizations, and university students. Beyond these tools, the government has incrementally developed additional layers of authoritarianism, usually in emergencies. Following the May 1969 riots, the government acting through the king suspended the constitution and Parliament and postponed elections in two provinces that had been scheduled for late May. Furthermore, the government transferred administrative powers during the emergency, which lasted a year and a half, to a "National Operations Council [which] consisted of the heads of the police, the armed forces, the public service, and the foreign service, plus three political leaders ... representing UMNO, ... MCA, and ... MIC" (Means 1991, p. 8). The government then promulgated an official ideology called the *Runkunegara*, based on five principles: belief in God, loyalty to king and country, dedication to the Constitution, adherence to the rule of law, and good behavior and morality (Means 1991, pp. 12–13). Before ending emergency rule, the government promulgated amendments to the Constitution "that were formulated '... to remove sensitive issues from the realm of public discussions...'" and to the Sedition Ordinance, making it an offence 'to question ... ' [matters dealing with] rights of citizenship; Malay special rights; the status and powers of Malay rulers; the status of Islam [as the official religion]; and the status of Malay as the sole National language. The new amendments also prohibited any act, speech, or publication that had a 'tendency to produce feelings of ill-will and enmity between different races....' (Means 1991, p. 13)

As a function of the emergency, thus, the government permanently had acquired additional powers that included the ability under the Internal Security Act to detain anyone "who might create public unrest or who might become a 'threat to internal security'" (Means 1991, pp. 15–16). These governmental mechanisms to control independent sources of power in society were supplemented in 1981 with the passage of amendments to the Societies Act under which groups could be removed from the register of allowed associations if they challenged the government, Islam or other religions, the national language, the special position of the Bumiputeras, or other legitimate communities (Means 1991, p. 85).

Although powers of suppression remain important tools to be invoked under extraordinary circumstances, the Malaysian government also follows policies to promote desired activities and to regulate undesirable ones. For example, as Islamic revival movements grew in the 1970s, the government extended its official sponsorship to approved *dakwah* (religious worship) organizations and placed unauthorized *dakwah* organizations under surveillance, holding in reserve the power to proscribe the latter (Means 1991, p. 72). For the most part, cultural leadership by the government was limited to the Malay, Islamic, Bumiputera portion of the citizenry. As Means (1991, pp. 130–131) notes, this emphasis and in particular the religious aspect tended to erode the legitimacy of governing institutions and ordinary processes of decision making and conflict resolution.

Criticism and initiatives from outside the government tend to be welcomed if done on a discrete private basis. On the other hand, it has become almost impossible to hold a broad public discussion on important issues of any kind—not just those dealing with sensitive national, linguistic, ethnic, and religious matters—because of licensing of the press and the Official Secrets Act. The former provides that both domestic and foreign media must be licensed on an annual basis. By including all information shared between officials, the latter covers all government activities (Means 1991, p. 139).

Prime Minister Mahathir Mohamed has considerably narrowed the scope for open public debate by introducing a style of governance characterized by bilateral negotiations rather than by broader debates and compromises. In addition, in the mid-1980s he also was able to reduce considerably the power of the traditional rulers and to emasculate the courts. As a ruthless political leader ready to employ all of the considerable means available, Mahathir "made himself the decisive arbiter of most of the major pending issues of politics" (Means 1991, p. 214). During the economic crisis of 1997 to 1998 when his heir apparent Anwar Ibrahim disagreed with him on economic strategy, Mahathir brought down his wrath on Anwar by sacking him from the position of deputy prime minister and bringing against him charges of both corruption and sodomy.

The political system that has evolved, then, relies on political patronage, unidirectional leadership of public opinion without broad debate, suppression, and bilateral political deals between the prime minister and partners isolated from others. Although the system produces a facade of unity, it also contains, as Means points out (1991, p. 306), "an implicit recognition of the potentially low level of legitimacy which supports the country's political institutions and its leaders."

What has held the system together and made it function effectively are the economic development strategies that have been followed under the New Economic Policy (NEP) since 1970. These have operated consistently with the principle of favoring the interests of Bumiputeras; indeed, they have often been referred to as a program of positive affirmative action. Thus the economy of Malaysia cannot possibly lend itself to a neoliberal interpretation, for the political and social agenda, to an exceptional degree, drives the economic one. Furthermore, economic prosperity supports the political system. Consequently, Malaysia offers an example of a developmental but not a liberal state.

In the face of economic crisis that occurred in 1997 to 1998 and political crisis associated with the ouster of Anwar in 1998 some intertwined questions arise. First, is it possible that the split in the ruling party will result in liberalization of political life and diminution of authoritarianism? A short-run answer to that turns out to be negative (Hwang 2000). Second, will the economic development strategy designed to serve mainly Bumiputera interests be able to sustain a growing economy within a developmental state, or will such economic programs as privatization be mired in cronyism, to be followed by descent into a predatory state? Above these questions looms the large social question of Malaysia of whether the society will evolve in the direction of multiracialism and egalitarianism, or will it continue to be characterized by the divisions of race?

The Malaysian Economy

Like many other countries, Malaysia has a broad national project that aims at economic development. Since moving from its colonial status, Malaysia has sought to industrialize; explicitly, the leadership laid out the objective of becoming a newly industrializing country first and then adopted the goal of becoming a developed country in the first quarter of the twenty-first century. In addition, Malaysia has attempted to redistribute wealth in such a way as to alleviate and end poverty, to ensure the dominant position of Bumiputeras, to maintain social peace, and to achieve an egalitarian and just society based on the principles of its official ideology, *Runkunegara*. Thus in Malaysia the two essential economic functions of the state, production and distribution, stand out with such transparency that one cannot mistake the political and state components of the national economy. Neither are the economic functions isolated in any conscious way from the overall political and social context. Stark neoliberalism does not apply; yet Malaysia, while acting to protect its autonomy, has linked itself fully with the international economy and with the dominant coalition that manages the international system.

The composition of the economy has changed over time. At independence, the economy exported mostly primary products, and its industrialization strategy was characterized by import substitution. In the following phase, Malaysia launched a combined import substitution/industrial export strategy, with growth driven by public investments, added labor, and foreign direct investment that brought accompanying technology. Malaysia's drive for developed country status has led to striving for an increasingly national economic base, an indigenous research and development capacity, growth driven by increased productivity, the export of national products both goods and services, and a bit of Malaysian investment in other countries.

Malaysia's thrust toward developed country status has been marked by indicative planning throughout, but the leadership has pointed the country in directions that have emphasized, at different times, all of the contributing components of economic growth. These include indigenous savings and investment, both public and private enterprise, education and training, foreign investment of both portfolio and direct types, and the promotion of trade and quest for financial resources and knowledge. To describe the main ingredients and evolution of Malaysia's economic development, the following description deals with (1) phases of the New Economic Plan (NEP), (2) broad development strategies, (3) industrialization policies, (4) foreign investment, and (5) acquisition of technology and promotion of proprietary knowledge.

Beginning in 1970 the country followed the NEP, which was designed to improve the situation of Bumiputeras in two ways: it aimed to reduce and eventually eliminate poverty, and it aspired to acquire for Bumiputeras 30 percent of the ownership of the country's wealth by 1990. Although the specific targets were not met, the Malaysian economy grew between 1971 and 1990 at an annual rate of 8.7 percent. That rate of growth led to "rapid improvements in poverty alleviation and restructuring of the society as well as raising the standard of living of all Malaysians (Malaysia, *Seventh Malaysia Plan 1996*, p. 5). Per capita income in the same period rose from RM1106 to RM9786. Still, the Bumiputera share of equity in publicly listed companies was 18 percent in 1983, 19 percent in 1990, and then 18 percent in 1992 (Jomo 1994, p. 1). Having fallen quite far short of the redistribution goals set twenty years earlier, the government shifted its emphasis from public acquisition of shares on behalf of Bumiputeras to education and training as mechanisms for raising the position of Malayans in the economy. Having previously emphasized increasing the capacity of educational institutions and access for all, in the mid-1990s Malaysian planners aimed to upgrade quality, particularly in science and technology (Malaysia, *Seventh Malaysia Plan 1996*, p. 329). In addition to training, the Seventh Plan aimed to employ institutions of higher education as instruments of consultancy to industry and to empower them to commercialize research findings (Malaysia, *Seventh Malaysia Plan 1996*, pp. 332–334).

Sloane (1999) indicates that the effects of the NEP have worked in the context of entrepreneurship more as an instrument for identity formation among its Bumiputera beneficiaries than it has as a blueprint or set of behaviors for business. She describes the merger of Vision 2020 with public Islam, shaped by both national politics and cultural evolution, which has produced both individual and community identities and an ideology that justifies the power position of the Bumiputera as determined by state policies.

Broad development strategies are generally characterized as import substitution or export-oriented industrialization. These directions are never exclusive, and one of the main challenges for developing countries lies in the area of integrating them by linking local economic activity with those segments connected with international markets. That is to say, a national economy may have a single structure, in which ISI and EOI combine to enhance wealth, or a dual structure, in which ISI serves only the domestic market and EOI serves only the international one. Despite its export orientation that predates the European colonial experience, Malaysia still faces the challenge of integrating its economy, for the post-independence period has seen the development of a dual structure (Drabble 2000, p. 239).

Another aspect of broad development strategies entails moving from reliance on the extraction of raw materials and growing of agricultural products to processing of those commodities. The next move leads to both light and heavy manufacturing. For developing countries, the shift to manufacturing often relies on foreign direct investment and technology. From there, the developing country seeks to sustain investment from its own savings and to develop its own base for technical innovation. Another step leads up a ladder of increasingly sophisticated and diverse industrialization. Another involves the growth of the service sector so that it occupies an increasingly larger segment of the national economy.

All of these components form parts of overall development from a less developed to an industrializing economy to the ranks of the developed countries. For Malaysia, these major stages form part of the leadership and mass consciousness. Aspirations to ascend the ranks of modern economies have formed part of the national mission since independence. It was in 1991 that Vision 2020 was announced. This vision, which is widely and popularly shared in Malaysia, aims to achieve developed country status by the year 2020. Achievement of that goal relies primarily on industrialization policies.

In its early years after independence Malaysia followed policies of import substitution but then shifted to an export-led growth strategy in the 1970s that relied to a large extent on sales of primary commodities. Increasingly, manufacturing has gained larger shares of total exports until the manufacturing sector accounted for "about one-third of GDP and more than three-quarters of merchandise exports" (Malaysia, *Seventh Malaysia Plan 1996*, p. 5). Two types of export-oriented industries developed after 1970: resource-based processing of primary commodities and nonresource-based manufacturing consisting largely of electrical and electronic components, much carried on in Free Trade Zones (Jomo 1993, p. 26). Although the first type has obviously developed on the basis of integration of the domestic and export contributors, the latter type forms one side of a dual manufacturing sector, with the "ISI sector producing for the domestic market almost entirely separate from the export-oriented industries in the EPZs" (Jomo 1993, p. 38).

Even while growth continued in the traditional electronic and electrical machinery and apparel and garment industries, Malaysia moved its industrialization policy in another direction in the early 1980s by investing in ISI-directed heavy industries. These included petrochemicals, automobiles, and iron and steel. Increasing government debt to finance these industries, together with some failures in these state-owned enterprises, led to a new emphasis on the private sector, beginning with the concept of "Malaysia Incorporated" introduced in 1983 to foster increased "collaboration between the public and private sectors" (Malaysia, *Seventh Malaysia Plan 1996*, p. 5).

In 1985 the government published an Industrial Master Plan designed to accelerate industrial development, and a Second Industrial Master Plan was promulgated in 1995. "The strategies adopted in the [first] Plan rapidly transformed the industrial sector into one with a broader base and greater sophistication" (Malaysia, *Seventh Malaysia Plan 1996*, p. 5), but it did so largely on the basis of extensive growth, that is, adding investments and components to production facilities. In contrast, the second plan indicates that the economy needs to move into a new phase of industrialization based more on high technology and knowledge-based industries. A quite visible aspect of this phase is the project called the Multi-media Super Corridor, which is designed to attract computer-related industries to Malaysia in order to reproduce a "Silicon Valley" phenomenon.

In promoting these industrialization goals, the government recognizes the ongoing need to provide infrastructure and increased education and training. At the same time, planning documents as well as academic commentators note the continuing problems and challenges. Drawing on government studies, for example, Edwards and Jomo (1993) point to five major problems: technological dependency, shortages of engineers and technicians, incentive-scheme deficiencies, lack of private sector initiative, and constraints from the NEP. The *Second Industrial Master Plan* (1996, p. 3), reflects not only awareness of such problems but also the shift in the NEP after 1990 and the need for flexibility in the face of change. It emphasizes clustering, which refers to the attempt to "enhance greater linkages between and within subsectors" and to "strengthen economic linkages ... through the further development and expansion of intermediate and supporting industries as well as to address the issue of high imports of intermediate and capital goods." The plan also stresses the aspiration to improve human resources and to strengthen indigenous R&D capability.

Although Malaysia clearly follows a strategy of integrating its economy in the international economy (Malaysia, *Seventh Malaysia Plan 1996*, p. 284), officials and observers recognize the weaknesses especially in indigenous R&D, the duality of the economy, and the need for strengthening both the quantity and quality of human resources. Indigenous research and development capabilities form an especially important ingredient of long-term development.

Amsden (2001, pp. 271–272 and Table 9.13) draws a sharp distinction between those countries that "buy" and those that "make" technology. Malaysia employs a broad strategy to try to transform its reliance on technology transfer from foreign firms to an indigenous R&D base. Thus the objective is to move from a buying economy to a making one. As pointed out by Jomo and Felker (1999), many obstacles stand in the way. In Malaysia itself, "most important is a relatively low level of skills" (Jomo and Felker 1999, p. 9); in addition, "the local technological base is remarkably shallow" (Felker 1999, p. 99). Furthermore, the knowledge needed to reach the goal of a fully developed country is proprietary knowledge (Amsden 2001), and multinational firms that have it are inclined not to share (Jomo and Felker 1999, p. 29). In addition, the general thrust of trading policy from the advanced countries aims to protect such knowledge under the rubric of intellectual property rights. Felker (1999, pp. 136–138) urges upon Malaysia a "highly internationalist 'Singapore-style' FDI-reliant industrial policy" and the use of its "bargaining leverage ... [to] accelerate the *indigenization* of technological capabilities without permanently alienating foreign capital." Lall (1999, p. 150) stresses that both local industry and MNC affiliates need to "'deepen'" their technological activity. As these arguments indicate, Malaysia faces the need to rely upon foreign investment but also the requirement to build its own indigenous strength if it hopes to compete in the long run in the international political economy to hold or enhance its position in the international system.

At the same time, one of the main reasons for acquiring and creating technology is that technology contributes to the productivity of the economy. A country's economy can grow by means of extensive development, that is, by adding factors of production, capital and labor, more machines and more workers. To move the economy toward increased productivity per unit of production factors, however, usually requires more efficiency, a good deal of which is added by technology. Although there is no direct means of measuring productivity, an approximation is provided by total factor productivity (TFP). The Malaysian Economic Planning Unit (Malaysia, *Seventh Malaysia Plan 1996*, p. 37 and Table 2–1) estimates TFP by applying the Cobb-Douglas Production Function, which subtracts from output growth the portion of growth that is accounted for by increases in capital and labor. By this estimate, productivity contributed 17.9 percent of the total 6.7 percent growth from 1971 to 1990 and 28.7 percent of the 8.7 percent growth from 1991 to 1995. The EPU projected TFP to contribute 41 percent of output growth expected during the Seventh Plan's five-year period beginning in 1996.

Although domestic educational, managerial, and innovative factors make an important contribution to such productivity gains, foreign direct investment remains a significant source of technology. In addition, FDI remains crucial to economic growth as a whole, which underlies Malaysia's power and position in the international system. Even though FDI will persist, as it does even in the most advanced industrial countries, the transition to developed status requires an indigenous industrial base of all the components of economic production: land, labor, capital, and technology. Over the long run, the ratio of domestic capital formation to FDI needs increasingly to be weighted in favor of the former.

The evidence concerning this trend is mixed. In the context of the NEP in which the government acquired corporate equity assets on behalf of the Bumiputera, the share of corporate equity held by foreigners fell "from 61.7 per cent to 24.6 per cent" from 1971 to 1988. At the same time, however, "foreign equity in the Malaysian corporate sector [rose] from M\$4.0 billion in 1971 to M\$24.1 billion in 1988" (Ariff

1991, p. 109). Ariff (1991, p. 110) further notes that wholly foreign-owned projects accounted in 1989 "for 48.8 percent of total approved capital investment, compared with" the wholly Malaysian-owned share of only 7.9 percent, leading him to conclude that "it is thus clear that foreign investment is playing an increasingly important role in the Malaysian economy." Part of the boom in foreign investment in the late 1980s may be attributed to the realignment of exchange rates through the Plaza Accord in 1985 (Yokoyama and Tamin 1991, p. 8).

Continuing to rely on foreign capital, the expanding Malaysian economy increased its investments which stood at 45.5 percent of GNP in 1995 (Malaysia, Ministry of Finance 1996, p. 31). In addition, Malaysia's planners worked to reduce the importation of capital and intermediate goods as components of the manufacturing sector and to increase local sources of such goods. Foreign direct investment rose as a portion of domestic capital formation from about 8 percent in the 1980s to "around 20 per cent by early 1990s. In terms of foreign equity share in manufacturing, it was estimated to be around 40 per cent in 1985, ... and 64.3 per cent in 1990 (Osman-Rani 1996, p. 22). By the mid-1990s, "foreign firms accounted for over 45 per cent of total manufacturing value added and they accounted for over three-quarters of total manufactured exports" (Athukorala 1998b, Ch. 8).

Still, the trend from the early 1990s until the onset of the 1997–1998 financial crisis inclined in favor of Malaysia's aspiration to become a fully developed economy. According to figures provided by the Malaysian Industrial Development Authority, in 1991 FDI formed 57.05 percent of investments in manufacturing, and this fell to 44 percent in 1997 (United States, Department of State 1998, 2002). Those proportions shifted significantly in 1999 when the foreign share of investment rose to 75 percent, as Malaysian domestic investment was drastically reduced as a result of the financial crisis. Signs of recovery appeared in the 2000 figures in which foreign investment had been lowered to 60 percent of total investment (United States, Department of State 2002). Recovery of the trend toward increasing Malaysian and diminishing foreign investment cannot be established by available data, although the will to do so is exhibited in Malaysian documents (Malaysia, Ministry of International Trade and Industry 2002).

At the same time, the high rate of domestic savings, which rose from about 27 percent in the second half of the 1980s to over 37 percent by the mid-1990s, underpinned Malaysia's high investment rate without incurring massive foreign debts, even while its gross domestic investment of over 40 percent in the mid-1990s and the difference between savings and investment was filled largely by FDI (Athukorala 2001, p. 17).

On the whole, then, Malaysia possesses a mature, robust, and diversified economy with many strengths and essentially secure fundamentals in its economic policies. At the same time, it remains somewhat dependent on the importation of capital and intermediate goods. To achieve its goal of becoming a full-fledged industrial and developed country, it has a variety of problems to overcome, but these tend to be faced forthrightly by the leadership and people.

Autonomy and Vulnerability

Malaysia responds to, uses, and resists globalization pressures. Although the pressures are many, in the post-Cold War period those most prominent may be expressed as political, economic, and social or cultural. There have been some major tendencies in the political realm. First, the dominant liberal international coalition led by the United States has attempted to manage the international system through interventions in unstable and fragmenting weak countries, often through multilateral, United Nations-sponsored peacekeeping forces. Malaysia has proven itself a committed supporter of this effort by contributing troops to every single post-Cold War, United Nations peacekeeping operation. In late 2001 the government moved decisively against international terrorists within the country's borders.

The second political tendency was the pressure against nationalism by which the leading states and the international institutions they employ promote a neoliberal agenda aimed at erasing national control over economic policy. In this realm, Malaysia held its own by rejecting assistance from the International Monetary Fund in the 1997–1998 financial crisis and adopting a national policy to set up a currency control board to manage foreign investment, especially hot money. In addition, Prime Minister Mahathir was often outspoken in his distinctive views about international developments. Malaysia also maintained contacts with other countries that hold independent political positions in the world. For example, Mahathir has long trumpeted a special relationship with Japan, and Malaysia has been in the forefront of maintaining and expanding the Association of Southeast Asian Nations. The country has continued to nurture ties with other Islamic countries; in 2003 Malaysia assumed the chairmanship of the Organization of the Islamic Conference and hosted its summit meeting.

When the 1997–1998 financial crisis drove many desperate workers from neighboring countries to more prosperous Malaysia, the government acted decisively and effectively to control its borders and to oust illegal immigrants. Within the country, distinctive national characteristics of language and customs are maintained; the official ideology of *Runkunegara* combined with suppression of dissent ensure unity; national symbols and the shared aspiration of achieving developed country status reinforce the sense of identity; and policies promote national coherence and direction. It is difficult in the context of these many indicators of national cohesion to envisage Malaysia's succumbing to anti-nationalist pressures and losing its national identity. At the same time, the country stands as an exemplar of interstate cooperation in building a more orderly, stable world.

Economic globalization pressures mainly fall under the rubrics of trade, investment, and finance. Developing countries such as Malaysia face pressures under the trade regimes of the General Agreement on Tariffs and Trade and the World Trade Organization to reduce protective subsidies and tariffs, to specialize according to comparative advantage, and to allow foreign goods to enter the domestic market on a freely competitive basis. At the same time, these pressures take place within a context in which the powerful countries follow their own interests in maintaining selected protective subsidies and tariffs to shield their own producers. For the most part, Malaysia has championed free trade by insisting that the United States and other rich countries adhere to the same free trade principles that they advocate and not add nontrade-related conditions such as environmental, labor, and human rights considerations to the trade agenda. In this contentious arena, each country looks out for itself, extending cooperation for advantage but also remaining committed to giving priority to the welfare of its own citizens.

With regard to investment, Malaysia has welcomed foreign investment, but it has been sufficiently diversified that no single country has gained dominance. For example, in 1989, 35 percent of FDI came from newly industrializing countries, with 24 percent from the European Community, 20 percent from Japan, and 6 percent from the United States (Lindblad 1998, p. 26, Table 2.3). In addition to garnering FDI for the purposes of building its industrial base and creating jobs, Malaysia seeks to acquire technology in order to form a base and then build up an autonomous research and development capacity. Although forming a logical and functional aspiration, the country has fallen short so far; the task of putting this essential pillar of autonomy into place, however, remains a critical priority.

Portfolio investment not only does not carry with it the potential for technology acquisition but also has the defect of volatility. The United States and the international financial institutions have exerted tremendous pressure on the less developed countries, particularly the emerging markets of which Malaysia is one, to open their economies to the free flow of finance. As the crisis of 1997–1998 showed, the massive flows of money that can be tapped as a resource for promoting economic growth can be withdrawn at a moment's notice and cause deep contraction and immense hardship. In the Asian crisis' turmoil, Malaysia was certainly injured, but the government did eventually establish a currency board to control the flow of foreign exchange, and it imposed controls on the flow of hot money, imposing a tax on funds that were withdrawn over short periods of time. Again, the country exhibited its ability to act autonomously, even in the vortex of a major world crisis. Continued strengthening of its banking and regulatory systems promise to assist in retaining that autonomy while also attracting FDI.

By drawing on the assets of the rest of the world to assist it in developing economically, Malaysia has succeeded to a large extent in promoting growth, alleviating poverty, redressing social inequalities, and acquiring the means for self-sustaining growth. As long as the country can continue to draw advantages from cooperation with others, it will be able to maintain its position. At the same time, the quest for autonomy and strength remain central to the national project, for the need to acquire capital and technology as well as to sell products implies a vulnerability to trends in the world over which the country exerts no control. This continued quest for autonomy in the context of vulnerability may be expected to characterize the country's economic position for the indefinite future, although success may be measured by gains in autonomy and reduction in vulnerability as well as increases in wealth.

Social and cultural pressures of globalization cover a substantial range, from air travel and hotel luxury and rich standards of living for the few to the more clichéd manifestations of popular culture in entertainment, food, music, and other dimensions. Undoubtedly, world standards have penetrated Malaysia as they have other countries. Simultaneously, with a distinctive culture, language, ethnic composition, traditions, and manners, Malaysia absorbs and adapts the cosmopolitan trends. Japan, a country buffeted by global pressures since the mid-nineteenth century, has remained distinctive culturally even while absorbing as much from others as any country has ever done. Malaysians may be expected to follow a similar path, perhaps even, as the Japanese have done, contributing some of their distinctive cultural traits to the global mix. The following section assesses the prospects for achieving Malaysia's economic ambitions and considers alternative lines along which Malaysia might develop its social and political life.

Future Prospects, Future Directions

Malaysia brought to independence several legacies. First, the traditional method of rule through an inherited aristocracy was carried forward and even enhanced in the *Agong* arrangement by which one of the rulers serves temporarily as king. Second, the colonial legacy—which featured top-down rulership, indirect rule, and a politics that served the interests of the elite before providing for citizens—had set a pattern for the ensuing independent state elites. Third, the Japanese occupation and the emergency that developed afterwards left a legacy of emergency laws that not only remained in force but that also offered a precedent upon which further to tighten the security laws that allowed further suppression of oppositions.

Although political bargaining and regulated elections brought a modicum of democratic character to the Malaysian political system, the suppressive features remained as most prominent. Ordinary debate about the most important matters of Malaysian society is forbidden, and nothing like a free press is allowed to operate. Added to these attributes, the strong personality of Prime Minister Mahathir made its mark on the authoritarian character of the state. In particular, the courts were undermined in the 1980s, and the absence of an independent judiciary enabled Mahathir to crush his previously designated successor, Anwar Ibrahim, by sustaining in the courts his charges of corruption and sodomy, when it appears that the matter was one of policy difference. In a free society, such policy differences would have been handled in debate and political processes.

Mahathir has now been succeeded by another prime minister, Abdullah Badawi. However, the prime minister's personality is the only contributing component to the authoritarian legacy that will inevitably change. With the traditional aristocracy, colonial, and emergency measures components, only an exceptional political leader is likely to counter and reverse, rather than employ, the tools that the political system gives him or her.

Despite the opening provided to opposition forces by the electoral and parliamentary system, the restrictions on speech and press will make it very difficult for an opposition to mount a successful campaign to strengthen democracy. In addition, the strongest opposition in recent years has come from the fundamentalist Islamic party, PAS, which seems unlikely to ride to power on a steed of pluralist democracy. Thus the most probable future for the Malaysian political system will retain the mixture of restriction, limited debate, and elections. That political system has been able, on the whole, to maintain social peace, to secure the country against threats, to promote a clear sense of national identity and common purpose, and to promote prosperity and equity.

Although other matters could conceivably disrupt the continuation of this successful system, the most probable cause of sustaining it lies in the continued strength of the economic system. If Malaysia retains the character of a developmental state, successfully promoting economic growth and equity, the political system is likely to last, even though there appears to be little hope for increased democracy and freedom. On the other hand, should the country move in the direction of a predatory state, then it is likely that the political system would also move toward a greater degree of authoritarianism.

Economic development tends to be heavily influenced by history. Thus once a country is launched on a course it tends to follow that trajectory. Naturally, as with any human enterprise, economic development can falter and tendencies can be reversed. In the case of Malaysia, economic development rests on a centuries-long tradition of production and trading for export. Since 1970 under the NEP, the country's development has been characterized by a strong state sector that promotes both growth and equity, seeks foreign investment and technology, contributes to the formation of human capital, and stimulates a very high level of domestic savings and investment. In the 1980s, the government shifted policy in the direction of privatization and away from state-owned enterprise.

Some critics have noted that elements of cronyism, nepotism, and favoritism have crept into the government-private nexus. Still, none has found evidence of the deep corruption characteristic of predatory states. At the same time, the government retains its role of indicative planning, and it intervenes to protect the national economy, as it did in creating a currency board during the 1997–1998 crisis. Thus it does not seem likely that Malaysia will veer very far off course from its historical tendency to maintain some combination of developmental state and a measure of reliance on the private sector to promote economic development. No imminent threat of turning the country into a predatory state seems to lurk.

Malaysia seems on track to achieve developed country status, if not by 2020, then not long after. Nonetheless, within the context of a developmental state, some weaknesses are apparent. A glaring one is the low level of indigenous research and development capacity needed to move toward adequate autonomy in technology and innovation. Another lies in a contradiction of educational policy in which a national aspiration to become a regional center of information technology and services is disserved by the policy of promoting education in *Bahasa Malaya* rather than in English. At the same time, building a massive airport to serve the Southeast Asian region and the Multi-media Super Corridor contribute a substantial base to the regional center aspiration.

A last major consideration for the future of Malaysia lies in the social realm in which tensions exist between race consciousness and privilege, on the one hand, and multiculturalism and equality. The major racial divisions among Malay, Chinese, and Indian have a one-hundred-year history and are thus ensconced in the society and politics. Moreover, Malayan fear of being overwhelmed provides a basic driving force that perpetuates race consciousness and is likely to continue to do so for the indefinite future. In response to that fear but also in consideration of the multiracial character of the country, the constitution embeds a privileged position for Malays while also extending fundamental protection to others. In response to the turmoil of May 1969, the Malayan privileged position was further reinforced by the national ideology. Beginning with the inauguration of the NEP the privileges of Malays have been extended to and enhanced by economic policy. Both party politics under *Barisan Nasional* and governmental policy, as well as political favoritism, add to these institutional props of privilege for the Malays. All of these establish a formidable edifice that seems unlikely to be dismantled.

The only apparent direction in which social policy might go is that of intensifying the privileged position of Malays should a fundamentalist Islamic party achieve power. As in the rest of the Islamic world, piety and custom have grown in Malaysia since the 1970s. Should the PAS ever come to national power in the context of a renewed Islamic resurgence and install *shari'a*, the privileged position of Malays would grow. Whether such a development would risk economic advance and the secure position of Malaysia in the world is difficult to foresee, but the question has to be asked. Had Anwar Ibrahim followed the trajectory envisaged for him before his downfall, it is likely that both economic development within globalized liberalism and an enhanced consciousness and practice of Islam would have occurred. Such a course might still be possible under his intellectual successors, but no basis for such a conjecture now exists. In addition, of course, it is impossible to forecast the direction of globalization.

Conclusion

As it is for any country, the future for Malaysia is uncertain. Nevertheless, authoritarianism tempered by elections and an elite bargaining political system seems likely to persist. The state is unlikely to stray from the path of promoting economic growth and equity for citizens. Economic development has such a strong base that it also seems likely to continue, absent a worldwide downturn of severe dimensions. Similarly, the base for the socially privileged position of Malays remains so deep and firm that radical change seems most unlikely. These characteristics have produced considerable wealth and strength in the past, and the country may be expected to continue to gain in the future. Malaysia remains quite vulnerable to larger powers and to international economic trends, but it also has considerable autonomy. That autonomy is more likely than not to grow in the future. Given its special characteristics, the country, its government, and its people seem destined to absorb modern and foreign influences, but they will do so in peculiarly Malaysian ways. It is beyond the imagination to conceive that the country will be absorbed in a globalized homogeneity. Thus, even while participating in globalization and drawing on the resources of the rest of the world, Malaysia may be expected to remain a strong autonomous state in charge of its own destiny.

12
Summary and Conclusion: Globalization and States

Introduction

In recent years, globalization has become a fashionable term used to characterize the increased connections that continue to grow across the world. Globalization is sometimes regarded as an inevitable phenomenon in which a fundamental transformation is occurring: the foundation of political economy is being shifted from a state-based to a market- and other nonstate-entity-based one. Observers often attribute inevitability to a technological cause; if the process stems from technological change, then it cannot be resisted. In this perspective there is no vision of what might replace the state-based system, only a vague notion that states will lose power and that other entities will gain power. In another version, inexorable globalizing trends contain a logic requiring a global governance system, possibly one based on a federation of existing states, in which law and administration emanate from a central authority.

This view of historical trends obscures the bedrock of power upon which developments in the world are built. It hides the human agency and policy decisions that have established arrangements within which interactions throughout the world occur. Additionally, this conventional perspective conceals the ideology and mindset of the most powerful shapers of international events. Despite its pretense of an ability to understand the future or its call for a logical solution to what are unforeseeable trends, this outlook also fails to look to the past in order to grasp how present arrangements have come into being.

The argument in this book has stressed the underlying power arrangements, philosophical positions, policy choices, ideological tendencies, and historical antecedents that have shaped the international system. Such an outlook has necessarily acknowledged the indispensability of states for the continued promotion of political cooperation, economic interactions, and suppression of disruptive forces. Instead of fading away, states remain essential to maintaining a stable international system and a prosperous political economy.

There are certain basic ways in which states are critical to globalization. First, the peace and stability that allow relatively free flows of people and commerce across international borders have been created by the military power of states. At the present time, the military domination of the United States provides the fundamental underpinning of stability in the world that enables the extensive and rapid transactions in information, finance, trade, and culture that represent the novel features of globalization. Second, developmental states remain critical to effective participation in the worldwide capitalist order, which drives the achievement of prosperity. Weak states are not in a position to take advantage of investment and trade flows. In addition, secure and prosperous states form the backbone of international cooperation.

Thus the analysis of this book leads to the clear conclusion that continued global cooperation with enhanced connections across national borders relies on strong states. To spread the beneficial effects of globalization to areas that they have hardly touched will rely upon continued military and political stability and the building of strong state institutions within units that are now characterized by weak capacities. Instead of fading away, states will remain essential to further globalization. Rather than diminishing in capacity, states will continue to acquire increased capacities.

Power, Politics, and Globalization

In much of the debate about globalization, politics is treated as a struggle for control of the future direction of an inexorable process of worldwide integration. Such a treatment often has the effect of ignoring the historical politics that put present arrangements in place and the politics of the present in which there is contention over many matters, both among the strong and between individual countries and prevailing norms and power arrangements.

Within the context of many background developments such as the rise of nationalism and democracy as well as the formation and spread of states since the fifteenth century, contemporary arrangements in the world stem from the rise of the United States and its defeat of challengers such as Nazi Germany, Imperial Japan, and the Soviet Union during the twentieth century, along with the decline of traditional powers such as Britain and France. Taking the lead after World War II the United States spearheaded the effort to establish institutions through which cooperative efforts in promoting its ideas and ways of thinking could be pursued. The kernel of American ideology is liberalism, specifically capitalism and democracy. But other ideas drawn from the American way of thinking also contributed to the discourse about ruling and managing the international system. These include pluralism and privatization, universal human rights, global governance, and international community. Stemming from an unexamined liberal consensus, these ideas are regarded by Americans as universal and comprehensive, not simply a set of concepts that exist in a broader array of thinking in the world.

Wedded to immense power, these ideas have gained widespread influence, particularly in the last quarter century or so.

Despite the importance of these liberal views which hardly reflect deeply on it, the state has remained central to the development of globalization. The state is both a coercive apparatus and an organ of deliberation; it provides both the underpinning and the surveillance mechanism for economic activities; and it offers both a focus for identity and the means for individuals and groups to gain freedom within the context of a larger purpose that surpasses individual and particular interests. Consequently, in examining the politics of globalization, one needs to pay extended attention to the state and to the politics that largely gets channeled through states.

There are many definitions of globalization, but the most useful working denotation is that it is a set of pressures emanating largely from the most powerful states with which individual countries need to cope. They have to do so within a system of political economy that is international rather than global and that is managed largely by a liberal coalition of powerful states led by the United States. Every state is constrained, but weaker ones face greater obstacles to their autonomy than stronger ones. Still, choices remain for everyone although always within a context of constraints.

Constraints emanate from power distributions, so the analysis treated distributions between states and markets, among states, and within states. As with any set of human arrangements, those involving globalization can potentially be disrupted or even wrecked. In the early twenty-first century there are no apparent forces that could inflict serious disruption. On the other hand, economic crises and political conflict have at times in human history hit very hard and very fast. The attacks on the United States by lightly armed terrorists provide an object lesson in how quickly events are able to transform perceptions of political situations.

Response to September 11, 2001 Attacks

The destruction of several tall buildings in downtown Manhattan and the severe damage inflicted on the Pentagon on September 11, 2001, by nineteen hijackers commandeering and crashing civilian aircraft formed a dramatic event, killing some 3000 civilians, and constituting a hit against the American economy. Americans were not only stunned but also immediately coalesced in support of one another as citizens in a state that transcended their particular interests and aspirations. Allies in the liberal coalition across the world, recognizing a common interest and shared danger, declared their unity with the leader. In response to the attacks, the United States launched a campaign to suppress the organization Al Qaeda, and to remove the Taliban regime in Afghanistan, which had provided the terrorist unit with a base. At the same time, the United States took action to reorganize and strengthen airline and shipping security, the first by dismantling the privatized passenger screening system and making it a government agency, the second by gaining the cooperation of other countries in inspecting shipments destined for American ports. In addition, new legislation was adopted to reorganize the national government, creating a new Homeland Security Agency, and to provide additional powers to law enforcement agencies. These actions resulted from a revised consciousness of power, of necessary functions of the state, and of the need to regulate private commerce.

At the same time, United States policy was driven by a flawed analysis and unilateral character, expressed in a Manichean rhetoric, that portended long-range difficulties. By casting the conflict as one of good versus evil and declaring a war on terrorism, the American leadership did not employ strategic thinking and political analysis; instead, it treated a nongovernmental organization as a state and did not set appropriate limits to its undertaking. An alternative conceptualization might have regarded Al Qaeda and associated organizations as groups that resist American domination in the Middle East and that aim at ousting liberal coalition influence from the area and at taking over governance of the various states in the region. These organizations might have been thought of as analogous to pirates in the nineteenth century that need to be suppressed, for they represent nonstate wielders of political violence. The Manichean rhetoric that cast others as either "for us or against us" excluded willing allies from consultation and declared a unilateral style that can potentially crack the hegemonic coalition. The unprovoked attack against Iraq in 2003 by the United States and Britain alone placed substantial stress on American relations with allies who did not support the invasion and who proved unwilling to submit to American authority during the occupation. It remains to be seen whether this conquest will remain an exception or whether the United States will in the long term drop its forbearance and employ military force in preventive wars against other foes.

Both situations in Afghanistan and Iraq evidence an inadequate conceptualization of state formation. Two years after the establishment of a central government in Kabul, local warlords ran most of the country and collected most of the taxes. In Iraq, as the successful military operation proceeded it became evident that whatever thought had been given to providing state services was not applied. Thus the Ba'ath government and army were dismantled down through the ranks of civil servants and ordinary soldiers, and public administration, such as it was, was provided largely by the United States military.

What the attacks on the United States and their aftermath bring to the fore is an awareness of the necessity to gain control of violence. Given the openness of the international economy and the greatly lowered costs of transport and communications, there is a need for international collaboration to suppress violence by nongovernmental organizations. That can be done most effectively through combined means of military, intelligence, and police operations by most states. The task is likely to become more manageable as more developmental states are built and ineffective states are transformed to reduce violence within their respective borders, both by suppression and by providing for citizens. Strategic thinking, with political goals and related means kept in mind—rather than Manichean moralistic conceptualizations—will more likely lead to the stability necessary for globalization processes to continue.

In both routine and crisis situations, human beings embroiled in political affairs make choices. With respect to globalization politics there are two especially important kinds of choices to be faced. Individual citizens and their governments choose whether to support specific policies on the grounds of their instrumental utility. One of the concerns that some have for globalization policies involves the instrumental function: citizens support those policies because they are beneficial. Should the policies fail to benefit citizens, they might withdraw their support. The other important kind of choice deals with normative and ethical considerations. Because of rapid communications, information about unfolding disasters is readily and nearly immediately available, so those who wield power have to make responses. Effectiveness in responding leads to popular support.

Management of Globalization

Given the vocabulary in which globalization tends to be discussed, particularly in the United States, it is important to distinguish between world problems and those of specific states. The liberal outlook inclines toward eliding these levels by discussing the views of the hegemonic powers as if they were universal. However, states are fundamentally unequal along four dimensions: material inequality, geographical location, cultural distinctiveness, and divergent vulnerability. When advocating a course of action, for example, the leading powers tend to cast their preferences in terms of the demands or wishes of a world community, but the effects on each country are highly divergent. States use international organizations to achieve coordination of their aims; within those organizations, a rhetoric of norms and commonality assists in achieving such coordination. At the same time, the disinterested observer notes that it is a rhetorical device and not a genuinely common set of interests that is being invoked.

Concurrently, certain areas of common endeavor and concern have become established at the international level. These include environmental concerns, migration, and war and turmoil. Such widespread and relatively common problems provide a focus for the attention of many countries that attempt to coordinate their actions in addressing such matters, even though each country endures such problems in its own way and with particular repercussions. Still, it is important to keep firmly in mind that countries vary; anyone who wishes to understand events and effects needs to recall that each country is unique and that its people are likely to view the common problem in a distinctive way.

Since the end of World War II international affairs have been managed by a hegemonic coalition led by the United States. Its characteristics have been implanted with an American style that can be traced through American history. For purposes of analysis, the arrangements can be thought of as regimes dealing, respectively, with security, trade, finance, and development. The security regime is centered on the United States and North America but has spread to Europe, the Middle East and the Persian Gulf area, to East Asia, and recently to Central Asia. The economic regimes are centered on international institutions, although the direct involvement of the United States in supplementary although consistent action on occasion is also apparent.

Management rests on three pillars: American policy commitment, stability provided by United States military strength, and developmental states with a strong capitalist economic component. Because management of the contemporary world aims at creating wealth through capitalism, human freedom, self-governance through democracy, and participation of citizens in civil society, it gains adherents who aspire to these goals. Such acceptance of the ruling ideology makes management much less difficult than it would otherwise be. Nonetheless, elements of resistance remain in many places.

With acceptance of the goals, people concede authority to political leaders pursuing the coalition's agenda. That authority, however, might be undermined either by power or ideas. Should the United States withdraw from active management or should a challenging state rise to a level of sufficient power to pose an alternative order, authority would disappear from the international realm. Should rightist ideas supporting the domination of the market or leftist ideas in favor of demolishing the state prevail, then globalization as it is understood in the early twenty-first century would come to an end. These are expressions of anti-politics; they might receive a hearing because of liberal tolerance and as a result of misunderstanding of how the world works. To provide insurance that they do not, it would be useful to employ a vocabulary of states, power, public good, and ethics in political discourse.

Developmental States in Globalization

Contemporary liberal thinking seeks to diminish the state, redefine citizenship, and substitute private for public and individual for community activity. It does so by means of neoliberal ideology, utopian assertions of an international community with claims to intervention on humanitarian grounds and assertion of rights not related to citizenship, and practices designed to strengthen individualism and nonstate organizations. Yet the project of globalization requires developmental states to implement it.

Developmental states provide order and security, collect taxes, invest in research and development and education, stop predatory activities in the private sector, and redistribute product among its citizens. In addition, a developmental state performs a number of other economic functions, such as providing a currency, enforcing contracts, and adopting macroeconomic policies. Developmental states do not simply support the economy but also provide a focus for identity of a citizenry, embody public purposes, and ensure security. Developmental states maintain a realm of public good, an arena of public space in which citizens can debate common problems and attempt to achieve a common good. This is what distinguishes them from states with centrally planned economies, and colonized, rentier, and predatory states.

An effective and autonomous state enables a society to participate in the international political economy or to resist pressures emanating from it. Without a strong state, a country will either be neglected by the powers that might otherwise offer it opportunities, or suffer intervention and domination by the same powers that impress their own interests upon it and intrude in its internal affairs.

Officials in developmental states still face tremendous pressures both from other states and from their own societies. These are encompassed analytically in sets of policy imperatives and dilemmas. For example, they face the imperative of strengthening their economies by devising and implementing a development strategy in order to achieve autonomy. To do so requires drawing investments and technology from abroad. Yet investors wish to control their proprietary knowledge and resist strengthening potential competitors. Another dilemma stems from the pressures from international financial institutions for inclusion of non-governmental groups in development and the need to build a strong state that can provide direction for development and override special interests. Developmental states need to build institutions, but they are pressed to emphasize individuals instead. Finally, political leaders need to build strong states in the midst of an international discourse that hardly includes the notion among its array of concepts.

These dilemmas lead to the problem for developing countries both to use opportunities offered by globalization pressures and to resist unwanted constraints. In seeking to follow such a contradictory course, leaders can emulate successful models, including the United States which regularly promotes cooperative action and simultaneously acts unilaterally. Western Europe offers yet another successful model, and Japan and the other East Asian developmental states demonstrate yet a third broad approach to development within the context of international pressures and opportunities. Contemporary China offers another model of successful development, one that includes a high level of nationalism. Furthermore, there is a substantial body of knowledge based on historical experience that points to alternative development strategies within the context of different international conditions.

In working toward economic development, political leaders also have to build their own states. Thus state formation remains essential to the achievement of the quest for wealth. But states have to do many things other than act as part of civil society for purposes of creating and distributing wealth. They must also provide security, order, and diplomacy. In order to command their societies, however, leaders must also build legitimacy. They can do so by ideology, but they also need to be effective in order to gain the consent of their constituents to their rule. These are formidable challenges.

Among the foremost of these challenges is the relationship between state and civil society. Considerable contention forms a debate over the meaning of civil society. One view holds civil society in opposition and an alternative to the state, whereas another regards civil society as an independent grouping in which citizens can debate public policies in a circumscribed arena without the politics of the state entering it. Both sides in this debate treat civil society as an independent force. However, civil society forms a component of the state.

This has become particularly apparent in the post-Cold War period in which advocates believe that a broad international civil society that transcends states is forming. Yet the proliferation of nongovernmental organizations that has occurred in recent years stems from the triumph of liberalism which allows and advocates citizen and group action without government direction. At the same time, the order and security that states provide establish the conditions for the functioning of private groups.

Some have carried the argument further by claiming that the activities of nongovernmental groups contribute to the causes of peace and stability. However, it is clear both from the evidence of such groups' dependency on governments, their nonrepresentative character, and their experiences in such activities as humanitarian relief that they rely for their effectiveness and for much of their existence on states. In addition, the arguments flow from traditional liberal contentions that do not seem warranted.

Establishing conditions of peace remains one of the most important functions of states. Civil society groups can contribute to advocacy and to deliberating in public spaces over ways their states can help to build the conditions, but traditional liberal ideas such as Wilsonian interventionism to instill democracy and liberal peace theory stem essentially from the prior existence of strong states.

In dominant discourses about globalization advocates present facts within ideological frameworks based on assumptions about trends in the world. Most assume that fundamental changes are in progress and that these entail the weakening or demise of the state and the nation as basic institutional means for organizing politics and public life. The right ideological position advocating markets without states remains untenable in the long run. The left approach which urges a strong international civil society would have to be built on a foundation of strong states, a stipulation unlikely to be accepted by advocates of new international identities.

A number of pressures carried forward in the discourses surrounding globalization have weakened the links between individuals and groups and have diminished the public space available for citizen deliberation. In the current discourses of deanchoring individuals, weakening nationalism, and disparaging states, new conceptions of citizenship have arisen. From the right comes a linkage between market-based activities, specifically jobs, and citizenship. From the left comes a variety of notions about cosmopolitan citizenship. Yet all stem from the power position of the dominant liberal coalition and, in particular, the United States. Without the protection of strong states individuals would be left to the wishes of the strong, whether predatory or criminal or simply powerful.

As an alternative to such conditions, I have advocated a broad conception of the state, political action that leads to empowerment, and a model of practical politics that gives a way of forming and reproducing a state. Effective states acting with and on behalf of their citizens and societies can benefit from certain of the globalization trends, but they can also oppose unwanted and undesirable pressures. In doing so, they will not only protect their citizens but will also strengthen their own abilities to participate effectively as autonomous units in the international system. Politics is about choices, and that truism applies to globalization, about which nothing is inevitable.

To illustrate the ways in which the general arguments of the book have worked in practice, I employed a study of Malaysia in particular with some references to other Southeast Asian states. Malaysia has enjoyed some of the advantages of globalization but also suffered some of its unwanted consequences. The history of the country shows insertion in and resistance to the international political economy.

Malaysians have made both good choices and erroneous ones. A survey of its history illustrates both the long-term historical nature of globalization and the new features that have made their appearance only in recent years. Perhaps most importantly, the Malaysian case reveals how basic are security and the state to the society's existence and how these relate to the economy. At the same time, the economy reciprocally affects the politics of the country.

Although much is not known about how the country will develop in the future, its past tends for the most part to illustrate that it works very closely along the lines that compose the argument of this book. Even though Malaysia is closely connected to other countries and depends upon those connections for its well-being and future growth, its strong state has proved essential for achieving the aspirations of its people. It is difficult to imagine that the state would diminish substantially. Yet at the same time the capitalist market remains a tremendous source for the ingredients by which Malaysians hope to build their autonomy and their strength so as to participate even more effectively in the world.

Conclusion

Throughout this extended essay I have criticized the tendency to predict the future and have endorsed attention to history and to actual conditions. Furthermore, my stress has remained on politics and power, specifically as manifested in states as the essential ingredients in globalization. These positions imply that the continuation of globalization requires the continued choice of the major powers, especially the United States, to remain committed to providing the stability required for economic and other peaceful intercourse throughout the world. It also requires that the liberal coalition remain dominant in the world, without a substantial challenger promoting different rules for managing the international system. To extend the benefits of globalization, in addition, requires the strengthening and capacitation of states in areas where they are weak, for production and the myriad activities associated with wealth cannot blossom in insecure and unstable circumstances. Markets are not antithetical to states: the two grow together.

Should states actually diminish, as some globalizers predict and advocate, the result will be the diminution of globalization's benefits and the rise of predators, terrorists, and criminals. Individuals need to have social systems in which to gain protection and scope for growth and development. Only within institutions and systems of power can individuals make major contributions to their societies and, thence, to humankind.

References

Abrahamian, Ervand 1982. *Iran Between Two Revolutions*. Princeton, NJ: Princeton University Press.

Albrow, Martin, and Elizabeth King, eds. 1990. *Globalization, Knowledge, and Society*. London: Sage.

Alias Mohamed 1991. *Malaysia's Islamic Opposition: Past, Represent* [sic] *and Future*. Kuala Lumpur: Gateway.

Amsden, Alice H. 2001. *The Rise of 'The Rest': Challenges to the West from Late-Industrializing Economies*. New York: Oxford University Press.

Arendt, Hannah 1959. *The Human Condition*. Chicago: University of Chicago Press.

Arendt, Hannah 1965. *On Revolution*. New York: Penguin Books.

Arendt, Hannah 1970. *On Violence*. New York: Harcourt, Brace & World.

Ariff, Mohamed 1991. *The Malaysian Economy: Pacific Connections*. New York: Oxford University Press.

Arnold, Wayne 2003. Singapore goes for biotech, *The New York Times*, August 26: W1.

Arts, Bas 2000. Political influence of NGOs on international environmental issues. *Power in Contemporary Politics: Theories, Practices, Globalizations*, edited by Henri Goverde, Philip G. Cerny, Mark Haugaard, and Howard H. Lentner. London: Sage.

Athukorala, Prema-chandra 1998a. Malaysia. *East Asia in Crisis: From Being a Miracle to Needing One?* edited by Ross H. McLeod and Ross Garnaut. London: Routledge.

Athukorala, Prema-chandra 1998b. *Trade Policy Issues in Asian Development*. London: Routledge.

Athukorala, Prema-chandra 2001. *Crisis and Recovery in Malaysia: The Role of Capital Controls*. Cheltenham, UK: Edward Elgar.

Attali, Jacques 1997. The crash of western civilization: The limits of the market and democracy. *Foreign Policy* 107 (Summer): 54–63.

Axelrod, Robert 1984. *The Evolution of Cooperation*. New York: Basic.

Axford, Barrie 1995. *The Global System: Economics, Politics and Culture*. New York: St. Martin's.

Ayoob, Mohammed, 1995. *The Third World Security Predicament: State Making, Regional Conflict, and the International System*. Boulder, CO: Lynne Rienner.

Baginda, Abdul Razak Abdullah, and Rohana Mahmood, eds. 1995. *Malaysia's Defence and Foreign Policies.* Petaling Jaya, Malaysia: Pelanduk.

Barber, Benjamin 1984. *Strong Democracy: Participatory Politics for a New Age.* Berkeley: University of California Press.

Barber, Benjamin 1999. Clansmen, consumers and citizens: Three takes on civil society. *Civil Society, Democracy, and Civic Renewal,* edited by Robert K. Fullinwider. Lanham: Rowman & Littlefield.

Barro, Robert J. 1997. *Determinants of Economic Growth: A Cross-Country Empirical Study.* Cambridge, Mass.: The MIT Press.

Barro, Robert J., and Xavier Sala-i-Martin 1995. *Economic Growth.* New York: McGraw-Hill.

Bauman, Zygmunt 1998. *Globalization: The Human Consequences.* New York: Columbia University Press.

Bauman, Zygmunt 2001. *The Individualized Society.* Cambridge, UK: Polity.

Bellah, Robert N., Richard Madsen, William M. Sullivan, Ann Swidler, and Steven M. Tipton 1985. *Habits of the Heart: Individualism and Commitment in American Life.* Berkeley: University of California Press.

Bennett, Jon, with Mark Duffield, Monika Kathina Juma, John Burton, Alan Burge, and Charlotte Benson 1995. *Meeting Needs: NGO Coordination in Practice.* London: Earthscan.

Berger, Suzanne, and Ronald Dore, eds. 1996. *National Diversity and Global Capitalism.* Ithaca, NY: Cornell University Press.

Berman, Marshall, 1992. Why modernism still matters. *Modernity and Identity,* edited by Scott Lash and Jonathan Friedman. Oxford: Blackwell.

Bhagwati, Jagdish 1998. Poverty and reforms: Friends or foes. *Journal of International Affairs.* Dow Jones Interactive Publications Library. Available at http://nrstg1s.djnr.com/cgi-bin/DJInter.

Bialer, Seweryn 1988. Gorbachev's program of change: Sources, significance, prospects. *Gorbachev's Russia and American Foreign Policy,* edited by Seweryn Bialer and Michael Mandelbaum. Boulder, CO: Westview.

Bobbio, Norberto 1988. Gramsci and the concept of civil society. *Civil Society and the State,"* edited by John Keane. London: Verso, 73–99.

Boroujerdi, Mehrzed 1996. *Iranian Intellectuals and the West: The Tormented Triumph of Nativism.* Syracuse, NY: Syracuse University Press.

Boutros-Ghali, Boutros 1992. *An Agenda for Peace: Preventive Diplomacy, Peacemaking and Peacekeeping.* New York: United Nations.

Boutros-Ghali, Boutros 1995. *An Agenda for Development 1995, with Related UN documents.* New York: United Nations.

Bracken, Paul 2000. The second nuclear age. *Foreign Affairs* 79 (January/February): 146–156.

Bradley, Stephen P., Jerry A. Hausman, and Richard L. Nolan, eds. 1993. *Globalization, Technology, and Competition: The Fusion of Computers and Telecommunications in the 1990s.* Boston: Harvard Business School Press.

Braman, Sandra, and Annabelle Sreberny-Mohammadi 1996. *Globalization, Communication and Transnational Civil Society.* Cresskill, NJ: Hampton.

Brown, Bernard E. 2000. NATO hits a land mine. *American Foreign Policy Interests* 22 (February): 1–15.

Brown, Gary, 1994. *Australia's Security: Issues for the New Century.* Canberra: Australian Defence Studies Centre, Australian Defence Force Academy.

Brown, Michael E., Sean M. Lynn-Jones, and Steven E. Miller, eds. 1995. *The Perils of*

Anarchy: Contemporary Realism and International Security. Cambridge, MA: MIT Press.

Bueno de Mesquita, Bruce, James D. Morrow, Randolph M. Siverson, and Alastair Smith 1999. An institutional explanation of the democratic peace. *American Political Science Review* 93: 791–807.

Bull, Hedley 1977. *The Anarchical Society: A Study of Order in World Politics.* New York: Columbia University Press.

Campbell, Robert 1988. The Soviet economic model. *Gorbachev's Russia and American Foreign Policy*, edited by Seweryn Bialer and Michael Mandelbaum. Boulder, CO: Westview.

Carr, Edward Hallett 1964/1939. *The Twenty Years' Crisis, 1919–1939: An Introduction to the Study of International Relations.* New York: Harper & Row/New York: St. Martin's.

Cerny, Philip G. 2000. Globalization and the disarticulation of power: Towards a new Middle Ages? *Power in Contemporary Politics: Theories, Practices, Globalizations*, edited by Henri Goverde, Philip G. Cerny, Mark Haugaard, and Howard H. Lentner. London: Sage.

Chin Kin Wah 1983. *The Defence of Malaysia and Singapore: The Transformation of a Security System 1957–1971.* Cambridge, UK: Cambridge University Press.

Clegg, Stewart 1989. *Frameworks of Power.* London: Sage.

Cohen, Jean L. 1999. American civil society talk. *Civil Society, Democracy, and Civic Renewal*, edited by Robert K. Fullinwider. Lanham: Rowman & Littlefield.

Cohen, Jean L., and Andrew Arato 1992. *Civil Society and Political Theory.* Cambridge, MA: MIT Press.

Commission on Global Governance 1995. *Our Global Neighborhood: The Report of the Commission on Global Governance.* Oxford: Oxford University Press.

Cox, Robert 1991. The global political economy and social choice. *The New Era of Global Competition: State Policy and Market Power*, edited by Daniel Drache and Meric S. Gertler. Montreal & Kingston: McGill-Queen's University Press.

Cox, Robert W. 1992. Post-hegemonic conceptualization of world order. *Governance Without Government: Order and Change in World Politics*, edited by James N. Rosenau and Ernst-Otto Cziempiel. Cambridge, UK: Cambridge University Press.

Cox, Robert W., with Timothy J. Sinclair 1996. *Approaches to World Order.* Cambridge, UK: Cambridge University Press.

Crossette, Barbara 1997. Agencies say U.N. ignored pleas on Hutu. *The New York Times*, May 28: A3.

Crouch, Harold 1996. *Government and Society in Malaysia.* Ithaca, NY: Cornell University Press.

Cumings, Bruce 1987. The origins and development of northeast Asian political economy: Industrial sectors, product cycles, and political consequences. *The Political Economy of the New Asian Industrialism*, edited by Frederic C. Deyo. Ithaca, NY: Cornell University Press.

Dahl, Robert A. 1957. The concept of power. *Behavioral Science* 2: 201–215.

Darcy de Oliveira, Miguel and Rajesh Tandon, coordinators 1994. *Citizens: Strengthening Global Civil Society.* Washington, DC: CIVICUS, World Alliance for Citizen Participation.

Diamond, Larry 1997. Civil society and democratic consolidation: Building a culture of democracy in a new South Africa. *Subsaharan Africa in the 1990s: Challenges to Democracy and Development*, edited by Rukhsana A. Siddiqui. Westport, CT: Praeger.

Dobbs-Higginson, Michael S. 1994. *Asia Pacific: Its Role in the New World Disorder.* London: Heinemann.

Dollar, David, and Aart Kraay 2000. Growth *is* good for the poor. Preliminary and incomplete paper. Washington, DC: Development Research Group, The World Bank (March).

Dombrowski, Peter 1996. *Policy Responses to the Globalization of American Banking.* Pittsburgh, PA: University of Pittsburgh Press.

Donnelly, Jack 1998. *International Human Rights*, 2nd ed. Boulder, CO: Westview.

Donnelly, Jack 2000. Human rights, security, and the dilemmas of humanitarian intervention: Reflections after Kosovo. *World Order and Peace in the New Millenium*, edited by Tai-joon Kwon and Dong-Sung Kim. Seoul: Korean National Commission for UNESCO.

Dower, John 1986. *War Without Mercy: Race and Power in the Pacific War.* New York: Pantheon.

Dower, John W. 1999. *Embracing Defeat: Japan in the Wake of World War II.* New York: W.W. Norton/ New Press.

Doyle, Michael W. 1983. Kant, liberal legacies and foreign affairs. *Philosophy and Public Affairs* 12, Part 1 (Summer) and Part 2 (Fall).

Doyle, Michael W. 1986. Liberalism and world politics. *American Political Science Review* 80 (December): 1151–1169.

Drabble, John H. 2000. *An Economic History of Malaysia, c. 1800–1990.* Houndsmills, UK: Macmillan Press.

Drèze, Jean, and Amartya Sen 1989. *Hunger and Public Action.* Oxford: Clarendon.

Dunning, John H. 1993. *The Globalization of Business: The Challenge of the 1990s.* London: Routledge.

Durkheim, Emile 1986. *Durkheim on Politics and the State*, edited by Anthony Giddens, translated by W.D. Halls. Cambridge, UK: Polity.

Edwards, Chris, and Jomo K.S. 1993. Policy options for Malaysian industrialization. *Industrializing Malaysia: Policy, Performance, Prospects*, edited by Jomo K.S. London: Routledge.

Ehrenberg, John 1999. *Civil Society: The Critical History of an Idea.* New York: New York University Press.

Ehrlich, Paul R. 1968. *The Population Bomb.* New York: Ballantine.

Eichengreen, Barry 1996. *Globalizing Capital: A History of the International Monetary System.* Princeton, NJ: Princeton University Press.

Eichengreen, Barry, and Peter B. Kenen 1994. Managing the world economy under the Bretton Woods system: An overview. *Managing the World Economy: Fifty Years After Bretton Woods.* Washington, DC: Institute for International Economics.

Evans, Peter 1995. *Embedded Autonomy: States and Industrial Transformation.* Princeton, NJ: Princeton University Press.

Evans, Peter 1997a. The eclipse of the state? Reflections on stateness in an era of globalization. *World Politics* 50 (October): 62–87.

Evans, Peter 1997b. State structures, government-business relations, and economic transformation. *Business and the State in Developing Countries*, edited by Sylvia Maxfield and Ben Ross Schneider. Ithaca, NY: Cornell University Press.

Evans, Peter B., Dietrich Rueschemeyer, and Theda Skocpol 1985. *Bringing the State Back In.* Cambridge, UK: Cambridge University Press.

Featherstone, Mike, ed. 1990. *Global Culture: Nationalism, Globalization and Modernity.* London: Sage.

Featherstone, Mike 1995. *Undoing Culture: Globalization, Postmodernism and Identity.* London: Sage.

Felker, Greg 1999. Malaysia's innovation system: Actors, interests and governance.

Technology, Competitiveness and the State: Malaysia's Industrial Technology Policies, edited by Jomo K.S. and Greg Felker. London: Routledge.

Ferguson, Adam 1995. *An Essay on the History of Civil Society*, edited by Fania Oz-Salzberger. Cambridge, UK: Cambridge University Press.

Finger, J. Michael, and L. Alan Winters 1998. What can the WTO do for developing countries? *The WTO as an International Organization*, edited by Anne O. Krueger, with the assistance of Chonira Aturupane. Chicago: University of Chicago Press.

Finkelstein, Lawrence S. 1995. What is global governance? *Global Governance* 1 (Sept.–Dec.): 367–372.

Friedman, Milton 1969. *The Optimum Quantity of Money and Other Essays*. New York: Aldine de Gruyter.

Friedman, Milton 1982. *Capitalism and Freedom*. Chicago: University of Chicago Press.

Friedman, Thomas L. 1999. *The Lexus and the Olive Tree*. New York: Farrar, Straus, Giroux.

Fukuyama, Francis 1989. The end of history. *The National Interest* 16 (Summer).

Fullinwider, Robert K., ed. 1999. *Civil Society, Democracy, and Civic Renewal*. Lanham: Rowman & Littlefield.

Fuss, Peter 1979. Hannah Arendt's conception of political community. *Hannah Arendt: The Recovery of the Public World*, edited by Melvyn A. Hill. New York: St. Martin's Press.

Gaffaney, Timothy J. 1999. Citizens of the market: The un-political theory of the new right. *Polity* 32 (Winter): 179–202.

Garten, Jeffrey E. 1995. Is America abandoning multilateral trade? *Foreign Affairs* 74 (November/December): 50–62.

Gellner, Ernest 1983. *Nations and Nationalism*. Ithaca, NY: Cornell University Press.

Giddens, Anthony 1987. *The Nation-State and Violence: Volume 2 of A Contemporary Critique of Historical Materialism*. Berkeley: University of California Press.

Giddens, Anthony 1990. *The Consequences of Modernity*. Cambridge, UK: Polity.

Giddens, Anthony 1991. *Modernity and Self-Identity*. Cambridge, UK: Polity.

Gilder, George 1981. *Wealth and Poverty*. New York: Basic.

Gill, Stephen 1997. *Globalization, Democratization and Multilateralism*. London: Macmillan.

Gilpin, Robert 1981. *War and Change in World Politics*. Cambridge, UK: Cambridge University Press.

Gilpin, Robert 1987. *The Political Economy of International Relations*. Princeton, NJ: Princeton University Press.

Gilpin, Robert, with the assistance of Jean Millis Gilpin 2000. *The Challenge of Global Capitalism: The World Economy in the 21st Century*. Princeton, NJ: Princeton University Press.

Gilpin, Robert, with the assistance of Jean M. Gilpin 2001. *Global Political Economy: Understanding the International Economic Order*. Princeton, NJ: Princeton University Press.

Goehler, Gerhard 2000. Constitution and use of power. *Power in Contemporary Politics: Theories, Practices, Globalizations*, edited by Henri Goverde, Philip G. Cerny, Mark Haugaard, and Howard H. Lentner. London: Sage.

Goldstein, Judith, and Robert O. Keohane, eds. 1993. *Ideas and Foreign Policy: Beliefs, Institutions, and Political Change*. Ithaca, NY: Cornell University Press.

Gomez, Edmund Terence, and Jomo K.S. 1997. *Malaysia's Political Economy: Politics, Patronage and Profits*. Cambridge, UK: Cambridge University Press.

Gordenker, Leon, and Thomas G. Weiss 1996. Pluralizing global governance: Analytical approaches and dimensions. *NGOs, the UN, and Global Governance*, edited by Thomas G. Weiss and Leon Gordenker. Boulder, CO: Lynne Rienner.

Gourevitch, Philip 1995. Letter from Rwanda: After the genocide. *The New Yorker*, December 18: 78–94.

Gourevitch, Philip 1998. *We Wish to Inform You that Tomorrow We Will Be Killed with Our Families: Stories from Rwanda.* New York: Farrar, Straus and Giroux.

Gowa, Joanne 1999. *Ballots and Bullets: The Elusive Democratic Peace.* Princeton, NJ: Princeton University Press.

Gramsci, Antonio 1971. *Prison Notebooks.* New York: International.

Green, Miriam, Margaret Grieco, and Len Holmes 2000. Archiving social practice: The management of transport boycotts. Paper presented at the Eighth Asian-Pacific Researchers in Organization Studies (APROS) Colloquium, Sydney, Australia, December 15–17.

Greenfeld, Liah 1992. *Nationalism: Five Roads to Modernity.* Cambridge, MA: Harvard University Press.

Greider, William 1997. *One World, Ready or Not: The Manic Logic of Global Capitalism.* New York: Simon & Schuster.

Grieco, Joseph M. 1988. Anarchy and the limits of cooperation. *International Organization* 42: 485–507.

Habermas, Jurgen 1987. *The Philosophical Discourse of Modernity: Twelve Lectures,* translated by Frederick Lawrence. Cambridge, MA: MIT Press.

Habermas, Juergen 1989. *The Structural Transformation of the Public Sphere: An Inquiry in a Category of Bourgeois Society.* Cambridge, MA: MIT Press.

Habermas, Juergen 1990a. *Moral Consciousness and Communicative Action,* translated by Christian Lenhardt and Shierry Weber Nicholsen. Cambridge, Mass.: MIT Press.

Habermas, Juergen 1990b. Discourse ethics: Notes on a program of a political ethic. *Moral Consciousness and Communicative Action.* Cambridge, MA: MIT Press.

Halinah Bamadhaj 1975. *The Impact of the Japanese Occupation of Malaya on Malay Society and Politics (1941–1945).* University of Auckland, M.A. Thesis in History.

Hann, Chris, and Elizabeth Dunn, eds. 1996. *Civil Society: Challenging Western Models.* London: Routledge.

Harries, Owen 2002. *Understanding America.* St. Leonards, NSW: CIS.

Hartz, Louis 1955. *The Liberal Tradition in America.* New York: Harcourt, Brace, Javonovich.

Haugaard, Mark 1997. *The Constitution of Power: A Theoretical Analysis of Power, Knowledge and Structure.* Manchester: Manchester University Press.

Hayek, Friedrich von 1960. *The Constitution of Liberty.* Chicago: University of Chicago Press.

Hayek, Friedrich von 1979. *Law, Legislation, and Liberty,* 3 vols. London: Routledge and Kegan Paul.

Hayek, Friedrich A. von 1944. *The Road to Serfdom.* Chicago: University of Chicago Press.

Hayek, Friedrich A. von 1972. *A Tiger by the Tail: A 40-Years Running Commentary on Keynesianism.* London: Institute of Economic Affairs.

Hegel, G.W.F. 1952. *Hegel's Philosophy of Right,* translated by T.M. Knox. London: Clarendon.

Heilbroner, Robert L. 1990. The future of capitalism. *Sea-Changes: American Foreign Policy in a World Transformed,* edited by Nicholas X. Rizopoulos. New York: Council on Foreign Relations Press.

Held, David, Anthony McGrew, David Goldblatt, and Jonathan Perraton 1999. *Global*

Transformations: Politics, Economics, and Culture. Stanford, CA: Stanford University Press.

Helleiner, Eric 1994. *States and the Reemergence of Global Finance: From Bretton Woods to the 1990s.* Ithaca, NY: Cornell University Press.

Hirst, Paul, and Grahame Thompson 1996. *Globalization in Question.* Cambridge, UK: Polity Press.

Hoekman, Bernard M., and Michel M. Kostecki 1995. *The Political Economy of the World Trading System: From GATT to WTO.* Oxford: Oxford University Press.

Hoffmann, Stanley 1995. The crisis of liberal internationalism. *Foreign Policy* Number 98 (Spring): 159–179.

Holm, Hans Henrik 1995. *Whose World Order? Uneven Globalization and the End of the Cold War.* Boulder, CO: Westview.

Holmes, Len, and Margaret Grieco 2000. Relational identity and relational technology: Distributed responsibility and action in modern commerce and administration. Paper presented at the Eighth Asian-Pacific Researchers in Organization Studies (APROS) Colloquium, Sydney, Australia, December 15–17.

Holsti, K.J. 1985. *The Dividing Discipline: Hegemony and Diversity in International Theory.* Boston: Allen & Unwin.

Hsiung, James C. 1993. *Asia Pacific in the New World Politics.* Boulder, CO: Lynne Rienner.

Huff, W.G. 1994. *The Economic Growth of Singapore: Trade and Development in the Twentieth Century.* Cambridge, UK: Cambridge University Press.

Hughes, Helen 1985. *Policy Lessons of the Development Experience,* Occasional Papers No. 16. New York: Group of Thirty.

Human Development Report 1997. New York: Oxford University Press for the United Nations Development Programme.

Huntington, Samuel P. 1968. *Political Order in Changing Societies.* New Haven, CT: Yale University Press.

Huntington, Samuel P. 1981. *American Politics: The Promise of Disharmony.* Cambridge, MA: The Belknap Press of Harvard University Press.

Huntington, Samuel P. 1991. *The Third Wave: Democratization in the Late Twentieth Century.* Norman, OK: University of Oklahoma Press.

Huntington, Samuel P., 1993. The clash of civilizations? *Foreign Affairs* 72 (Summer): 22–49.

Huntington, Samuel P. 1996. *The Clash of Civilizations and the Remaking of World Order.* New York: Simon & Schuster.

Huntley, Wade L. 1996. Kant's third image: Systemic sources of the liberal peace. *International Studies Quarterly* 40: 45–76.

Hwang, In-Won 2000. UMNO's factional conflicts and political liberalization in Malaysia. Unpublished draft manuscript.

Ikenberry, G. John 2001. *After Victory: Institutions, Strategic Restraint, and the Rebuilding of Order After Major Wars.* Princeton, NJ: Princeton University Press.

Jackson, Robert H., and Carl Rosberg, 1982. Why Africa's weak states persist. *World Politics* 45 (October).

Jackson, Robert H., and Alan James 1993. The character of independent statehood. *States in a Changing World: A Contemporary Analysis,* edited by Robert H. Jackson and Alan James. Oxford: Clarendon.

Johnson, Chalmers 1982. *MITI and the Japanese Miracle: The Growth of Industrial Policy, 1925–1975.* Stanford, CA: Stanford University Press.

Johnson, Chalmers 1987. Political institutions and economic performance: The government-business relationship in Japan, South Korea, and Taiwan. *The Political*

Economy of the New Asian Industrialism, edited by Frederic C. Deyo. Ithaca, NY: Cornell University Press.

Johnson, Chalmers 1995. *Japan: Who Governs? The Rise of the Developmental State.* New York: Norton.

Johnson, Chalmers 1999. The developmental state. *The Developmental State*, edited by Meredith Woo-Cumings. Ithaca, NY: Cornell University Press.

Johnson, Hazel 1991. *Dispelling the Myth of Globalization: The Case for Regionalization.* New York: Praeger.

Jomo K.S., ed. 1993. *Industrializing Malaysia: Policy, Performance, Prospects.* London: Routledge.

Jomo K.S. 1994. *U-Turn? Malaysian Economic Development Policy After 1990.* Townsville, Queensland, Australia: James Cook University North Queensland Centre for East and Southeast Asian Studies.

Jomo K.S., and Greg Felker, eds. 1999. *Technology, Competitiveness and the State: Malaysia's Industrial Technology Policies.* London: Routledge.

Jones, Eric 1996. Extensive growth. *The Course of Human History: Economic Growth.* Armonk, NY: M.E. Sharp.

Kamarck, Elaine Ciulla 2000. Globalization and public administration reform. *Governance in a Globalizing World*, edited by Joseph S. Nye Jr. and John D. Donahue. Washington, DC: Brookings Institution Press.

Kant, Immanuel 1957. *Perpetual Peace*, edited by Lewis White Beck. New York: Liberal Arts.

Kant, Immanuel n.d. On the common saying: "This may be true in theory, but it does not apply in practice," cited by Ehrenberg 1999, 116.

Kapstein, Ethan B. 1991/1992. We are us: The myth of the multinational. *National Interest* 26 (Winter): 55–62.

Kapstein, Ethan B. 1994. Governing global finance. *The Washington Quarterly* 17 (Spring): 77–87.

Kapstein, Ethan B. 1994. *Governing the Global Economy: International Finance and the State.* Cambridge, MA: Harvard University Press.

Katzenstein, Peter J., ed. 1996. *The Culture of National Security: Norms and Identity in World Politics.* New York: Columbia University Press.

Katzenstein, Peter J., Robert O. Keohane, and Stephen D. Krasner 1998. International organization and the study of world politics. *International Organization* 52 (Autumn): 645–685.

Kaul, Inge 2001. The international financial architecture: A global public goods perspective. Talking points for the seminar on *Global Finance and Civil Society*, New York, 3 April.

Keane, John 1998. *Civil Society: Old Images, New Visions.* Stanford, CA: Stanford University Press.

Kelly, George Armstrong 1979. Who needs a theory of citizenship? *Daedalus*, Fall: 21–36.

Kennedy, Paul 1993. *Preparing for the Twenty-First Century.* New York: Random House.

Keohane, Robert O. 1984. *After Hegemony: Cooperation and Discord in the World Political Economy.* Princeton, NJ: Princeton University Press.

Keohane, Robert O. 1989. *International Institutions and State Power: Essays in International Relations Theory.* Boulder, CO: Westview.

Keohane, Robert O. 1994. Comment. *Managing the World Economy: Fifty Years After Bretton Woods*, edited by Barry Eichengreen and Peter B. Kenen. Washington, DC: Institute for International Economics.

Keohane, Robert O., and Lisa L. Martin 1995. The promise of institutionalist theory. *International Security* 20 (Summer): 39–51.

Keohane, Robert O., and Joseph S. Nye 1989. *Power and Interdependence*, 2nd ed. Glenview, IL: Scott, Foresman/Little, Brown.

Kindleberger, Charles P. 1973. *The World in Depression, 1929–1939*. Berkeley: University of California Press.

Kindleberger, Charles P. 1981. Dominance and leadership in the international economy: Exploitation, public goods, and free rides. *International Studies Quarterly* 25: 242–254.

Kohli, Atul 1999. Japan's colonial legacy on Korea. *The Developmental State*, edited by Meredith Woo-Cumings. Ithaca, NY: Cornell University Press.

Koo, Hagen 1987. The interplay of state, social class, and world system in East Asian development: The cases of South Korea and Taiwan. *The Political Economy of the New Asian Industrialism*, edited by Frederic C. Deyo. Ithaca, NY: Cornell University Press.

Koo, Hagen, ed. 1993. *State and Society in Contemporary Korea*. Ithaca: Cornell University Press.

Korten, David C. 1998. *Globalizing Civil Society: Reclaiming Our Right to Power*. New York: Seven Stories.

Krasner, Stephen D., ed. 1983. *International Regimes*. Ithaca, NY: Cornell University Press.

Krasner, Stephen D. 1993. Economic interdependence and independent statehood. *States in a Changing World: A Contemporary Analysis*, edited by Robert H. Jackson and Alan James. Oxford: Clarendon.

Krasner, Stephen D. 1999. *Sovereignty: Organized Hypocrisy*. Princeton, NJ: Princeton University Press.

Krueger, Anne O., with the assistance of Chonira Aturupane, ed. 1998. *The WTO as an International Organization*. Chicago: University of Chicago Press.

Krugman, Paul 1994. *Peddling Prosperity*. New York: W.W. Norton.

Kupchan, Charles A., 1996. Reviving the west. *Foreign Affairs* 75 (May/June): 92–104.

Kuznets, Simon 1973. Modern economic growth: Findings and reflections. *American Economic Review* 63, 3 (November): 247–258.

Lake, Anthony 1993. From containment to enlargement. Address September 21. *Vital Speeches of the Day* 60 (October 15): 13–19.

Lall, Sanjaya 1999. Technology policy and competitiveness in Malaysia. *Technology, Competitiveness and the State: Malaysia's Industrial Technology Policies*, edited by Jomo K.S. and Greg Felker. London: Routledge.

Layne, Christopher 1994. Kant or cant: The myth of the democratic peace. *International Security* 19: 5–44.

Lee Kuan Yew 2000. *From Third World to First, The Singapore Story: 1965–2000*. New York: HarperCollins.

LeHeron, Richard, and Sam Ock Park, eds. 1995. *The Asian Pacific Rim and Globalization: Enterprise, Governance, and Territoriality*. Aldershot, UK: Avebury.

Lehmann, David 1990. *Democracy and Development in Latin America: Economics, Politics and Religion in the Post-War Period*. Cambridge, UK: Polity.

Leipziger, Danny M., and Vinod Thomas, 1994. Roots of East Asia's success. *Finance and Development* 31 (March): 6–9.

Lentner, Howard H. 1996. The political underpinning: United Nations' contributions to state formation as a prerequisite to economic and social development. Paper presented at the Ninth Annual Meeting of the Academic Council on the United Nations System. Turin, Italy. June 25.

Lentner, Howard H. 2000a. Globalization and power. *Rethinking Globalization(s): From*

Corporate Transnationalism to Local Interventions, edited by Michael G. Schechter and Preet Aulakh. London: Macmillan.

Lentner, Howard H. 2000b. Politics, power, and states in globalization. *Power in Contemporary Politics: Theories, Practices, Globalizations*, edited by Henri Goverde, Philip G. Cerny, Mark Haugaard, and Howard H. Lentner. London: Sage.

Lentner, Howard H. 2000c. Developmental states and global pressures: Accumulation, production, distribution. Paper presented at Eighth Asian-Pacific Researchers in Organization Studies (APROS) Colloquium. Sydney, Australia, December 15–17.

Lentner, Howard H. 2003. Modernization and foreign policy: An alternative approach to the global south. *Foreign Policies of the Global South: Rethinking Conceptual Frameworks*, edited by Jacqueline Braveboy-Wagner. Boulder, CO: Lynne Rienner.

Lewis, W. Arthur 1955. *The Theory of Economic Growth*. London: George Allen & Unwin.

Lindblad, J.T. 1998. *Foreign Investment in Southeast Asia in the Twentieth Century*. London: Macmillan.

Luard, Evan 1990. *The Globalization of Politics: The Changed Focus of Political Action in the Modern World*. London: Macmillan.

Lundestad, Geir 1998. *"Empire" by Integration : The United States and European Integration, 1945–1997*. New York: Oxford University Press.

Macdonald, Laura 1997. *Supporting Civil Society: The Political Role of Non-Governmental Organizations in Central America*. New York: St. Martin's.

Mackay, Donald 1997. *The Malayan Emergency 1948–60: The Domino that Stood*. London: Brassey's.

Maddison, Angus 1995. *Monitoring the World Economy, 1820–1991*. Paris: Development Centre of the Organisation for Economic Cooperation and Development.

Mahathir Mohamed 1970. *The Malay Dilemma*. Singapore: Donald Moore for Asia Pacific Press.

Malaysia, *Seventh Malaysia Plan 1996–2000* 1996. Kuala Lumpur: Economic Planning Unit, Prime Minister's Department.

Malaysia, Ministry of International Trade and Industry 1996. *Second Industrial Master Plan (1996–2005), Executive Summary*. Kuala Lumpur: MIDA.

Malaysia, Ministry of International Trade and Industry 2002. Government Policies to Promote Industrial Development: The Second Industrial Master Plan (IMP2) 1996–2005. Available at http://www.miti.gov.my/trd-indpolicy.html.

Mandelbaum, Michael, ed. 1995. *The Strategic Quadrangle: Russia, China, Japan, and the United States in East Asia*. New York: Council on Foreign Relations Press.

Mandelbaum, Michael 1996a. *The Dawn of Peace in Europe*. New York: Twentieth Century Fund Press.

Mandelbaum, Michael 1996b. The Russian Regime. *The Dawn of Peace in Europe*. New York: Twentieth Century Fund Press.

Maoz, Zeev, and Bruce M. Russett 1993. Normative and structural causes of the democratic peace. *American Political Science Review* 87: 624–638.

Markovitz, Irving Leonard 2000. Civil society, pluralism, Goldilocks, and other fairy tales in Africa. *Contested Terrains and Constructed Categories: Contemporary Africa in Focus*, edited by George Bond and Nigel Gibson. Boulder, CO: Westview .

Marx, Karl 1857–1858. Economic Manuscripts of 1857–58 (First Version of *Capital*) or *Grundisse*.

Marx, Karl n.d. Contribution to the critique of Hegel's philosophy of law. *Collected Works* by Karl Marx and Frederick Engels. New York: International, 1975, 3, p.48.

May, Radmilla 1999.The Yugoslav war crimes tribunal. *Contemporary Review* 275: "Part One" (September): 123–128; "Part Two" (October): 174–179.

Meadows, Donella H., et al 1974. *The Limits to Growth: A Report for the Club of Rome's Project on the Predicament of Mankind*, 2d ed. New York: Universe Books.

Means, Gordon P. 1991. *Malaysian Politics: The Second Generation*. Singapore: Oxford University Press.

Mearsheimer, John J. 1990. Back to the future: Instability in Europe after the cold war. *International Security* 15 (Summer): 5–56.

Mearsheimer, John J. 1994/95. The false promise of international institutions. *International Security* 19 (Winter): 5–49.

Milne, R.S., and Diane K. Mauzy 1999. *Malaysian Politics under Mahathir*. London: Routledge.

Milner, Anthony 1998. Ideological work in constructing the Malay majority. *Making Majorities: Constituting the Nation in Japan, Korea, China, Malaysia, Fiji, Turkey, and the United States*, edited by Dru C. Gladney. Stanford, CA: Stanford University Press.

Milward, Alan S. 1984. *The Reconstruction of Western Europe, 1945–51*. London: Methuen.

Minear, Larry, and Philippe Guillot 1996. *Soldiers to the Rescue: Humanitarian Lessons from Rwanda*. Paris: Development Centre of the Organisation for Economic Co-operation and Development.

Mittelman, James H., ed. 1996. *Globalization: Critical Reflections*. Boulder, CO: Lynne Rienner.

Mittelman, James H. 2000. *The Globalization Syndrome: Transformation and Resistance*. Princeton, NJ: Princeton University Press.

Mlinar, Zdravko 1992. *Globalization and Territorial Identities*. Aldershot, UK: Avebury.

Murray, Charles 1984. *Losing Ground: American Social Policy 1950–1980*. New York: Basic.

Mussington, David 1994. *Arms Unbound: The Globalization of Defense Production*. Washington, DC: Brassey's.

Nathan, K.S. 1998. Malaysia: Reinventing the nation. *Asian Security Practice: Material and Ideational Influences*, edited by Muthiah Alagappa. Stanford, CA: Stanford University Press.

Nayyar, Harish, and P. Ramaswamy, eds. 1995. *Globalization and Agricultural Marketing*. Jaipur: Rawat.

North, Douglass C., and Robert Paul Thomas 1973. *The Rise of the Western World: A New Economic History*. Cambridge, UK: Cambridge University Press.

Novak, Michael, ed. 1979. *The Family, America's Hope*. Rockford: Rockford College Institute.

Novak, Michael, et al. 1987. *The New Consensus on Welfare and the Family*. Washington, DC: American Enterprise Institute.

Nozick, Robert 1974. *Anarchy, State and Utopia*. New York: Basic.

Nussbaum, Martha C. 2000. Duties of justice, duties of material aid: Cicero's problematic legacy. *Journal of Political Philosophy* 8: 176–206.

Nye, Joseph S. Jr. 1988. Neorealism and neoliberalism. *World Politics* 60: 235–251.

Nye, Joseph S. Jr. 1990. *Bound To Lead: The Changing Nature of American Power*. New York: Basic.

Nye, Joseph S. Jr. 1993. *Understanding International Conflicts: An Introduction to Theory and History*. New York: HarperCollins College.

Nye, Joseph S. Jr. 2002. *The Paradox of American Power: Why the World's Only Superpower Can't Go It Alone*. New York: Oxford University Press.

Nye, Joseph S. Jr., and William A. Owens 1996. America's information edge. *Foreign Affairs* 75 (March/April): 20–36.

Offe, Claus, 1996. *Modernity and the State: East, West*. Cambridge, UK: Polity.

Ohmae, Kenichi 1990. *The Borderless World.* New York: Collins.

Ohmae, Kenichi 1995. Putting global logic first. *Harvard Business Review* 73 (1): 119–125.

Ohmae, Kenichi, ed. 1995. *The Evolving Global Economy: Making Sense of the New World Order.* Cambridge, MA: Harvard Business Review series.

Omaar, Rakiya and Alex de Waal 1994. *Humanitarianism Unbound?* Discussion Paper No. 5. London: African Rights.

Ongkili, James P. 1985. *Nation-building in Malaysia 1946–1974.* Singapore: Oxford University Press.

Onis, Ziya 1991. The logic of the developmental state. *Comparative Politics* 24 (October): 109–126.

Osman-Rani, H. 1996. *Alternative Perspectives in Third-World Development: The Case of Malaysia,* edited by Masudul Alam Choudhury, Uzir Abdul Malik, and Mohammad Anuar Adnan. New York: St. Martin's.

Paarlberg, Robert 1997. Earth in abeyance: Explaining weak leadership in U.S. international environmental policy. *Eagle Adrift: American Foreign Policy at the End of the Century,* edited by Robert J. Lieber. New York: Longman.

Panitch, Leo 1996. Rethinking the role of the state. *Globalization: Critical Reflections,* edited by James H. Mittelman. Boulder, CO: Lynne Rienner.

Panitch, Leo, and Colin Leys 1997. *The End of Parliamentary Socialism: From New Left to New Labour.* London: Verso.

Parsons, Talcott 1971. *The System of Modern Societies.* Englewood Cliffs, NJ: Prentice-Hall.

Pelczynski, Z.A. 1984. *The State and Civil Society: Studies in Hegel's Political Philosophy.* Cambridge, UK: Cambridge University Press.

Pempel, T.J. 1999. The developmental regime in a changing world economy. *The Developmental State,* edited by Meredith Woo-Cumings. Ithaca, NY: Cornell University Press.

Penttinen, Elina 2000. Capitalism as a system of global power. *Power in Contemporary Politics: Theories, Practices, Globalizations,* edited by Henri Goverde, Philip G. Cerny, Mark Haugaard, and Howard H. Lentner. London: Sage.

Perlez, Jane 2003. "Mahathir, Malaysia's Autocratic Modernizer, Steps Down," *The New York Times,* November 1.

Polanyi, Karl 1944. *The Great Transformation.* New York: Farrar & Rinehart.

Putnam, Robert D. 1993. *Making Democracy Work: Civic Traditions in Modern Italy.* Princeton, NJ: Princeton University Press.

Putnam, Robert D. 1995. Bowling alone: America's declining social capital. *Journal of Democracy* 6: 65–78.

Robertson, Roland 1990. Mapping the global condition: Globalization as the central concept. *Global Culture: Nationalism, Globalization and Modernity,* edited by Mike Featherstone. London: Sage.

Robertson, Roland 1992. *Globalization: Social Theory and Global Culture.* London: Sage.

Roche, John P. 1961. The founding fathers: A reform caucus in action. *American Political Science Review* LV (December): 799–816.

Rodrik, Dani 1997a. *Has Globalization Gone Too Far?* Washington, DC: Institute for International Economics.

Rodrik, Dani 1997b. Sense and nonsense in the globalization debate. *Foreign Policy* 107 (Summer): 19–36.

Rodrik, Dani 2000. Governance of economic globalization. *Governance in a Globalizing World,* edited by Joseph S. Nye Jr. and John D. Donahue. Washington, DC: Brookings Institution Press.

Roff, William R. 1967. *The Origins of Malay Nationalism*. New Haven, CT: Yale University Press.

Rosecrance, Richard 1986. *The Rise of the Trading State: Commerce and Conquest in the Modern World*. New York: Basic.

Rosenau, James N. 1990. *Turbulence in World Politics: A Theory of Change and Continuity*. Princeton, NJ: Princeton University Press.

Rousseau, Jean-Jacques 1973. *The Social Contract and Discourses*, translated by G.D.H. Cole, revised by J.H. Brumfitt and John C. Hall. London: J.M. Dent.

Ruggie, John Gerard 1982. International regimes, transactions, and change: Embedded liberalism in the postwar economic order. *International Organization* 36 (Spring): 379–415.

Ruggie, John Gerard, ed. 1983. *The Antinomies of Interdependence*. New York: Columbia University Press.

Ruggie, John Gerard 1993. Territoriality and beyond: Problematizing modernity in international relations. *International Organization* 47 (Winter): 139–174.

Ruggie, John Gerard 1996. *Winning the Peace: America and World Order in the New Era*. New York: Columbia University Press.

Ruggie, John Gerard 1998. *Constructing the World Polity: Essays on International Institutionalization*. London: Routledge.

Russett, Bruce M. 1995. *Grasping the Democratic Peace: Principles for a Post-Cold War World*. Princeton, NJ: Princeton University Press.

Sanger, David E. 1997. Big industrial nations warn dollar rise must be halted. *The New York Times*, April 28, D2.

Sassen, Saskia 1996. *Losing Control? Sovereignty in an Age of Globalization*. New York: Columbia University Press.

Schelling, Thomas C. 1960. *The Strategy of Conflict*. Cambridge, MA: Harvard University Press.

Schelling, Thomas C. 1966. *Arms and Influence*. New Haven, CT: Yale University Press.

Scholte, Jan Aart 2000. Can globality bring a good society? *Rethinking Globalization(s): From Corporate Transnationalism to Local Interventions*, edited by Preet S. Aulakh and Michael G. Schechter. New York: St. Martin's.

Schumpeter, Joseph 1950. *Capitalism, Socialism and Democracy*. New York: Harper and Row.

Segal, Gerald 1996. East Asia and the "constrainment" of China. *International Security* 20, Spring: 107–135.

Seligman, Adam B. 1992. *The Idea of Civil Society*. New York: Free Press.

Sen, Amartya 1999. *Development as Freedom*. New York: Knopf.

Simon, Denis Fred, ed. 1995. *The Emerging Technological Trajectory of the Pacific Rim*. Armonk, NY: M.E. Sharpe.

Simon, Julian L. 1981. *The Ultimate Resource*. Princeton, NJ: Princeton University Press.

Singer, Max, and Aaron Wildavsky 1993. *The Real World Order: Zones of Peace/Zones of Turmoil*. Chatham, NJ: Chatham House.

Sloane, Patricia 1999. *Islam, Modernity and Entrepreneurship among the Malays*. New York: St. Martin's.

Smith, Adam 1970/1776. *The Wealth of Nations*. Harmondsworth, UK: Penguin.

Smith, Anthony D. 1986. *The Ethnic Origins of Nations*. Oxford: Blackwell.

Smith, Steven B. 1989. *Hegel's Critique of Liberalism: Rights in Context*. Chicago: University of Chicago Press.

Somjee, A.H. 1982. *Political Capacity in Developing Societies*. New York: St. Martin's.

Spiro, David 1994. The insignificance of the liberal peace. *International Security* 19: 50–86.

Steel, Ronald 1998. Instead of NATO. *The New York Review of Books* XLV, January 15: 21–24.

Stewart, Frances, and Albert Barry 1999. Globalization, liberalization, and inequality: Expectations and experience. *Inequality, Globalization, and World Politics*, edited by Andrew Hurrell and Ngaire Woods. Oxford: Oxford University Press.

Stiglitz, Joseph E. 2002. *Globalization and Its Discontents.* New York: W.W. Norton.

Stopford, John M., and Susan Strange with John S. Henley 1991. *Rival States, Rival Firms: Competition for World Market Shares.* Cambridge, UK: Cambridge University Press.

Strange, Susan 1988. *States and Markets.* London: Pinter.

Strange, Susan 1996. *The Retreat of the State: The Diffusion of Power in the World Economy.* Cambridge, UK: Cambridge University Press.

Stubbs, Richard, and Geoffrey R.D. Underhill 1994. *Political Economy and the Changing Global Order.* New York: St. Martin's.

Tanahashi, T. Keisei 1992. *Asian Alternative for Regional Cooperation: A Quest of Asian Strategy for Globalization.* Bangkok: Institute of Asian Studies, Chulalongkorn University.

Thomas, Henk, ed. 1995. *Globalization and Third World Trade Unions: The Challenge of Rapid Economic Development.* Atlantic Highlands, NJ: Zed.

Thomson, Janice E. 1995. State sovereignty in international relations: Bridging the gap between theory and empirical research, *International Studies Quarterly* 39 (June): 213–233.

Thomson, Janice E., and Stephen D. Krasner, 1989. Global transactions and the consolidation of sovereignty. *Global Changes and Theoretical Challenges*, edited by Ernst-Otto Czempiel and James N. Rosenau. New York: Lexington.

Thurow, Lester C. 1999. Building wealth: The rules for individuals, companies, and nations. *Atlantic Monthly* 283, No. 6.

Tismaneanu, Vladimir 1992. *Reinventing Politics: Eastern Europe After Communism.* New York: Free Press.

Tocqueville, Alexis de 1945. *Democracy in America.* 2 volumes. New York: Knopf.

Tunku Abdul Rahman Putra 1984. *Malaysia: The Road to Independence.* Petaling Jaya: Pelanduk.

Ul Haq, Mahbub 1994, The Bretton Woods institutions and global governance. *Managing the World Economy: Fifty Years After Bretton Woods*, edited by Barry Eichengreen and Peter B. Kenen. Washington, DC: Institute for International Economics.

United Nations 1992. *World Investment Directory 1992, Volume 1 Asia and the Pacific.* New York: United Nations.

UNDP 2000. *Overcoming Human Poverty: UNDP Poverty Report 2000.* Available at http://www.undp.org/povertyreport/.

UNHCR United Nations High Commissioner for Refugees Website "Basic Facts" 2002. Available at http://www.unhcr.ch/cgi-bin/texis/vtx/home?page=basics.

U.S. Agency for International Development, Bureau for Humanitarian Response, Office of U.S. Foreign Disaster 1997. *Great Lakes—Complex Emergency, Situation Report #34,* Fiscal Year 1997, May 9.

United States, Department of State 1998. *Country Commercial Guide 1996.* Washington, DC: Bureau of Economic and Business Affairs.

United States, Department of State 2002. *Country Commercial Guide for Malaysia.* Kuala Lumpur: United States Embassy. Available at http://usembassymalaysia.org.my/cog-2002.html.

Vernon, Raymond 1996. The U.S. government at Bretton Woods and after. *The Bretton*

Woods-GATT System: Retrospect and Prospect After Fifty Years. Armonk, NY: M.E. Sharpe.

Vines, David 1998. The WTO in relation to the Fund and the Bank: Competencies, agenda, and linkages. *The WTO as an International Organization,* edited by Anne O. Krueger, with the assistance of Chonira Aturupane. Chicago: University of Chicago Press.

Wade, Robert 1990. *Governing the Market: Economic Theory and the Role of Government in East Asian Industrialization.* Princeton, NJ: Princeton University Press.

Waldner, David 1999. *State Building and Late Development.* Ithaca, NY: Cornell University Press.

Waltz, Kenneth N. 1959. *Man, the State and War: A Theoretical Analysis.* New York: Columbia University Press.

Waltz, Kenneth N. 1979. *Theory of International Politics.* Reading, MA: Addison-Wesley.

Waltz, Kenneth N. 1986. Reflections on *Theory of International Politics:* A response to my critics. *Neorealism and Its Critics,* edited by Robert O. Keohane. New York: Columbia University Press.

Waltz, Kenneth N. 1993. The emerging structure of international politics. *International Security* 18 (Fall): 44–79.

Waltz, Kenneth N. 2000. Structural realism after the cold war. *International Security* 25 (Summer): 5–41.

Warkentin, Craig, and Karen Mingst 2000. International institutions, the state, and global civil society in the age of the World Wide Web. *Global Governance* 6: 237–257.

Washington, George 1796. Farewell address. Cited in *A Diplomatic History of the United States,* 4th edition, by Samuel Flagg Bemis 1963. New York: Holt, Rinehart and Winston, 109.

Waters, Malcolm 1995. *Globalization.* London: Routledge.

Weber, Max 1948. *The Theory of Social and Economic Organization,* translated by Talcott Parsons and A.M. Henderson. New York: Free Press.

Weber, Max 1978. *Economy and Society: An Outline of Interpretive Sociology.* 2 volumes. Edited by Guenther Roth and Claus Wittich. Berkeley: University of California Press.

Weede, Erich 1996. *Economic Development, Social Order, and World Politics: With Special Emphasis on War, Freedom, the Rise and Decline of the West, and the Future of East Asia.* Boulder, CO: Lynne Rienner.

Weiss, Linda 1998. *The Myth of the Powerless State.* Ithaca, NY: Cornell University Press.

Wendt, Alexander 1994. Collective identity formation and the international state. *American Political Science Review* 88 (June): 384–398.

Wendt, Alexander 1995. Constructing international politics. *International Security* 20 (Summer): 71–81.

Wendt, Alexander 1999. *Social Theory of International Politics.* New York: Cambridge University Press.

White, Randall, 1995. *Global Spin: Probing the Globalization Debate: Where in the World Are We Going?* Toronto: Dundurn.

Williamson, John, 1990. Assessment. *The Progress of Policy Reform in Latin America.* Washington, DC: Institute for International Economics.

Williamson, John 2003. From reform agenda to damaged brand name: A short history of the Washington Consensus and suggestions for what to do next. *Finance and Development* 40 (September): 10–13.

Wolf, Martin 2001. Will the nation-state survive globalization? *Foreign Affairs* 80 (January/February).

Woo-Cumings, Meredith 1999. *The Developmental State.* Ithaca, NY: Cornell University Press.

World Bank 1990. *Financial Systems and Development.* Washington, DC: The World Bank.

World Bank 1993. *The East Asian Miracle: Economic Growth and Public Policy,* a World Bank Policy Research Report. New York: Oxford University Press for the World Bank.

World Bank 1996. *World Development Report 1996: From Plan to Market.* New York: Oxford University Press.

World Bank 1997. *World Development Report 1997: The State in a Changing World.* New York: Oxford University Press.

World Bank 2000. *World Development Report 2000/2001: Attacking Poverty.* New York: Oxford University Press for the World Bank.

World Commission on Environment and Development 1987. *Our Common Future.* Oxford: Oxford University Press.

Yang, Xiaohua 1995. *Globalization of the Automobile Industry: The United States, Japan, and the People's Republic of China.* Westport, CT: Praeger.

Yokoyama, Hisashi, and Mokhtar Tamin, eds. 1991. *Malaysian Economy in Transition.* Tokyo: Institute of Developing Economies.

Interviews

3/11/98. Ministry of Defense, Kuala Lumpur.
3/17/98. Foreign Ministry, Kuala Lumpur.

Index